The Art of Data-Driven Business

Transform your organization into a data-driven one with the power of Python machine learning

Alan Bernardo Palacio

BIRMINGHAM—MUMBAI

The Art of Data-Driven Business

Publishing Product Manager: Siddharth Mandal

Content Development Editor: Joseph Sunil

Technical Editor: Rahul Limbachiya

Copy Editor: Safis Editing

Project Coordinator: Farheen Fathima

Proofreader: Safis Editing

Indexer: Sejal Dsilva

Production Designer: Vijay Kamble

Marketing Coordinator: Shifa Ansari

First published: December 2022

Production reference: 1301122

Published by Packt Publishing Ltd.

Livery Place

35 Livery Street

Birmingham

B3 2PB, UK.

ISBN 978-1-80461-103-6

www.packt.com

Contributors

About the author

Alan Bernardo Palacio is a data scientist and engineer with vast experience in different engineering fields. His focus has been the development and application of state-of-the-art data products and algorithms in several industries. He has worked for companies such as Ernst & Young and Globant and is now the head of data engineering at Ebiquity Media, helping the company to create a scalable data pipeline. Alan graduated with a mechanical engineering degree from the National University of Tucuman in 2015, participated in founding several start-ups, and later earned a master's degree from the Faculty of Mathematics in the Autonomous University of Barcelona in 2017. Originally from Argentina, he now works and resides in the Netherlands.

About the reviewer

Marwa is an agile and inspirational Egyptian data scientist, clinical pharmacist, data analytics mentor, and medical researcher with more than 8 years of experience in a range of fields, including the medical, telecom, financial, and technology sectors. She has a background in clinical pharmacy with a bachelor's degree and a PharmD (Master's), and she has pursued her enthusiasm for DS, AI, and ML by teaching herself a variety of programming languages before completing a Data Science and Big Data Analytics diploma and becoming certified as an AWS Machine Learning Engineer. She is now pursuing an MBA while working as a senior business operations analyst and data scientist. Visit Marwa Eshra's LinkedIn and GitHub pages to learn more about her.

Table of Contents

Part 2: Market and Customer Insights

3

4

5

Part 3: Operation and Pricing Optimization

10

Web Analytics Optimization   233

11

Creating a Data-Driven Culture in Business   257

Preface

One of the most valuable contributions of data science is toward helping businesses make the right decisions. Understanding this complicated confluence of two disparate worlds, as well as a fiercely competitive market, calls for all the guidance you can get.

The Art of Data-Driven Business is your invaluable guide to gaining a data-driven perspective, as well as leveraging the power of **machine learning** (**ML**) to guide decision-making in your business. This book provides a common ground of discussion for several profiles within a company.

You'll begin by looking at how to use Python and its many libraries for ML. Experienced data scientists may want to skip this short introduction, but you'll soon get to the meat of the book and explore the many and varied ways ML with Python can be applied to the domain of business decisions through real-world business problems that you can tackle by yourself. As you advance, you'll gain practical insights into the value that ML can provide to your business, as well as the technical ability to apply a wide variety of tried-and-tested ML methods.

By the end of this Python book, you'll have learned the value of basing your business decisions on data-driven methodologies and developed the Python skills needed to apply what you've learned in the real world.

Who this book is for

This book is for data scientists, ML engineers and developers, data engineers, and business decision-makers who want to apply data science to business process optimization and develop the skills needed to implement data science projects in marketing, sales, pricing, customer success, ad tech, and more from a business perspective. Other professionals looking to explore how data science can be used to improve business operations, as well as individuals with technical skills who want to back their technical proposal with a strong business case, will also find this book useful.

What this book covers

Chapter 1, Analyzing and Visualizing Data with Python, serves as an introduction to data analytics with pandas and data analytics with Seaborn. You will learn how to transform, visualize, and analyze data, as these are the fundamental tools that will be used throughout the book. You will be introduced to these libraries through examples based on real-life example applications.

Chapter 2, Using Machine Learning in Business Operations, introduces scikit-learn, the most popular ML framework for applying ML algorithms using Python. You will learn about the basic concepts of

ML, how to perform training, and the inference of supervised and unsupervised algorithms. These concepts will be reinforced through exercises and used in later chapters in real-life applications regarding the optimization of various business applications.

Chapter 3, Finding Business Opportunities with Market Insights, focuses on the use of Python and search trends analysis in order to obtain valuable information from search engine data. You will learn how to obtain information about search engine trends using Python, structure and visualize the results to validate assumptions, expand queries with similar ones, and analyze the content of the results using NLP and scikit-learn.

Chapter 4, Understanding Customer Preferences with Conjoint Analysis, will introduce you to conjoint analysis, which involves analyzing user preference survey data, applying methods to determine how users weigh each attribute, and predicting how new combinations will be ranked.

Chapter 5, Selecting the Optimal Price with Price Demand Elasticity, will introduce you to the concept of price elasticity and it will use it to find the best price for different products using sales data. By the end of the chapter, you will be able to find the price that maximizes revenue and understand the demand curve.

Chapter 6, Product Recommendation, demonstrates two methods for creating product recommendations and performing market basket analysis. You will learn about collaborative filtering and a priori algorithms and how to implement them to create product recommendations using sales data.

Chapter 7, Predicting Customer Churn, will show you how to predict the subtle changes in consumer behavior using Python and scikit-learn.

Chapter 8, Grouping Users with Customer Segmentation, will help you learn about and practice, with real-life cases, methods that can be applied to model the data and which unsupervised ML methods can be used to find these groups, as well as to find their key characteristics. Finally, you will learn how to capitalize on this knowledge by learning to analyze these segments in terms of sales, and how to convey these findings in clearly defined dashboards using Seaborn.

Chapter 9, Using Historical Markdown Data to Predict Sales, will allow you to analyze the impact of promotions on historic time-series sales data using pandas and Seaborn, as well as optimize stock and storage using scikit-learn to analyze the impact of promotions and optimize storage costs.

Chapter 10, Web Analytics Optimization, will show you how to analyze digital marketing data using Python by analyzing the result of digital advertising campaigns, calculate the return on investment based on the customer lifetime value prediction, and optimize the investments being done in programmatic advertising platforms.

Chapter 11, Creating a Data-Driven Culture in Business, reaches out to business leaders to learn how they have applied data science and analytics to improve business operations. We will reach out to several chief data officers and lead data scientists to gather concrete examples of how they have applied these methods throughout several companies.

To get the most out of this book

Software/hardware covered in the book	Operating system requirements
Python 3.x	Windows, macOS, or Linux

If you are using the digital version of this book, we advise you to type the code yourself or access the code from the book's GitHub repository (a link is available in the next section). Doing so will help you avoid any potential errors related to the copying and pasting of code.

Download the example code files

You can download the example code files for this book from GitHub at `https://github.com/PacktPublishing/The-Art-of-Data-Driven-Business-Decisions`. If there's an update to the code, it will be updated in the GitHub repository.

We also have other code bundles from our rich catalog of books and videos available at `https://github.com/PacktPublishing/`. Check them out!

Conventions used

There are a number of text conventions used throughout this book.

`Code in text`: Indicates code words in text, database table names, folder names, filenames, file extensions, pathnames, dummy URLs, user input, and Twitter handles. Here is an example: "Mount the downloaded `WebStorm-10*.dmg` disk image file as another disk in your system."

A block of code is set as follows:

```
results_df = pd.DataFrame(results).dropna()
results_df.columns = ['client','slope','std']
results_df.index = results_df.client
results_df = results_df.drop(['client'],axis=1)
results_df.head()
```

When we wish to draw your attention to a particular part of a code block, the relevant lines or items are set in bold:

```
df.columns.tolist()
>>> ['period', 'sub_market', 'client_class', 'division',
'brand','cat', 'product', 'client_code', 'client_name', 'kgs_
sold']
```

Any command-line input or output is written as follows:

```
!pip install --upgrade openpyxl scikit-surprise
```

Bold: Indicates a new term, an important word, or words that you see onscreen. For instance, words in menus or dialog boxes appear in **bold**. Here is an example: "Select **System info** from the **Administration** panel."

> **Tips or important notes**
> Appear like this.

Get in touch

Feedback from our readers is always welcome.

General feedback: If you have questions about any aspect of this book, email us at customercare@packtpub.com and mention the book title in the subject of your message.

Errata: Although we have taken every care to ensure the accuracy of our content, mistakes do happen. If you have found a mistake in this book, we would be grateful if you would report this to us. Please visit www.packtpub.com/support/errata and fill in the form.

Piracy: If you come across any illegal copies of our works in any form on the internet, we would be grateful if you would provide us with the location address or website name. Please contact us at copyright@packt.com with a link to the material.

If you are interested in becoming an author: If there is a topic that you have expertise in and you are interested in either writing or contributing to a book, please visit authors.packtpub.com.

Share Your Thoughts

Once you've read *The Art of Data-Driven Business*, we'd love to hear your thoughts! Scan the QR code below to go straight to the Amazon review page for this book and share your feedback.

https://packt.link/r/1-804-61103-4

Your review is important to us and the tech community and will help us make sure we're delivering excellent quality content.

Download a free PDF copy of this book

Thanks for purchasing this book!

Do you like to read on the go but are unable to carry your print books everywhere?

Is your eBook purchase not compatible with the device of your choice?

Don't worry, now with every Packt book you get a DRM-free PDF version of that book at no cost.

Read anywhere, any place, on any device. Search, copy, and paste code from your favorite technical books directly into your application.

The perks don't stop there, you can get exclusive access to discounts, newsletters, and great free content in your inbox daily

Follow these simple steps to get the benefits:

1. Scan the QR code or visit the link below

https://packt.link/free-ebook/9781804611036

2. Submit your proof of purchase
3. That's it! We'll send your free PDF and other benefits to your email directly

Part 1:
Data Analytics and
Forecasting with Python

The first part will introduce the main tools used to analyze, predict, and visualize the data using Python. Core frameworks such as Pandas, Scikit-learn, and Seaborn will be introduced, ensuring that you learn how to properly explore and manipulate data, learn about the basics of machine learning algorithms to predict and cluster data, and effective visualization for data storytelling.

This part covers the following chapters:

- *Chapter 1, Analyzing and Visualizing Data with Python*
- *Chapter 2, Using Machine Learning in Business Operations*

1
Analyzing and Visualizing Data with Python

Advanced analytics and data science now play a major role in the majority of businesses. It supports organizations in tracking, managing, and gathering performance metrics to enhance organizational decision-making. Business managers can utilize innovative analysis and machine learning to help them decide how to best engage customers, enhance business performance, and increase sales. Data science and analytics can be utilized to create user-centric products and make wise choices. This can be achieved by comparing various product aspects and studying consumer feedback and market trends to develop goods and services that can draw clients and keep them around for an extended period.

This book is intended for everyone who wants to have an introduction to the techniques and methods of data science, advanced analytics, and machine learning for studying business cases that have been impacted by the use of these methods. The cases shown are heavily based on real use cases, with a demonstrated positive impact in various companies of different sectors. So, anyone who might be considering the application of data science in business operations, regardless of whether they are a seasoned business analyst seeking to enhance their list of skills, or a manager looking for methods that can be applied to maximize certain operations, can benefit from the examples discussed in this book.

In this chapter, we will lay down the initial components that will be used throughout this book to manage the data, manipulate it, and visualize it. Specifically, we will discuss the following:

- The use of data science in business and the main differences with roles such as business or data analysts
- The use of statistical programming libraries such as NumPy to apply matrix algebra and statical methods
- Storing the data in pandas, a library for data analysis and manipulation that is widely used in the context of data science
- Visualization with Seaborn and how the different types of charts can be used in different kinds of situations

Next, we will discuss the technical requirements that you will need to be able to follow the examples presented in this chapter.

Technical requirements

To be able to follow the steps in this chapter, you will need to meet the following requirements:

- A Jupyter notebook instance running Python 3.7 and above. You can use the Google Colab notebook to run the steps as well if you have a Google Drive account.

- A basic understanding of math and statistical concepts.

Using data science and advanced analytics in business

Most of the, time the question of what differentiates a data scientist from a business analyst arises, as both roles focus on attaining insight from data. From a certain perspective, it can be considered that data science involves creating forecasts by analyzing the patterns behind the raw data. Business intelligence is backward-looking and discovers the previous and current trends, while data science is forward-looking and forecasts future trends.

Business decision-making strongly relies on data science and advanced analytics because they help managers understand how decisions affect outcomes. As a result, data scientists are increasingly required to integrate common machine learning technologies with knowledge of the underlying causal linkages. These developments have given rise to positions like that of the decision scientist, a technologist who focuses on using technology to support business and decision-making. When compared to a different employment description known as a "data scientist" or "big data scientist," however, the phrase "decision scientist" becomes truly meaningful.

Most times, there might be confusion between the roles of business analysts, data scientists, and data analysts. Business analysts are more likely to address business problems and suggest solutions, whereas data analysts typically work more directly with the data itself. Both positions are in high demand and are often well paid, but data science is far more engaged in forecasting since it examines the patterns hidden in the raw data.

Using NumPy for statistics and algebra

NumPy is a Python library used for working with arrays. Additionally, it provides functions for working with matrices, the Fourier transform, and the area of linear algebra. Large, multi-dimensional arrays and matrices are now supported by NumPy, along with a wide range of sophisticated mathematical operations that may be performed on these arrays. They use a huge number of sophisticated mathematical functions to process massive multidimensional arrays and matrices, as well as basic scientific computations in machine learning, which makes them highly helpful. It gives the n-dimensional array, a straightforward yet effective data structure. Learning NumPy is the first step on every Python data scientist's path because it serves as the cornerstone on which nearly all of the toolkit's capabilities are constructed.

The array, which is a grid of values all of the same type that's indexed by a tuple of nonnegative integers, is the fundamental building block utilized by NumPy. Similar to how the dimensions of a matrix are defined in algebra, the array's rank is determined by its number of dimensions. A tuple of numbers indicating the size of the array along each dimension makes up the shape of an array:

```
import numpy as np
arr = np.array([1, 2, 3, 4, 5])
print(arr)
print(type(arr))
```

A NumPy array is a container that can house a certain number of elements, all of which must be of the same type, as was previously specified. The majority of data structures employ arrays to carry out their algorithms. Similar to how you can slice a list, you can also slice a NumPy array, but in more than one dimension. Similar to indexing, slicing a NumPy array returns an array that is a view of the original array.

Slicing in Python means taking elements from one given index to another given index. We can select certain elements of an array by slicing the array using [start:end], where we reference the elements of the array from where we can start and where we want to finish. We can also define the step using [start:end:step]:

```
print('select elements by index:',arr[0])
print('slice elements of the array:',arr[1:5])
print('ending point of the array:',arr[4:])
print('ending point of the array:',arr[:4])
```

There are three different sorts of indexing techniques: field access, fundamental slicing, and advanced indexing. Basic slicing is the n-dimensional extension of Python's fundamental slicing notion. By passing start, stop, and step parameters to the built-in slice function, a Python slice object is created. Writing understandable, clear, and succinct code is made possible through slicing. An iterable element is referred to by its position within the iterable when it is "indexed." Getting a subset of elements from an iterable, depending on their indices, is referred to as "slicing."

To combine (concatenate) two arrays, we must copy each element in both arrays to result by using the np.concatenate() function:

```
arr1 = np.array([1, 2, 3])
arr2 = np.array([4, 5, 6])
arr = np.concatenate((arr1, arr2))
print(arr)
```

Arrays can be joined using NumPy stack methods as well. We can combine two 1D arrays along the second axis to stack them on top of one another, a process known as stacking. The `stack()` method receives a list of arrays that we wish to connect with the axis:

```
arr = np.stack((arr1, arr2), axis=1)
print(arr)
```

The `axis` parameter can be used to reference the axis over which we want to make the concatenation:

```
arr = np.stack((arr1, arr2), axis=0)
print(arr)
```

The NumPy `mean()` function is used to compute the arithmetic mean along the specified axis:

```
np.mean(arr,axis=1)
```

You need to use the NumPy `mean()` function with `axis=0` to compute the average by column. To compute the average by row, you need to use `axis=1`:

```
np.mean(arr,axis=0)
```

In the next section, we will introduce pandas, a library for data analysis and manipulation. pandas is one of the most extensively used Python libraries in data science, much like NumPy. It offers high-performance, simple-to-use data analysis tools. In contrast to the multi-dimensional array objects provided by the NumPy library, pandas offers an in-memory 2D table object called a DataFrame.

Storing and manipulating data with pandas

pandas is an open-source toolkit built on top of NumPy that offers Python programmers high-performance, user-friendly data structures, and data analysis capabilities. It enables quick analysis, data preparation, and cleaning. It performs and produces at a high level.

pandas is a package for data analysis, and because it includes many built-in auxiliary functions, it is typically used for financial time series data, economic data, and any form of tabular data. For scientific computing, NumPy is a quick way to manage huge multidimensional arrays, and it can be used in conjunction with the SciPy and pandas packages.

Constructing a DataFrame from a dictionary is possible by passing this dictionary to the `DataFrame` constructor:

```
import pandas as pd
d = {'col1': [1,5,8, 2], 'col2': [3,3,7, 4]}
```

```
df = pd.DataFrame(data=d)
df
```

The pandas `groupby` function is a powerful and versatile function that allows us to split data into separate groups to perform computations for better analysis:

```
df = pd.DataFrame({'Animal': ['Dog', 'Dog',
                            'Rat', 'Rat','Rat'],
                 'Max Speed': [380., 370., 24., 26.,25.],
                 'Max Weight': [10., 8.1, .1, .12,.09]})
df
```

The three steps of "split," "apply," and "combine" make it the simplest to recall what a "groupby" performs. Split refers to dividing your data into distinct groups based on a particular column. As an illustration, we can divide our sales data into months:

```
df.groupby(['Animal']).mean()
```

pandas' `groupby` technique is extremely potent. Using value counts, you can group by one column and count the values of a different column as a function of this column value. We can count the number of activities each person completed using `groupby` and `value` counts:

```
df.value_counts()
```

We can also aggregate data over the rows using the `aggregate()` method, which allows you to apply a function or a list of function names to be executed along one of the axes of the DataFrame. The default is 0, which is the index (row) axis. It's important to note that the `agg()` method is an alias of the `aggregate()` method:

```
df.agg("mean", axis="rows",numeric_only=True)
```

We can also pass several functions to be used in each of the selected columns:

```
df.agg({'Max Speed' : ['sum', 'min'], 'Max Weight' : ['mean',
'max']})
```

The quantile of the values on a given axis is determined via the `quantile()` method. The row-level axis is the default. The `quantile()` method calculates the quantile column-wise and returns the mean value for each row when the column axis is specified (`axis='columns'`). The following line will give us the 10% quantile across the entire DataFrame:

```
df.quantile(.1)
```

We can also pass a list of quantiles:

```
df.quantile([.1, .5])
```

The `pivot()` function is used to reshape a given DataFrame structured by supplied index or column values and is one of the different types of functions that we can use to change the data. Data aggregation is not supported by this function; multiple values produce a `MultiIndex` in the columns:

```
df = pd.DataFrame(
{'type': ['one', 'one', 'one', 'two', 'two',  'two'],
 'cat': ['A', 'B', 'C', 'A', 'B', 'C'],
'val': [1, 2, 3, 4, 5, 6],
'letter': ['x', 'y', 'z', 'q', 'w', 't']})
df.pivot(index='type', columns='cat', values='val')
```

Pivot tables are one of pandas' most powerful features. A pivot table allows us to draw insights from data. pandas provides a similar function called `pivot_table()`. It is a simple function but can produce a very powerful analysis very quickly.

The next step for us will be to learn how to visualize the data to create proper storytelling and appropriate interpretations.

Visualizing patterns with Seaborn

Seaborn is a Python data visualization library based on Matplotlib. It offers a sophisticated drawing tool for creating eye-catching and educational statistical visuals.

The primary distinction between Seaborn and Matplotlib is how well Seaborn handles pandas DataFrames. Beautiful graphics are provided in Python by using simple sets of functions. When dealing with DataFrames and arrays, Matplotlib performs well. It views axes and figures as objects. There are several stateful plotting APIs in it.

Here, we will start our examples using the "tips" dataset, which contains a mixture of numeric and categorical variables:

```
import seaborn as sns
import matplotlib.pyplot as plt
tips = sns.load_dataset("tips")
f, ax = plt.subplots(figsize=(12, 6))
sns.scatterplot(data=tips, x="total_bill", y="tip", hue="time")
```

In the preceding code snippet, we have imported Seaborn and Matplotlib; the latter allows users to control certain aspects of the plots created, such as the figure size, which we defined as a 12 by 6 inches size. This creates the layout in which Seaborn will place the visualization.

We are using the `scatterplot()` function to create a visualization of points where the *X*-axis refers to the `total_bill` variable and the *Y*-axis refers to the `tip` variable. Here, we are using the `hue` parameter to color the different dots according to the `time` categorical variable, which allows us to plot numerical data with a categorical dimension:

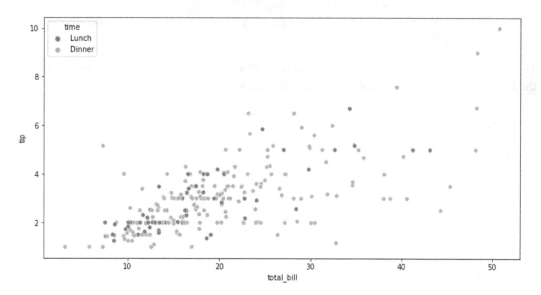

Figure 1.1: Seaborn scatterplot with the color depending on the categorical variable

This generated figure shows the distribution of the data according to the color codes that we have specified, which in our case are the tips that were received, their relationship with the total bill amount, and whether it was during lunch or dinner.

The interpretation that we can make is that there might be a linear relationship between the total amount of the bill and the tip received. But if we look closer, we can see that the highest total bill amounts are placed during dinner, also leading to the highest values in tips.

This information can be really useful in the context of business, but it first needs to be validated with proper hypothesis testing approaches, which can be a t-test to validate these hypotheses, plus a linear regression analysis to conclude that there is a relationship between the total amount and the tip distribution, accounting for the differences in the time in which this occurred. We will look into these analyses in the next chapter.

We can now see how a simple exploration graph can help us construct the hypothesis over which we can base decisions to better improve business products or services.

We can also assign hue and style to different variables that will vary colors and markers independently. This allows us to introduce another categorical dimension in the same graph, which in the case of Seaborn can be used with the `style` parameter, which will assign different types of markers according to our referenced categorical variable:

```
f, ax = plt.subplots(figsize=(12, 6))
sns.scatterplot(data=tips, x="total_bill", y="tip", hue="day",
style="time")
```

The preceding code snippet will create a layout that's 12 x 6 inches and will add information about the `time` categorical variable, as shown in the following graph:

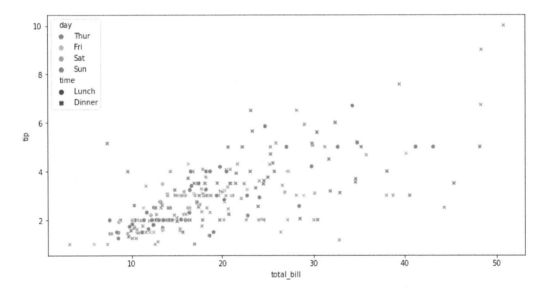

Figure 1.2: Seaborn scatterplot with color and shape depending on the categorical variable

This kind of graph allows us to pack a lot of information into a single plot, which can be beneficial but also can lead to a cluttering of information that can be difficult to digest at once. It is important to always account for the understanding of the information that we want to show, making it easier for the stakeholders to be able to see the relationships at a glance.

Here, it is much more difficult to see any kind of interpretation of the days of the week at first glance. This is because a lot of information is already being shown. These differences that cannot be obtained by simply looking at a graph can be achieved through other kinds of analysis, such as statistical tests, correlations, and causations.

Another way to add more dimensions to the graphics created with Seaborn is to represent numerical variables as the size of the points in the scatterplot. Numerical variables can be assigned to `size` to apply a semantic mapping to the areas of the points.

We can control the range of marker areas with sizes, and set the legend parameter to `full` to force every unique value to appear in the legend:

```
f, ax = plt.subplots(figsize=(12, 6))
sns.scatterplot(
    data=tips, x="total_bill", y="tip", hue="size",
    size="size", sizes=(20, 200), legend="full"
)
```

The preceding code snippet creates a scatterplot where the points have a size and color that depends on the `size` variable. This can be useful to pack another numerical dimension into these kinds of plots:

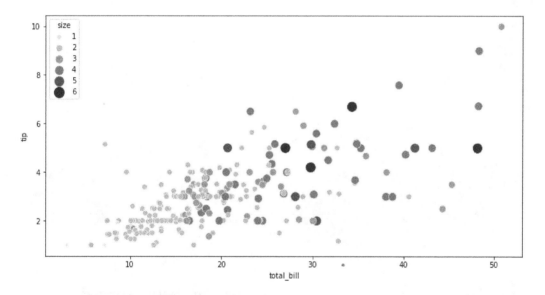

Figure 1.3: Seaborn scatterplot with size depending on a third variable

Another important way to represent data is by looking at time series information. We can use the Seaborn package to display time series data without the need to give the data any special treatment.

In the following example, we are creating a pandas DataFrame with dates, using Matplotlib to create a figure that's 15 x 8 inches, and then using the Seaborn `lineplot` function to display the information:

```
df = pd.DataFrame({"Dates":
['01/01/2019','01/02/2019','01/03/2019','01/04/2019',
'01/05/2019','01/06/2019','01/07/2019','01/08/2019'],
"Count": [727,716,668,710,718,732,694,755]})
plt.figure(figsize = (15,8))
sns.lineplot(x = 'Dates', y = 'Count',data = df)
```

The preceding example creates a wonderful plot with the dates on the *x* axis and the count variable on the *y* axis:

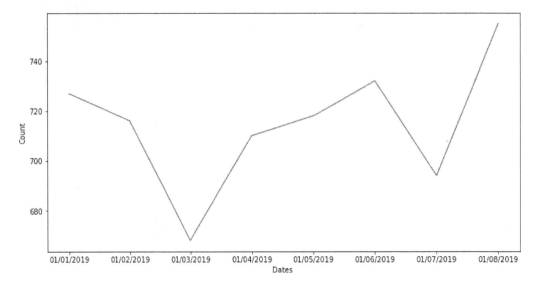

Figure 1.4: Seaborn line plot with a time-based axis

For the following example, we will load a pre-defined dataset from Seaborn known as the FMRI dataset, which contains time series data.

First, we will load an example dataset with long-form data and then plot the responses for different events and regions. To do this, we will create a 15 x 8 inches Matplotlib figure and use the `lineplot` function to show the information, using the `hue` parameter to display categorical information about the region, and the `style` parameter to show categorical information about the type of event:

```
fmri = sns.load_dataset("fmri")
f, ax = plt.subplots(figsize=(15, 8))
```

```
sns.lineplot(x="timepoint", y="signal", hue="region",
style="event",data=fmri)
```

The preceding code snippet creates a display of the information that allows us to study how the variables move through time according to the different categorical aspects of the data:

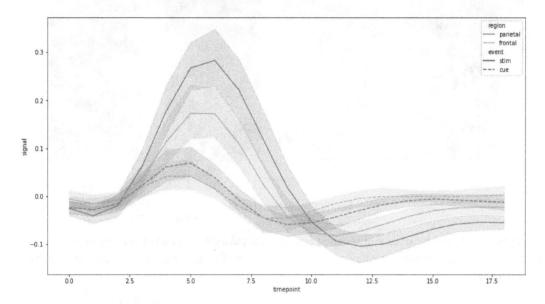

Figure 1.5: Seaborn line plot with confidence intervals

One of the features of the Seaborn `lineplot` function is that it shows us the confidence intervals of all points within a range of 95% confidence; the solid line represents the main. This way of showing us the information can be really useful when showing time series data that contains multiple data points for each point in time. Trends can be visualized by the mean as well as to give us a sense of the degree of dispersion, which is something that can be important when analyzing behavior patterns.

One of the ways we can visualize data is through bar plots. Seaborn uses the `barplot` function to create bar plots:

```
f, ax = plt.subplots(figsize=(12, 6))
ax = sns.barplot(x="day", y="total_bill", data=tips,ci=.9)
```

The preceding code uses Matplotlib to create a 12 x 6 inches figure where the Seaborn bar plot is created. Here, we will display the days on the *x* axis and the total bill on the *y* axis, showing the confidence bars as whiskers above the bars. The preceding code generates the following graph:

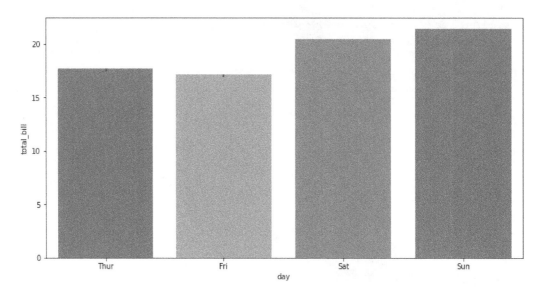

Figure 1.6: Seaborn bar plot

In the preceding graph, we cannot see the whiskers in detail as the data has a very small amount of dispersion. We can see this in better detail by drawing a set of vertical bars while grouping them by two variables:

```
f, ax = plt.subplots(figsize=(12, 6))
ax = sns.barplot(x="day", y="total_bill", hue="sex", data=tips)
```

The preceding code snippet creates a bar plot on a 12 x 6-inch Matplotlib figure. The difference is that we use the hue parameter to show gender differences:

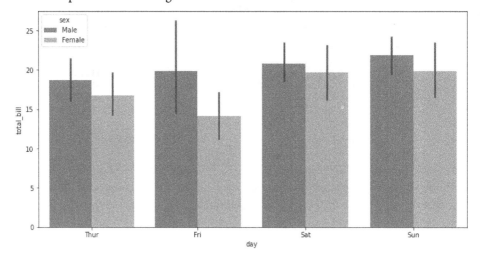

Figure 1.7: Seaborn bar plot with categorical data

One of the conclusions that can be extracted from this graph is that females get to have total bills that are lower than males on average, with Saturday being the only day when there's a difference between the means, though there's a much lower basepoint for the dispersion.

We can add another categorical dimension to the visualization using `catplot` to combine a `barplot` with a FacetGrid to create multiple plots. This allows us to group within additional categorical variables. Using `catplot` is safer than using FacetGrid to create multiple graphs as it ensures synchronization of variable order across different facets:

```
sns.catplot(x="sex", y="total_bill",hue="smoker",
col="time",data=tips, kind="bar",height=6, aspect=.7)
```

The preceding code snippet generates a categorical plot that contains the different bar plots. Note that the size of the graph is controlled using the `height` and `aspect` variables instead of via a Matplotlib figure:

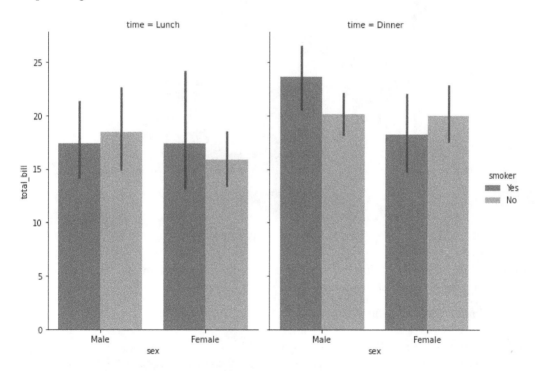

Figure 1.8: Seaborn bar plot with two categorical variables

Here, we can see an interesting trend during lunch, where the mean of the male smokers is lower than the non-smokers, while the female smoker's mean is higher than those of non-smokers. This tendency is inverted during dinner when there are more male smokers on average than female smokers.

Analyzing trends using histograms is a wonderful tool to be used while analyzing patterns. We can use them with the Searbon `hisplot` function. Here, we will use the `penguins` dataset and create a Matplotlib figure that's 12 x 6 inches:

```
penguins = sns.load_dataset("penguins")
f, ax = plt.subplots(figsize=(12, 6))
sns.histplot(data=penguins, x="flipper_length_mm", bins=30)
```

The preceding code creates a histogram of the flipper length grouping data in 30 bins:

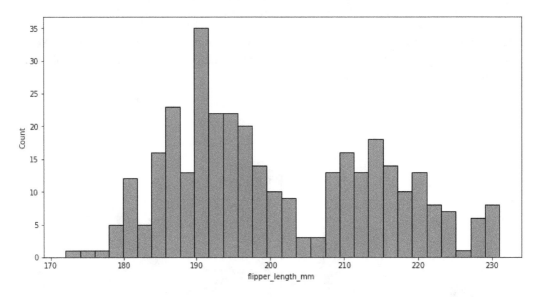

Figure 1.9: Seaborn histogram plot

Here, we can add a kernel density line estimate, which softens the histogram, providing more information about the shape of the data distribution.

The following code adds the `kde` parameter set to `True` to show this line:

```
f, ax = plt.subplots(figsize=(12, 6))
sns.histplot(data=penguins, x="flipper_length_mm", kde=True)
```

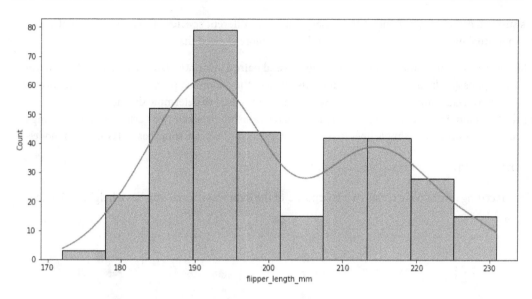

Figure 1.10: Seaborn histogram plot with KDE estimated density

Here, we can see that the data approaches some superimposed standard distribution, which can mean that we are looking at different kinds of data.

We can also add more dimensions to the graph by using the hue parameter on the categorical species variable:

```
f, ax = plt.subplots(figsize=(12, 6))
sns.histplot(data=penguins, x="flipper_length_mm",
hue="species")
```

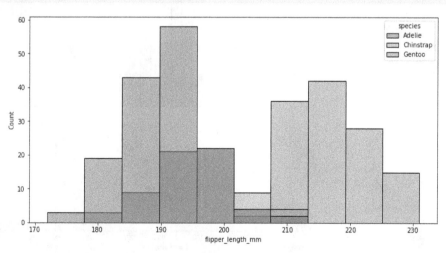

Figure 1.11: Seaborn histogram plot with categorical data

As suspected, we were looking at the superposition of different species of penguins, each of which has a normal distribution, though some of them are more skewed than others.

The `pairplot` function can be used to plot several paired bivariate distributions in a dataset. The diagonal plots are the univariate plots, and this displays the relationship for the (n, 2) combination of variables in a DataFrame as a matrix of plots. `pairplot` is used to determine the most distinct clusters or the best combination of features to explain the relationship between two variables. Constructing a linear separation or some simple lines in our dataset also helps to create some basic classification models:

```
sns.pairplot(penguins,height=3)
```

The preceding line of code creates a `pairplot` of the data where each box has a height of 3 inches:

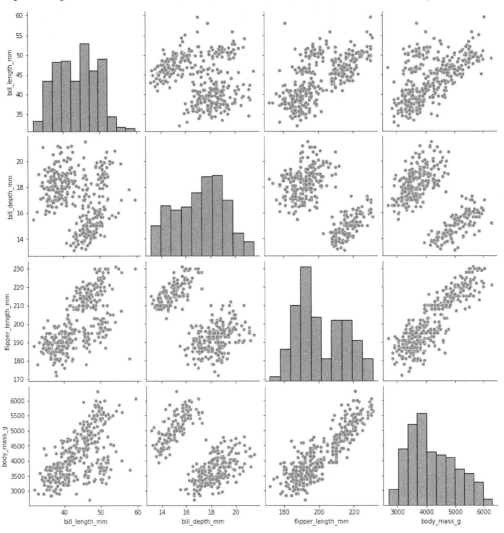

Figure 1.12: Variable relationship and histogram of selected features

The variable names are shown on the matrix's outer borders, making it easy to comprehend. The density plot for each variable is shown in the boxes along the diagonals. The scatterplot between each variable is displayed in the boxes in the lower left corner.

We can also use the hue parameter to add categorical dimensions to the visualization:

```
sns.pairplot(penguins, hue="species", diag_
kind="hist",height=3)
```

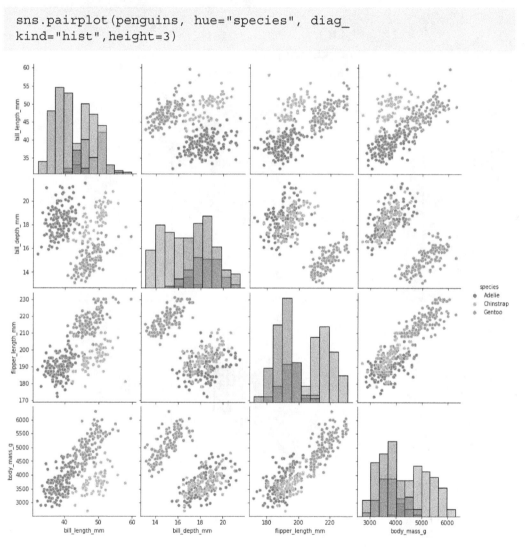

Figure 1.13: Variable relationship and histogram with categorical labels

Although incredibly useful, this graph can be very computationally expensive, which can be solved by looking only at some of the variables instead of the whole dataset.

We can reduce the time required to render the visualization by reducing the number of graphs shown. We can do this by specifying the types of variables we want to show in each axis, as shown in the following block of code:

```
sns.pairplot(
    penguins,
    x_vars=["bill_length_mm", "bill_depth_mm",
        "flipper_length_mm"],
    y_vars=["bill_length_mm", "bill_depth_mm"],
    height=3
)
```

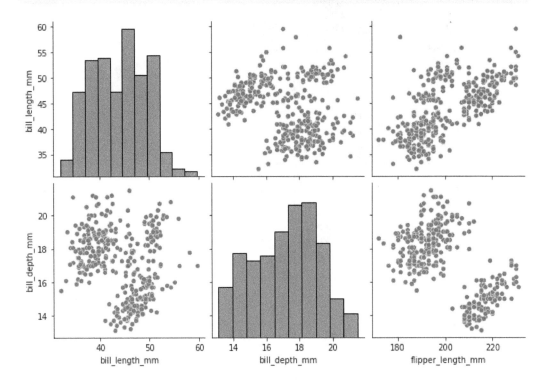

Figure 1.14: Variable relationship and histogram of selected features

A box plot, sometimes referred to as a box-and-whisker plot in descriptive statistics, is a type of chart that is frequently used in explanatory data analysis. Box plots use the data's quartiles (or percentiles) and averages to visually depict the distribution of numerical data and skewness.

We can use them in Seaborn using the `boxplot` function, as shown here:

```
f, ax = plt.subplots(figsize=(12, 6))
ax = sns.boxplot(x="day", y="total_bill", data=tips)
```

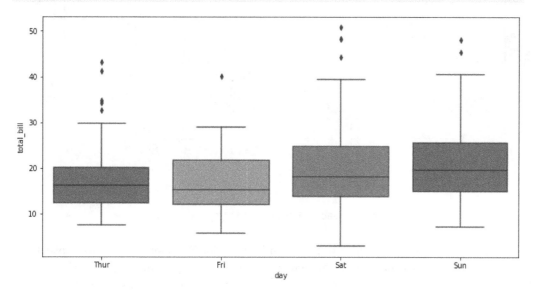

Figure 1.15: Seaborn box plot

The seaborn box plot has a very simple structure. Distributions are represented visually using box plots. When you want to compare data between two groups, they are helpful. A box plot may also be referred to as a box-and-whisker plot. Any box displays the dataset's quartiles, and the whiskers extend to display the remainder of the distribution.

Here, we can specify a type of categorical variable we might want to show using the hue parameter, as well as specify the palette of colors we want to use from Seaborn's default options:

```
f, ax = plt.subplots(figsize=(12, 6))
ax = sns.boxplot(x="day", y="total_bill",
hue="smoker",data=tips, palette="Set3")
```

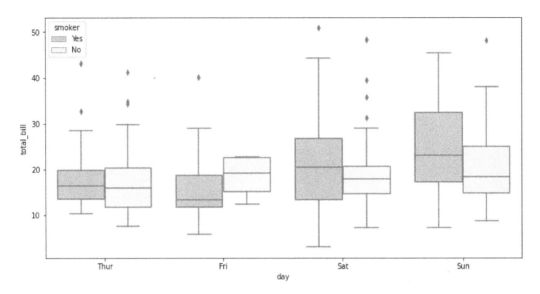

Figure 1.16: Seaborn box plot with categorical data

There is always the question of when you would use a box plot. Box plots are used to display the distributions of numerical data values, particularly when comparing them across various groups. They are designed to give high-level information at a glance and provide details like the symmetry, skew, variance, and outliers of a set of data.

Summary

In this chapter, we introduced the initial concepts of how we can store and manipulate data with pandas and NumPy, and how to visualize data patterns using Seaborn. These elements are used not only to explore the data but to be able to create visual narratives that allow us to understand patterns in the data and to be able to communicate simply and practically.

In the next chapter, we will build upon this to understand how machine learning and descriptive statistics can be used to validate hypotheses, study correlations and causations, as well as to make predictive models.

2

Using Machine Learning in Business Operations

Machine learning is an area of research focused on comprehending and developing "learning" processes, or processes that use data to enhance performance on a given set of tasks. It is considered to be a component of artificial intelligence. Among them, machine learning is a technology that enables companies to efficiently extract knowledge from unstructured data. With little to no programming, machine learning—and more precisely, machine learning algorithms—can be used to iteratively learn from a given dataset and comprehend patterns, behaviors, and so on.

In this chapter, we will learn how to do the following:

- Validate the difference of observed effects with statistical analysis
- Analyze the correlation and causation as well as model relationships between variables
- Prepare the data for clustering and machine learning models
- Develop machine learning models for regression and classification

Technical requirements

In order to be able to follow the steps in this chapter, you will need to meet the next requirements:

- Have a Jupyter notebook instance running Python 3.7 and above. You can use the Google Colab notebook to run the steps as well if you have a Google Drive account.
- Have an understanding of basic math and statistical concepts.
- Download the example datasets provided in the book's GitHub page, and the original source is `https://python.cogsci.nl/numerical/statistics/`.

Validating the effect of changes with the t-test

When measuring the effects of certain actions applied to a given population of users, we need to validate that these actions have actually affected the target groups in a significant manner. To be able to do this, we can use the t-test.

A t-test is a statistical test that is used to compare the means of two groups to ascertain whether a method or treatment has an impact on the population of interest or whether two groups differ from one another; it is frequently employed in hypothesis testing.

When the datasets in the two groups don't relate to identical values, separate t-test samples are chosen independently of one another. They might consist of two groups of randomly selected, unrelated patients to study the effects of a medication, for example. While the other group receives the prescribed treatment, one of the groups serves as the control group and is given a placebo. This results in two separate sample sets that are unpaired and unconnected from one another. Simply put, the t-test is employed to compare the means of two groups. It is frequently employed in hypothesis testing to establish whether a procedure or treatment truly affects the population of interest or whether two groups differ from one another.

The t-test is used in the context of businesses to compare two different means and determine whether they represent the exact same population, and it's especially useful in validating the effects of promotions applied in the uplift of sales. Additionally, it enables firms to comprehend the likelihood that their outcomes are the product of chance.

We will learn how to make an independent-samples t-test using the SciPy package and the Matzke et al. dataset (2015). Participants in this dataset underwent a memory challenge in which they had to recollect a list of words. One group of participants focused on a central fixation dot on a display during the retention interval. Another group of volunteers continuously moved their eyes horizontally, which some people think helps with memory.

To determine whether memory performance (`CriticalRecall`) was better for the horizontal eye movement group than the fixation group, we can utilize the `ttest_ind` function from the SciPy library:

```
from scipy.stats import ttest_ind
import pandas as pd
dm = pd.read_csv('matzke_et_al.csv')
dm_horizontal = dm[dm.Condition=='Horizontal']
dm_fixation = dm[dm.Condition=='Fixation']
t, p = ttest_ind(dm_horizontal.CriticalRecall, dm_fixation.
CriticalRecall)
print('t = {:.3f}, p = {:.3f}'.format(t, p))
```

t = -2.845, p = 0.007

Figure 2.1: T-test result

The test's p-value, which may be found on the output, is all you need to evaluate the t-test findings. Simply compare the output's p-value to the selected alpha level to conduct a hypothesis test at the desired alpha (significance) level:

```
import seaborn as sns
import matplotlib.pyplot as plt # visualization

sns.barplot(x='Condition', y='CriticalRecall', data=dm)
plt.xlabel('Condition')
plt.ylabel('Memory performance')
plt.show()
```

You can reject the null hypothesis if the p-value is less than your threshold for significance (for example, 0.05). The two means' difference is statistically significant. The data from your sample is convincing enough to support the conclusion that the two population means are not equal:

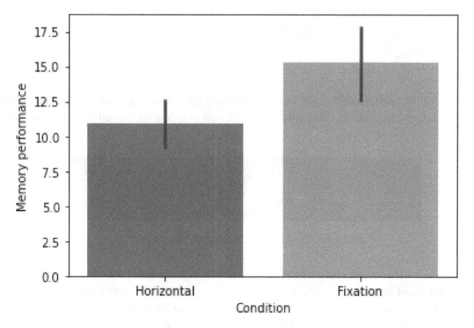

Figure 2.2: Population distribution

A high t-score, also known as a t-value, denotes that the groups are distinct, whereas a low t-score denotes similarity. Degrees of freedom, or the values in a study that can fluctuate, are crucial for determining the significance and veracity of the null hypothesis.

In our example, the results indicate a noteworthy difference (p =.0066). The fixation group, however, outperformed the other groups, where the effect is in the opposite direction from what was anticipated.

Another way to test the difference between two populations is using the paired-samples t-test, which compares a single group's means for two variables. To determine whether the average deviates from 0, the process computes the differences between the values of the two variables for each occurrence. The means of two independent or unrelated groups are compared using an unpaired t-test. An unpaired t-test makes the assumption that the variance in the groups is equal. The variance is not expected to be equal in a paired t-test. The process also automates the calculation of the t-test effect size. The paired t-test is used when data are in the form of matched pairs, while the two-sample t-test is used when data from two samples are statistically independent.

Let's use the Moore, McCabe, and Craig datasets. Here, aggressive conduct in dementia patients was assessed during the full moon and another lunar phase. This was a within-subject design because measurements were taken from every participant at both times.

You can use the `ttest_rel` SciPy function to test whether aggression differed between the full moon and the other lunar phase:

```python
from scipy.stats import ttest_rel
dm = pd.read_csv('moon-aggression.csv')
t, p = ttest_rel(dm.Moon, dm.Other)
print('t = {:.3f}, p = {:.3f}'.format(t, p))
```

As you can see in the figure below, there was an interesting effect that was substantial, as the p values are never 0 as the output implies. This effect was such that people were indeed most violent during full moons:

```
print('t = {:.3f}, p = {:.3f}'.format(t, p))

t = 6.452, p = 0.000
```

Figure 2.3: T-test result of the aggression dataset

Another way in which we can compare the difference between two groups is the statistical method known as **analysis of variance (ANOVA)**, which is used to examine how different means differ from one another. Ronald Fisher created this statistical test in 1918, and it has been in use ever since. Simply put, an ANOVA analysis determines whether the means of three or more independent groups differ statistically. So does ANOVA replace the t-test, then? Not really. ANOVA is used to compare the means among three or more groups, while the t-test is used to compare the means between two groups.

When employed in a business setting, ANOVA can be used to manage budgets by, for instance, comparing your budget against costs to manage revenue and inventories. ANOVA can also be used to manage budgets by, for instance, comparing your budget against costs to manage revenue and inventories. For example, in order to better understand how sales will perform in the future, ANOVA can also be used to forecast trends by examining data patterns. When assessing the multi-item scales used frequently in market research, ANOVA is especially helpful. Using ANOVA might assist you as a market researcher in comprehending how various groups react. You can start the test by accepting the null hypothesis, or that the means of all the groups that were observed are equal.

For our next example, let's revisit the heart rate information provided by Moore, McCabe, and Craig. Gender and group are two subject-specific factors in this dataset, along with one dependent variable (heart rate). You need the following code to see if gender, group, or their interactions have an impact on heart rate.

We will use a combination of **ordinary least squares** (**OLS**) and an ANOVA test (anova_lm), which isn't very elegant, but the important part is the formula:

```
from statsmodels.stats.anova import anova_lm
dm = pd.read_csv('heartrate.csv')
dm = dm.rename({'Heart Rate':'HeartRate'},axis=1)   #
statsmodels doesn't like spaces
df = anova_lm(ols('HeartRate ~ Gender * Group', data=dm).fit())
print(df)
```

The results show us that heart rate is related to all factors: gender (F = 185.980, p < .001), group (F = 695.647, p < .001), and the gender-by-group interaction (F = 7.409, p = .006).

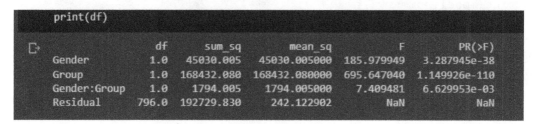

Figure 2.4: ANOVA test results

Now that we have validated that there is in fact difference between multiple groups, we can start to model these relationships.

Modeling relationships with multiple linear regression

The statistical method known as multiple linear regression employs two or more independent variables to forecast the results of a dependent variable. Using this method, analysts may calculate the model's variance and the relative contributions of each independent variable to the overall variance. Regressions involving numerous explanatory variables, both linear and nonlinear, fall under the category of multiple regression.

The purpose of multiple regression analysis is so that researchers can evaluate the strength of the relationship between an outcome (the dependent variable) and a number of predictor variables, as well as the significance of each predictor to the relationship using multiple regression analysis frequently with the effect of other predictors statistically eliminated.

Multiple regression includes multiple independent variables, whereas linear regression only takes into account one independent variable to affect the relationship's slope.

Businesses can use linear regressions to analyze trends and generate estimates or forecasts. For instance, if a firm's sales have been rising gradually each month for the previous several years, the corporation may anticipate sales in the months to come by doing a linear analysis of the sales data with monthly sales.

Let's use the dataset from Moore, McCabe, and Craig, which contains grade point averages and SAT scores for mathematics and verbal knowledge for high-school students. We can use the following code to test whether satm and satv are (uniquely) related to gpa.

We will use the OLS SciPy function to evaluate this relationship, which is passed as a combination of the variables in question, and then fitted to the data:

```
from statsmodels.formula.api import ols
dm = pd.read_csv('gpa.csv')
model = ols('gpa ~ satm + satv', data=dm).fit()
print(model.summary())
```

```
                          OLS Regression Results
================================================================================
Dep. Variable:                  gpa    R-squared:                       0.063
Model:                          OLS    Adj. R-squared:                  0.055
Method:               Least Squares    F-statistic:                     7.476
Date:              Mon, 05 Sep 2022    Prob (F-statistic):           0.000722
Time:                      14:06:57    Log-Likelihood:                 -254.18
No. Observations:               224    AIC:                             514.4
Df Residuals:                   221    BIC:                             524.6
Df Model:                         2
Covariance Type:            nonrobust
================================================================================
                 coef    std err          t      P>|t|      [0.025      0.975]
--------------------------------------------------------------------------------
Intercept      1.2887      0.376      3.427      0.001       0.548       2.030
satm           0.0023      0.001      3.444      0.001       0.001       0.004
satv       -2.456e-05      0.001     -0.040      0.968      -0.001       0.001
================================================================================
Omnibus:                     23.688    Durbin-Watson:                   1.715
Prob(Omnibus):                0.000    Jarque-Bera (JB):               27.838
Skew:                        -0.809    Prob(JB):                     9.02e-07
Kurtosis:                     3.601    Cond. No.                     5.85e+03
================================================================================

Notes:
[1] Standard Errors assume that the covariance matrix of the errors is correctly specified.
[2] The condition number is large, 5.85e+03. This might indicate that there are
strong multicollinearity or other numerical problems.
```

Figure 2.5: OLS results

The result shows us that only SAT scores for mathematics, but not for verbal knowledge, are uniquely related to the grade point average.

In the next section, we will look at the concepts of correlation, which is when variables behave in a similar manner, and causation, which is when a variable affects another one.

Establishing correlation and causation

The statistical measure known as correlation expresses how closely two variables are related linearly, which can be understood graphically as how close two curves overlap. It's a typical technique for describing straightforward connections without explicitly stating cause and consequence.

The correlation matrix displays the correlation values, which quantify how closely each pair of variables is related linearly. The correlation coefficients have a range of -1 to +1. The correlation value is positive if the two variables tend to rise and fall together.

The four types of correlations that are typically measured in statistics are the Spearman correlation, Pearson correlation, Kendall rank correlation, and the point-biserial correlation.

In order for organizations to make data-driven decisions based on forecasting the result of events, correlation and regression analysis are used to foresee future outcomes. The two main advantages of correlation analysis are that it enables quick hypothesis testing and assists businesses in deciding which variables they wish to look into further. To determine the strength of the linear relationship between two variables, the primary type of correlation analysis applies Pearson's r formula.

Using the `corr` method in a pandas data frame, we can calculate the pairwise correlation of columns while removing NA/null values. The technique can be passed as a parameter with the `pearson` or `kendall` values for the standard correlation coefficient, `spearman` for the Spearman rank correlation, or `kendall` for the Kendall Tau correlation coefficient.

The `corr` method in a pandas data frame returns a matrix of floats from 1 along the diagonals and symmetric regardless of the callable's behavior:

```
import numpy as np
import pandas as pd
df = pd.DataFrame([(.2, .3,.8), (.0, .6,.9), (.6, .0,.4),
(.2, .1,.9),(.1, .3,.7), (.1, .5,.6), (.7, .1,.5), (.3,
.0,.8),],columns=['dogs', 'cats','birds'])
corr_mat = df.corr()
```

We can plot the results correlation matrix using a seaborn heatmap:

```
import seaborn as sn
sn.heatmap(corr_mat, annot=True)
```

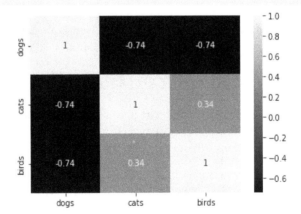

Figure 2.6: Correlation matrix

Finding groups of highly correlated features and only maintaining one of them is the main goal of employing pairwise correlation for feature selection, which aims to maximize the predictive value of your model by using the fewest number of features possible.

Pairwise correlation is calculated between rows or columns of a DataFrame and rows or columns of a Series or DataFrame. The correlations are calculated after DataFrames have been aligned along both axes. Next, we can see an example that might make it more clear:

```
df1=pd.DataFrame( np.random.randn(3,2), columns=['a','b'] )
df2=pd.DataFrame( np.random.randn(3,2), columns=['a','b'] )
```

Use `corr` to compare numerical columns within the same data frame. Non-numerical columns will automatically be skipped:

```
corr_mat = df1.corr()
sn.heatmap(corr_mat, annot=True)
plt.show()
```

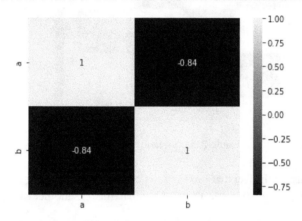

Figure 2.7: Correlation matrix

We can also compare the columns of `df1` and `df2` with `corrwith`. Note that only columns with the same names are compared:

```
df1.corrwith(df2)
```

To make things easier, we can rename the columns of `df2` to match the columns of `df1` if we would like for pandas to disregard the column names and only compare the first row of `df1` to the first row of `df2`:

```
df1.corrwith(df2.set_axis( df1.columns, axis='columns',
inplace=False))
```

It's important to note that `df1` and `df2` need to have the same number of columns in that case.

Last but not least, you could also just horizontally combine the two datasets and utilize `corr`. The benefit is that this essentially functions independently of the quantity and naming conventions of the columns, but the drawback is that you can receive more output than you require or want:

```
corr_mat = pd.concat([df1,df2],axis=1).corr()
sn.heatmap(corr_mat, annot=True)
plt.show()
```

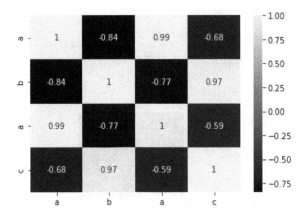

Figure 2.8: Correlation heatmap

Now that we have established the fact that two variables can be correlated using correlation analysis, we can seek to validate whether the variables are actually impacting one another using causation analysis.

The ability of one variable to impact another is known as causality. The first variable might create the second or might change the incidence of the second variable.

Causality is the process by which one event, process, state, or object influences the development of another event, process, condition, or object, where the cause and effect are both partially reliant on each other. So what distinguishes correlation from causation? Correlation does not automatically imply causation, even if causality and correlation might coexist. In situations where action A results in outcome B, causation is expressly applicable. Correlation, on the other hand, is just a relationship.

We can use the next dataset to study the causation between variables:

```
import numpy as np
import pandas as pd
import random
ds = pd.DataFrame(columns = ['x','y'])
ds['x'] = [int(n>500) for n in random.sample(range(0, 1000),
```

```
        100)]
ds['y'] = [int(n>500) for n in random.sample(range(0, 1000),
        100)]
ds.head()
```

To study the causation, we can seek to estimate the difference in means between two groups. The absolute difference between the mean values in two different groups is measured by the mean difference, often known as the difference in means. It offers you a sense of how much the averages of the experimental group and control groups differ from one another in clinical studies.

In the next example, we will estimate the uplift as a quantified difference in means along with the determined standard error. We will use 90 as the confidence interval in the range of the normal, which yields a z-score of 1.96:

```
base,var  = ds[ds.x == 0], ds[ds.x == 1]
delta = var.y.mean() - base.y.mean()
delta_dev = 1.96 * np.sqrt(var.y.var() / var.shape[0]
        +base.y.var() / base.shape[0])
print("estimated_effect":,delta, "standard_error": delta_dev)
```

```
{'estimated_effect': -0.02101723413198825, 'standard_error': 0.20312418042730232}
```

Figure 2.9: Estimated differences between populations

We can also use the contingency chi-square for the comparison of two groups with a dichotomous dependent variable. For example, we might contrast males and females using a yes/no response scale. The contingency chi-square is built on the same ideas as the straightforward chi-square analysis, which compares the anticipated and actual outcomes.

This statistical technique is used to compare actual outcomes with predictions. The goal of this test is to establish whether a discrepancy between observed and expected data is the result of chance or a correlation between the variables you are researching. The results create a contingency matrix from which we can infer that your variables are independent of one another and have no association with one another if C is close to zero (or equal to zero). There is a relationship if C is not zero; C can only take on positive values:

```
from scipy.stats import chi2_contingency
contingency_table = (
        ds
        .assign(placeholder=1)
```

```
        .pivot_table(index="x", columns="y",
            values="placeholder", aggfunc="sum")
        .values)
_, p, _, _ = chi2_contingency(contingency_table,
    lambda_="log-likelihood")
```

Here, we will just seek to interpret the p-values:

```
print("P-value:",p)
```

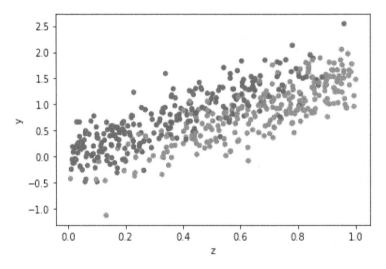

Figure 2.10: Resulting p-value

Now we will use a set of datasets that were synthetically generated:

```
data_1 = pd.read_csv('observed_data_1.csv' )
data_1.plot.scatter(x="z", y="y", c="x", cmap="rainbow",
colorbar=False)
```

Figure 2.11: Plot of data distribution

The probability density function of a continuous random variable can be estimated using the **kernel density estimation** (**KDE**) seaborn method. The area under the depicted curve serves as a representation of the probability distribution of the data values:

```
import seaborn as sns
sns.kdeplot(data_1.loc[lambda df: df.x == 0].y,
label="untreated")
sns.kdeplot(data_1.loc[lambda df: df.x == 1].y,
label="treated")
```

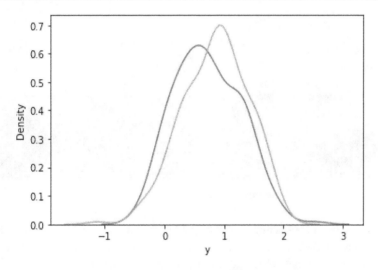

Figure 2.12: Density graph

To study causation, the researcher must build a model to describe the connections between ideas connected to a particular phenomenon in causal modeling.

Multiple causality—the idea that any given outcome may have more than one cause—is incorporated into causal models. For instance, social status, age, sex, ethnicity, and other factors may influence someone's voting behavior. In addition, some of the independent or explanatory factors might be connected.

External validity can be addressed using causal models (whether results from one study apply to unstudied populations). In some cases, causal models can combine data to provide answers to questions that no single dataset alone is able to address.

We can use the `est_via_ols` function of the `causalinference` package to estimate average treatment effects using least squares.

Here, *y* is the potential outcome when treated, D is the treatment status, and X is a vector of covariates or individual characteristics.

The parameter to control is adj, an int which can be either 0, 1, or 2. This parameter indicates how covariate adjustments are to be performed. Setting adj to 0 will not include any covariates. Set adj to 1 to include treatment indicator D and covariates X separately, or set adj to 2 to additionally include interaction terms between D and X. The default is 2.

```
!pip install causalinference
from causalinference import CausalModel
cm = CausalModel(
    Y=data_1.y.values,
    D=data_1.x.values,
    X=data_1.z.values)
cm.est_via_ols(adj=1)
print(cm.estimates)
```

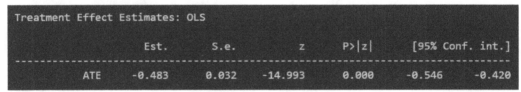

Treatment Effect Estimates: OLS

	Est.	S.e.	z	P>|z|	[95% Conf. int.]	
ATE	-0.483	0.032	-14.993	0.000	-0.546	-0.420

Figure 2.13: Causal model results

The estimates show us that there is a negative relationship between the variables. The negative estimate might be an indication that the application of D reduces the probability of Y by 48%. It's really important to look at the entire set of estimate distributions to draw any conclusions.

The analysis of a hypothetical or counterfactual reality is causal analysis, because we must make claims about the counterfactual result that we did not witness in order to assess the treatment effect:

```
data_2 = pd.read_csv('observed_data_2.csv')
data_2.plot.scatter(x="z", y="y", c="x", cmap="rainbow",
colorbar=False)
```

The data previously loaded will show us different values in the causal model:

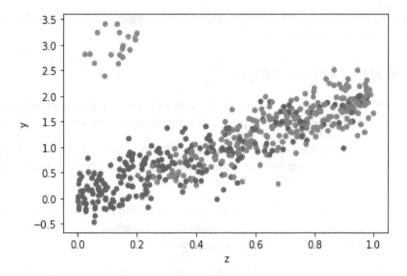

Figure 2.14: Data distribution

We will build the new causal model using the new loaded values:

```
cm = CausalModel(
    Y=data_2 .y.values,
    D=data_2 .x.values,
    X=data_2 .z.values)
cm.est_via_ols(adj=1)
```

We can print the treatment effect estimates to validate whether our causal model is valid:

```
print(cm.estimates)
```

```
Treatment Effect Estimates: OLS

                Est.        S.e.           z        P>|z|      [95% Conf. int.]
--------------------------------------------------------------------------------
        ATE    0.472       0.090       5.236        0.000       0.295       0.648
```

Figure 2.15: Causal model results with new data

The estimates inform us that the relationship has become positive.

Causal models are a great way to validate the modeling and direction of relationships between the variables in data.

In the next section, we will dive into how we can use scaling to prepare our data for machine learning, depending on the distribution that it has.

Scaling features to a range

When working with machine learning models, it is important to preprocess data so certain problems such as an explosion of gradients or lack of proper distribution representation can be solved.

To transform raw feature vectors into a representation that is better suited for the downstream estimators, the `sklearn.preprocessing` package offers a number of common utility functions and transformer classes.

Many machine learning estimators used in `scikit-learn` frequently require dataset standardization; if the individual features do not more or less resemble standard normally distributed data, they may behave poorly: Gaussian with a mean of 0 and a variation of 1.

In general, standardizing the dataset is advantageous for learning algorithms. Robust scalers or transformers are preferable if there are any outliers in the collection. On a dataset with marginal outliers, the actions of several scalers, transformers, and normalizers are highlighted in the analysis of the impact of various scalers on data containing outliers.

In reality, we frequently ignore the distribution's shape and simply adapt the data to scale by dividing non-constant features by their standard deviation and centering it by subtracting each feature's mean value.

For instance, several components of a learning algorithm's objective function (such as the RBF kernel of SVMs or the l1 and l2 regularizers of linear models) may make the assumption that all features are centered around zero or have variance in the same order. A feature may dominate the objective function and prevent the estimator from successfully inferring from other features as expected if its variance is orders of magnitude greater than that of other features.

The `StandardScaler` utility class, which the preprocessing module offers, makes it quick and simple to carry out the following operation on an array-like dataset:

```
from sklearn import preprocessing
x_train = pd.DataFrame([[ 1., -1.,  2.],
                        [ 2.,  0.,  0.],
                        [ 0.,  1., -1.]],columns=['x','y','z'])
scaler = preprocessing.StandardScaler().fit(x_train)
```

The following code will fit the scaler to the data, assuming that our distribution is standard:

```
scaler.mean_
```

We can visualize now the mean of the data:

```
array([0.81649658, 0.81649658, 1.24721913])
```

Figure 2.16: Mean of the data

We can visualize the scale as well:

```
scaler.scale_
```

The data is shown as an array of values:

```
array([0.81649658, 0.81649658, 1.24721913])
```

Figure 2.17: Scale of the columns

Finally, we can scale the data using the `transform` method:

```
x_scaled = scaler.transform(x_train)
```

A different method of standardization is to scale each feature's maximum absolute value to one unit, or to a value between a predetermined minimum and maximum value, usually zero and one. `MaxAbsScaler` or `MinMaxScaler` can be used to do this.

The robustness to very small standard deviations of features and the preservation of zero entries in sparse data are two reasons to employ this scaling.

To scale a toy data matrix to the [0, 1] range, consider the following example:

```
min_max_scaler = preprocessing.MinMaxScaler()
x_train_minmax = min_max_scaler.fit_transform(x_train)
```

In case our distribution differs from the standard Gaussian, we can use non-linear transformations. There are two different kinds of transformations: power and quantile transform. The rank of the values along each feature is preserved by both quantile and power transforms because they are based on monotonic transformations of the features.

Based on the formula, which is the cumulative distribution function of the feature and the quantile function of the desired output distribution, quantile transformations place all features into the same desired distribution. These two facts are used in this formula: it is uniformly distributed if it is a random variable with a continuous cumulative distribution function, and it has distribution if it is a random variable with a uniform distribution on. A quantile transform smoothes out atypical distributions using a rank transformation and is less susceptible to outliers than scaling techniques. Correlations and distances within and between features are, however, distorted by it.

Sklearn provides a series of parametric transformations called power transforms that aim to translate data from any distribution to one that resembles a Gaussian distribution as closely as possible.

We can map our data to a uniform distribution using `QuantileTransformer`, which provides a non-parametric transformation to map the data to a uniform distribution with values between 0 and 1:

```
from sklearn.datasets import load_iris
data = load_iris()
x, y = data['data'],data['target']
quantile_transformer = preprocessing.QuantileTransformer(
n_quantiles=5)
x_train_qt = quantile_transformer.fit_transform(x)
x_train_qt[:5]
```

We can see the resulting array:

```
array([[0.25      , 0.79545455, 0.16666667, 0.125     ],
       [0.1875    , 0.5       , 0.16666667, 0.125     ],
       [0.125     , 0.66666667, 0.125     , 0.125     ],
       [0.09375   , 0.58333333, 0.20833333, 0.125     ],
       [0.21875   , 0.81818182, 0.16666667, 0.125     ]])
```

Figure 2.18: Transformed data

It is also possible to map data to a normal distribution using `QuantileTransformer` by setting `output_distribution='normal'`. The following example uses the earlier example with the `iris` dataset:

```
quantile_transformer = preprocessing.QuantileTransformer(
n_quantiles=5,output_distribution='normal')
x_trans_qt = quantile_transformer.fit_transform(x)
quantile_transformer.quantiles_
```

```
array([[4.3 , 2.  , 1.  , 0.1 ],
       [5.1 , 2.8 , 1.6 , 0.3 ],
       [5.8 , 3.  , 4.35, 1.3 ],
       [6.4 , 3.3 , 5.1 , 1.8 ],
       [7.9 , 4.4 , 6.9 , 2.5 ]])
```

Figure 2.19: Transformed data through the quantiles method

The preceding code will scale the data using a quantile transformation, defining five quantiles and looking to have a normal distribution in the output.

To determine the proper distribution to be utilized, we need to analyze in depth the distribution of our variables, as the wrong transformation can make us lose details that might be important to take into account.

In the next section, we will dive into unsupervised learning by looking at clustering algorithms using scikit-learn.

Clustering data and reducing the dimensionality

The process of clustering involves grouping the population or data points into a number of groups so that the data points within each group are more similar to one another than the data points within other groups. Simply said, the goal is to sort any groups of people who share similar characteristics into clusters. It is frequently used in business analytics. How to arrange the enormous volumes of available data into useful structures is one of the issues that organizations are currently confronting.

Image segmentation, grouping web pages, market segmentation, and information retrieval are four examples of how clustering can help firms better manage their data. Data clustering is beneficial for retail firms since it influences sales efforts, customer retention, and customer shopping behavior.

The goal of the vector quantization technique known as "K-means clustering," which has its roots in signal processing, is to divide a set of n observations into k clusters, each of which has as its prototype in the observation with the closest mean. K-means clustering is an unsupervised technique that uses the input data as is and doesn't require a labeled response. A popular method for clustering is K-means clustering. Typically, practitioners start by studying the dataset's architecture. Data points are grouped by K-means into distinct, non-overlapping groups.

In the next code, we can use KMeans to fit the data in order to label each data point to a given cluster:

```
from sklearn.cluster import KMeans
kmeans = KMeans(n_clusters=len(set(y)), random_state=0).fit(x)
kmeans.labels_
```

```
array([1, 1, 1, 1, 1, 1, 1, 1, 1, 1, 1, 1, 1, 1, 1, 1, 1, 1, 1, 1, 1,
       1, 1, 1, 1, 1, 1, 1, 1, 1, 1, 1, 1, 1, 1, 1, 1, 1, 1, 1, 1, 1,
       1, 1, 1, 1, 1, 1, 0, 0, 2, 0, 0, 0, 0, 0, 0, 0, 0, 0, 0, 0, 0, 0,
       0, 0, 0, 0, 0, 0, 0, 0, 0, 0, 0, 2, 0, 0, 0, 0, 0, 0, 0, 0, 0, 0,
       0, 0, 0, 0, 0, 0, 0, 0, 0, 0, 0, 2, 0, 2, 2, 2, 2, 0, 2, 2, 2,
       2, 2, 2, 0, 0, 2, 2, 2, 2, 0, 2, 0, 2, 0, 2, 2, 0, 0, 2, 2, 2, 2,
       2, 0, 2, 2, 2, 2, 0, 2, 2, 2, 0, 2, 2, 2, 0, 2, 2, 0], dtype=int32)
```

Figure 2.20: Cluster data

We can predict to which cluster each new instance of data belongs:

```
kmeans.predict(x[0].reshape(1,-1))
```

```
array([1], dtype=int32)
```

Figure 2.21: Predicted data

We can also visualize the cluster centers:

```
kmeans.cluster_centers_
```

```
array([[5.9016129 , 2.7483871 , 4.39354839, 1.43387097],
       [5.006      , 3.428      , 1.462      , 0.246      ],
       [6.85       , 3.07368421, 5.74210526, 2.07105263]])
```

Figure 2.22: Cluster centers

KMeans allows us to find the characteristics in common data when the number of variables is too high and it's useful for segmentation. But sometimes, there is the need to reduce the number of dimensions to a set of grouped variables with common traits.

In order to project the data into a lower dimensional environment, we can use **principal component analysis (PCA)**, a linear dimensionality reduction technique. Before using the SVD, the input data is scaled but not centered for each feature. Depending on the structure of the input data and the number of components to be extracted, it employs either a randomized truncated SVD or the complete SVD implementation as implemented by LAPACK. You should be aware that this class does not accept sparse input. For a sparse data alternative, use the TruncatedSVD class.

Up next, we fit data into two components in order to reduce the dimensionality:

```
from sklearn.decomposition import PCA
pca = PCA(n_components=2)
pca.fit(x)
```

We should strive to account for the maximum amount of variance possible, which in simple terms can be understood as the degree to which our model can explain the whole dataset:

```
print(pca.explained_variance_ratio_)
print(pca.singular_values_)
```

```
[0.92461872 0.05306648]
[25.09996044  6.01314738]
```

Figure 2.23: PCA singular values

After we have worked our data to preprocess it, reducing the number of dimensions and clustering, we can now build machine learning models to make predictions of future behavior.

In the next section, we will build machine learning models that we can use to predict new data labels for regression and classification tasks.

Building machine learning models

One of the most simple machine learning models we can construct to make a forecast of future behaviors is linear regression, which reduces the residual sum of squares between the targets observed in the dataset and the targets anticipated by the linear approximation, fitting a linear model using coefficients.

This is simply ordinary least squares or non-negative least squares wrapped in a predictor object from the implementation perspective.

We can implement this really simply by using the `LinearRegression` class in Sklearn:

```python
from sklearn.linear_model import LinearRegression
from sklearn.datasets import load_diabetes
data_reg = load_diabetes()
x,y = data_reg['data'],data_reg['target']
reg = LinearRegression().fit(x, y)
reg.score(x, y)
```

```
0.5177494254132934
```

Figure 2.24: Model regression score

The preceding code will fit a linear regression model to our data and print the score of our data.

We can also print the coefficients, which give us a great estimation of the contribution of each variable to explain the variable we are trying to predict:

```python
reg.coef_
```

```
array([ -10.01219782, -239.81908937, 519.83978679, 324.39042769,
        -792.18416163, 476.74583782, 101.04457032, 177.06417623,
         751.27932109,  67.62538639])
```

Figure 2.25: Regression coefficients

We can also print the intercept variables:

```
reg.intercept_
```

```
152.1334841628965
```

Figure 2.26: Regression intercepts

Finally, we can use the model to make predictions:

```
print('Predicted:',reg.predict(x[10].reshape(
1,-1)),'Actual:',y[10])
```

```
[66] print('Predicted:',reg.predict(x[10].reshape(1,-1)),'Actual:',y[10])

     Predicted: [97.07853583] Actual: 101.0
```

Figure 2.27: Predicted regression values

Here we are predicting a continuous variable, but we can also predict categorical variables using a classifier instead of a regression.

Sklearn gives us the option of using the logistic regression (logit and MaxEnt) classifier, in which in the multiclass case, the training algorithm uses the one-vs-rest (OvR) scheme if the 'multi_class' option is set to 'ovr' and uses the cross-entropy loss if the 'multi_class' option is set to 'multinomial'. This class uses the 'liblinear' library, 'newton-cg', 'sag', 'saga', and the 'lbfgs' solvers to implement regularized logistic regression. Keep in mind that regularization is used by default. Both dense and sparse input can be handled by it. For best speed, only use matrices with 64-bit floats; all other input formats will be transformed.

The sole regularization supported by the "newton-cg," "sag," and "lbfgs" solvers is the L2 regularization with the primal formulation. The "liblinear" solver supports both the L1 and L2 regularizations, however, only the L2 penalty has a dual formulation. The only solver that supports the elastic net regularization is the "saga" solver.

When fitting the model, the underlying C program chooses features using a random number generator. Thus, slightly varied outputs for the same input data are common. Try using a smaller `tol` parameter if it occurs:

```
from sklearn.pipeline import make_pipeline
from sklearn.preprocessing import StandardScaler
from sklearn.linear_model import LogisticRegression
from sklearn.datasets import load_digits

data_class = load_digits()
x,y = data_class['data'],data_class['target']
clf = make_pipeline(StandardScaler(),
    LogisticRegression(penalty='l2',C=.1))
clf.fit(x, y)
clf.predict(x[:2, :])
```

```
array([0, 1])
```

Figure 2.28: Logistic regression results

We can also score the model to assess the precision of our predictions:

```
clf.score(x, y)
```

```
0.988313856427379
```

Figure 2.29: User data

In order to validate the model, we can use cross-validation, which allows us to evaluate the estimator's performance. This is a methodological error in learning the parameters of a prediction function and evaluating it on the same set of data. A model that simply repeats the labels of the samples it has just seen would score well but be unable to make any predictions about data that has not yet been seen. Overfitting is the term for this circumstance. It is customary to reserve a portion of the available data as a test set (x test, y test) when conducting a (supervised) machine learning experiment in order to avoid this problem.

It should be noted that the term "experiment" does not just refer to academic purposes because machine learning experiments sometimes begin in commercial contexts as well. Grid search methods can be used to find the optimal parameters.

In `scikit-learn`, a random split into training and test sets can be quickly computed with the `train_test_split` helper function. Let's load the `iris` dataset to fit a linear support vector machine on it:

```
x, y = load_iris(return_X_y=True)
x.shape, y.shape
```

```
((150, 4), (150,))
```

Figure 2.30: Data shape

We can now quickly sample a training set while holding out 40% of the data for testing (evaluating) our classifier:

```
from sklearn.model_selection import train_test_split
from sklearn import svm
x_train, x_test, y_train, y_test = train_test_split(x, y,
test_size=0.4, random_state=0)
```

We can validate the shape of the generated train dataset by looking at the numpy array shape:

```
x_train.shape, y_train.shape
```

```
((90, 4), (90,))
```

Figure 2.31: Train data shape

We can repeat the same with the `test` dataset:

```
x_test.shape, y_test.shape
```

```
((60, 4), (60,))
```

Figure 2.32: Test data shape

Finally, we can train our machine learning model on the training data and score it using the `test` dataset, which holds data points not seen by the model during training:

```
clf = svm.SVC(kernel='linear', C=.7).fit(x_train, y_train)
clf.score(x_test, y_test)
```

Figure 2.33: Logistic regression scores

There is still a chance of overfitting on the test set when comparing various settings of hyperparameters for estimators, such as the C setting that must be manually selected for an SVM. This is because the parameters can be adjusted until the estimator performs at its best. In this method, the model may "leak" information about the test set, and evaluation measures may no longer reflect generalization performance. This issue can be resolved by holding out a further portion of the dataset as a "validation set": training is conducted on the training set, followed by evaluation on the validation set, and when it appears that the experiment has succeeded, a final evaluation can be conducted on the test set.

However, by dividing the available data into three sets, we dramatically cut down on the number of samples that can be used to train the model, and the outcomes can vary depending on the randomization of the pair of (train and validation) sets.

Cross-validation is an approach that can be used to address this issue (CV for short). When doing CV, the validation set is no longer required, but a test set should still be kept aside for final assessment. The fundamental strategy, known as a k-fold CV, divides the training set into k smaller sets (other approaches are described below, but generally follow the same principles). Every single one of the k "folds" is done as follows:

The folds are used as training data for a model, and the resulting model is validated using the remaining portion of the data (as in, it is used as a test set to compute a performance measure such as accuracy).

The average of the numbers calculated in the loop is then the performance indicator supplied by k-fold cross-validation. Although this method can be computationally expensive, it does not waste a lot of data (unlike fixing an arbitrary validation set), which is a significant benefit in applications such as inverse inference where there are few samples.

We can compute the cross-validated metrics by calling the `cross_val` score helper function on the estimator and the dataset is the simplest approach to apply cross-validation. The example that follows shows how to split the data, develop a model, and calculate the score five times in a row (using various splits each time) to measure the accuracy of a linear kernel support vector machine on the `iris` dataset:

```
from sklearn.model_selection import cross_val_score
scores = cross_val_score(clf, x, y, cv=5)
```

The mean score and the standard deviation are hence given by the following:

```
print('Mean:',scores.mean(),'Standard Deviation:',
scores.std())
```

The estimator's scoring technique is by default used to calculate the score at each CV iteration:

```
Mean: 0.9866666666666667 Standard Deviation: 0.01632993161855452
```

Figure 2.34: CV mean scores

This can be altered by applying the `scoring` parameter:

```
from sklearn import metrics
scores = cross_val_score(clf, x, y, cv=5, scoring='f1_macro')
scores
```

Since the samples in the iris dataset are distributed evenly throughout the target classes, the accuracy and F1 score are nearly equal:

```
array([0.96658312, 1.        , 1.        , 0.96658312, 1.        ])
```

Figure 2.35: CV scores

The CV score defaults to using the `KFold` or `StratifiedKFold` strategies when the cv parameter is an integer, with the latter being utilized if the estimator comes from `ClassifierMixin`.

It is also possible to use other CV strategies by passing a CV iterator using the `ShuffleSplit` Sklearn class instead:

```
from sklearn.model_selection import ShuffleSplit
n_samples = x.shape[0]
cv = ShuffleSplit(n_splits=5, test_size=0.3, random_state=0)
cross_val_score(clf, x, y, cv=cv)
```

The preceding code will show us the CV scores on multiple folds of test samples, which can be used to prevent the overfitting problem:

```
array([0.97777778, 0.97777778, 1.        , 0.95555556, 1.        ])
```

Figure 2.36: Results using shuffle split

The preceding results show us the results of the CV score.

Summary

In this chapter, we have learned how descriptive statistics and machine learning models can be used to quantify the difference between populations, which can later be used to validate business hypotheses as well as to assess the lift of certain marketing activities. We have also learned how to study the relationship of variables with the use of correlation and causation analysis, and how to model these relationships with linear models. Finally, we have built machine learning models to predict and classify variables.

In the next chapter, we will learn how to use results from web searches and how to apply this in the context of market research.

Part 2:
Market and Customer Insights

In this part, you will learn how to obtain and analyze market data by leveraging certain tools. This part will teach you how to obtain search trends, enrich trends with similar queries, use scraping tools to obtain data, and structure the results to drive better decisions using effective visualizations to monitor key business performance KPIs.

This part covers the following chapters:

- *Chapter 3, Finding Business Opportunities with Market Insights*
- *Chapter 4, Understanding Customer Preferences with Conjoint Analysis*
- *Chapter 5, Selecting the Optimal Price with Price Demand Elasticity*
- *Chapter 6, Product Recommendation*

Finding Business Opportunities with Market Insights

In recent years, the word insight has been used with more frequency among innovation market testers. Most of the time it's utilized without a clear definition, sometimes implying that there are hidden patterns in the data that is being utilized, or it can be used in the context of business to create new sources of revenue streams, to define more clearly the conditions and preferences of a given market, or how the different customer preferences vary across different geographies or groups.

In this chapter, we will use search engine trends to analyze the performance of different financial assets in several markets. Overall, we will focus on the following:

- Gathering information about the relative performance of different terms using the Google Trends data with the Pytrends package

- Finding changes in the patterns of those insights to identify shifts in consumer preferences

- Using information about similar queries to understand the search patterns associated with each one of the financial products we are studying

After that, we will go through the different stages of the analysis, and by the end of the chapter, you will be able to do the following:

- Use search engine trends to identify regions that might be susceptible to liking/buying/subscribing to a given product or service

- Understand that these relationships are changing in their behavior and adapt to those changes

- Expand the search space analysis with terms that relate to the original queries to gather a better understanding of the underlying market needs

This chapter covers the following topics:

- Understanding search trends with Pytrends
- Installing Pytrends and ranking markets
- Finding changes in search trend patterns
- Using similar queries to get insights on new trends
- Analyzing the performance of similar queries in time

Let's start the analysis of trends using the Google Trends API with a given set of examples and some hypothetical situations that many companies and businesses might face. An example of this is gathering intelligence about a given market to advertise new products and services.

Technical requirements

In order to be able to follow the steps in this chapter you will need to meet the following requirements:

- A Jupyter Notebook instance running Python 3.7 and above. You can also use a Google Colab notebook to run the steps if you have a Google Drive account.
- An understanding of basic math and statistical concepts.

Understanding search trends with Pytrends

In marketing, market research refers to finding relevant, actionable, and novel knowledge about a given target market, which is always important when planning commercial strategies. This means that the intention is to find information that allows us to know more about the needs of a given market and how the business can meet them with its products and services. We access this knowledge by running data analysis to find previously unseen patterns. This new insight allows companies to do the following:

- Be able to innovate by actually meeting needs
- Gain a better understanding of the customers in a given market
- Monitor brand awareness, and more

In this chapter, we will analyze a set of financial assets and how they perform in different markets, and what people are searching for when they search for these assets. The four assets we will be tracking in particular are bitcoin, real estate, bonds, and stocks. These assets are financial assets in the form of cryptocurrencies, the housing market, bonds, which are loans to a given company or government, as well as bonds which are a company's partial ownership. In this case, we will simulate a company that is looking to have a particular set of assets and wants to target certain markets with information that better meets their search patterns.

We will use the Pytrends package, which accesses the data from the Google Trends API, which is freely accessible with some exceptions.

The Google Trends API retrieves the same information as the one shown in the web interface on any browser, but it makes it easier to access the data through the API in cases where we have large amounts of data.

There are some limitations to this data that have to be carefully considered, which are the following:

- The API has a limitation on the number of responses that it can retrieve in a given amount of time. This means that you cannot make a huge number of requests in a short amount of time.

- The results are shown in relative terms. The queries used will yield different results if we remove one of them and make a new request. This is because the results are relative.

- The units of measure according to Google are calculated between zero and 100, considering the fraction of total searches for a given query in that location.

- The requests are limited in the number of terms that you can provide at the same time. You can only compare up to five terms in the same request. This limitation does not apply to the results, which can be quite extensive sometimes.

Now that we understand what we are looking for, let's start the analysis.

Installing Pytrends and ranking markets

As a first step, we need to install the package that we will use to analyze the web search data. We will install the Pytrends package, which is a wrapper around the Google Trends API. To do this, open a new Jupyter notebook running Python 3.7, and in a new cell run the following command to install the package:

```
pip install pytrends
```

After the package has been installed, we can start the analysis. We can run several types of queries to the API, which are as follows:

- Interest over time

- Historical hourly interest

- Interest by region

- Related topics

- Related queries

- Trending searches

- Real-time search trends

- Top charts

- Suggestions

In this case, we want to obtain information about where the interest per region in a given set of terms is. These are steps that we will follow:

1. Import the pandas package for storing the results and plotting the data.

2. Initialize the Pytrends API and we will pass a set of search terms and build the payload using the last 12 months as a parameter of the search.

3. Finally, we will store the results in a pandas DataFrame named regiondf_12m:

```
import pandas as pd
from pytrends.request import TrendReq
pytrend = TrendReq()
#provide your search terms
kw_list=['bitcoin',
         'stocks',
         'real estate',
         'bonds']
#search interest per region
pytrend.build_payload(kw_list, timeframe='today 12-m')
# Interest by Region
regiondf_12m = pytrend.interest_by_region()
```

In the result, it might be the case that some regions will have no results for the search terms that we are looking for, so we can remove them by summing the rows and checking whether the sum equals zero. If it does, we will remove this row. If you try to make too many requests in a given amount of time, Google will restrict you from making new queries and you will receive an error with code 429, which indicates that you might need to wait until you make can more queries.

4. Now, we can use this logic to create the mask between brackets that is passed to the regiondf_12m DataFrame to remove the rows with no results:

```
# #looking at rows where all values are not equal to 0
regiondf_12m = regiondf_12m[regiondf_12m.sum(axis=1)!=0]
```

5. Finally, we can visualize the results by using the `plot` method of the `pandas` DataFrame to
    create a bar chart showing the results:

```
# visualize
regiondf_12m.plot(figsize=(14, 8), y=kw_list,
    kind ='bar')
```

Executing the previous block of code will prompt us with a result similar to this one:

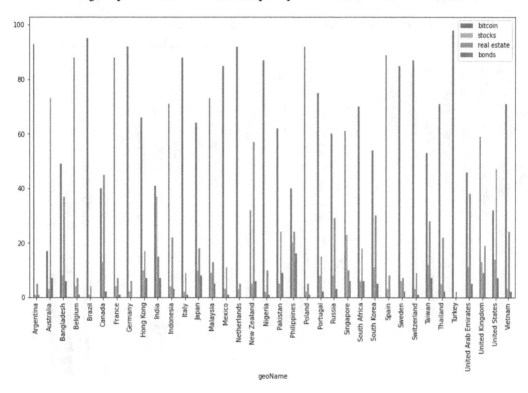

Figure 3.1: Relative search trend importance by region in the last 12 months

Here, it is important to remember that the search trend is modeled as a fraction of the total
searches in a given area, so all these results are relative only to the region that they indicate.

Trying to analyze the results from only this bar chart might be a little difficult, so we will dive
into the specifics of each one of the search terms we analyzed.

6. We will now plot the regions where the search term `bitcoin` has performed better in the last 12 months. To do this, we need to select the column, sort the values in ascending order, and use the `plot` method to draw a bar chart indicating the regions where the search term was a larger relative fraction of the total regional searches:

```
regiondf_12m['bitcoin'].sort_values(ascending= False).
plot(figsize=(14, 8),
y=regiondf_12m['bitcoin'].index,kind ='bar')
```

This code generates the following result:

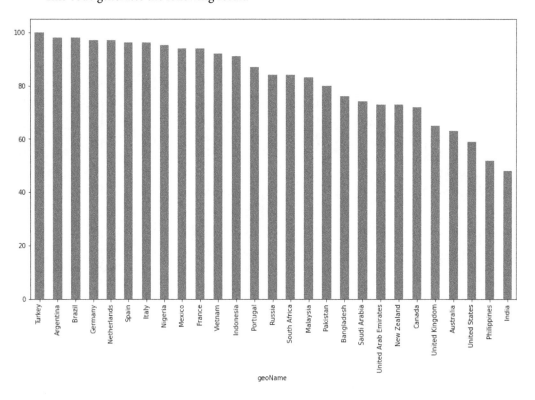

Figure 3.2: Countries where bitcoin was a top search trend in the last 12 months

This graph shows us the countries where `bitcoin` has been a popular search trend in the last 12 months. This can be an indicator of the maturity of a given trend in a market because it means that there has been a constant search relative to other search trends for these locations for a period of at least a year.

7. Next, we will do the same for the rest of the search terms and we will compare the difference between the given markets.

The next block of code filters, sorts, and plots the data in the same way but in this case for the `real estate` search term:

```
regiondf_12m['real estate'].sort_values(ascending=
    False).plot(figsize=(14, 8),
        y=regiondf_12m['real estate'].index,kind ='bar')
```

The result of this block is a bar chart showing the results of searches for this term in different regions:

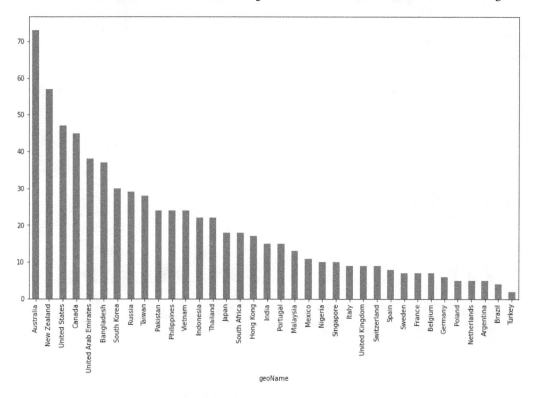

Figure 3.3: Countries where real estate was a top search trend in the last 12 months

As a first difference, we can see that the results for real estate differ in the distribution of the results. While we can see in *Figure 3.1* that the results tend to be more evenly distributed among the results, in the real estate results the data shows that only a certain number of countries have a relatively large number of searches for this term. This might be an indication that this type of investment is much tighter to the local regulations and conditions. We can see that Australia, New Zealand, the USA, and Canada are the only countries that represent more than 40 points.

8. The next block of code will show us the performance of the search term stocks:

```
regiondf_12m['stocks'].sort_values(ascending= False).
plot(figsize=(14, 8),
     y=regiondf_12m['stocks'].index,kind ='bar')
```

This shows us the results of the stocks search term in the last 12 months:

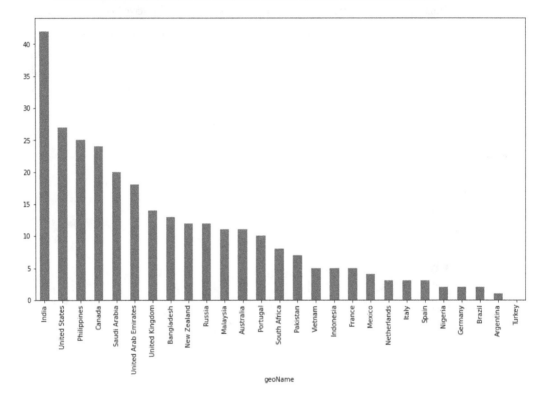

Figure 3.4: Countries where stocks were a top search trend in the last 12 months

Here, the tendency tends to repeat but in different countries. In this case, the top five countries are India, the USA, the Philippines, Canada, and Saudi Arabia. Here, the difference lies in the fact that India is the only country that surpasses the mark of 40 points. This might be a good way to infer how the people in these regions are thinking in terms of investment options.

9. Finally, we need to repeat the same process but for the bonds search term by changing the column in the code used before:

```
regiondf_12m['bonds'].sort_values(ascending= False).
plot(figsize=(14, 8),
     y=regiondf_12m['bonds'].index, kind ='bar')
```

Executing this code will return the following result:

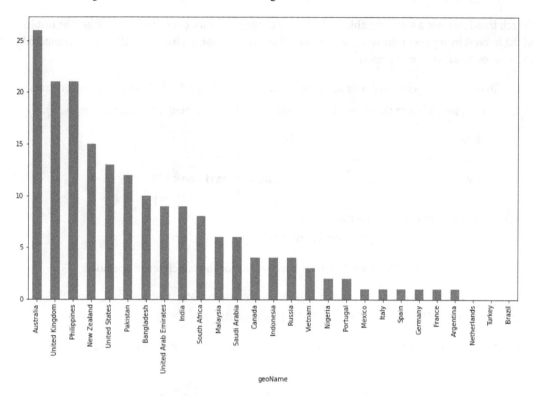

Figure 3.5: Countries where bonds were a top search trend in the last 12 months

It can be seen that bonds seem to be an option less used by the users searching for investment options on Google. The fact that Australia is the leading country in terms of the proportion of searches for bonds along with real estate suggests that bonds and real estate seem to be an option that is more attractive than stocks or bitcoin in Australia.

Now that we have determined the regions where each of the assets performs best in terms of popularity, we will study the change in patterns of these trends.

Finding changes in search trend patterns

Search trends are not a static variable; in fact, they change and vary over time. We will get the results of the interest by region in the last 3 months and then we will look at changes in the results compared to the ones obtained over a period of 12 months:

1. To find the changes in search trends patterns, we will build the payload within a different timeframe.

2. Finally, we will store the results in a `pandas` DataFrame named `regiondf_3m`:

```
#search interest per region
pytrend = TrendReq()
pytrend.build_payload(kw_list, timeframe='today 3-m')


# Interest by Region
regiondf_3m = pytrend.interest_by_region()
```

3. We need to remove the rows that don't have results for the search terms specified:

```
# #looking at rows where all values are not equal to 0
regiondf_3m = regiondf_3m[regiondf_3m.sum(axis=1)!=0]
```

4. Now, we can visualize the results using the `plot` method of the `pandas` DataFrame:

```
# visualize
regiondf_3m.plot(figsize=(14, 8), y=kw_list, kind ='bar')
```

This code yields the next visualization:

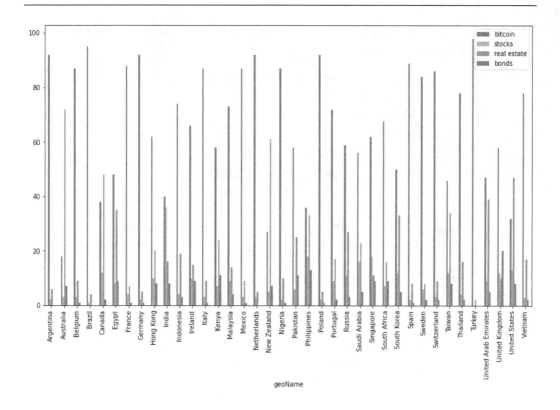

Figure 3.6: Interest over time in the last 3 months

At a glance, it would be very complicated to find any possible changes in the results so we will arrange the data in such a way that we will just display the changes in these trends:

1. The first step is to create a DataFrame that contains the information from both the last 12 months and the last 3 months:

```
df = pd.DataFrame([regiondf_3m['stocks'],
                   regiondf_12m['stocks'],
                   regiondf_3m['bitcoin'],
                   regiondf_12m['bitcoin'],
                   regiondf_3m['real estate'],
                   regiondf_12m['real estate'],
                   regiondf_3m['bonds'],
                   regiondf_12m['bonds']
                   ]).T
```

Here, the DataFrame is constructed by concatenating the results of the different search terms.

2. Next, we need to rename the columns and create columns that are the differences in the interest in the search terms over time:

```
cols = ['stocks_3m','stocks_12m','bitcoin_3m',
'bitcoin_12m','real_estate_3m','real_estate_12m','bonds_3
m','bonds_12m']
df.columns = cols
df['diff_stocks'] = df['stocks_12m'] - df['stocks_3m']
df['diff_bitcoin'] = df['bitcoin_12m'] - df['bitcoin_3m']
df['diff_real_estate'] = df['real_estate_12m'] -
df['real_estate_3m']
df['diff_bonds'] = df['bonds_12m'] - df['bonds_3m']
# Inspect the new created columns
df.head()
```

3. Now, we can limit the values to the newly created columns:

```
n_cols = ['diff_stocks','diff_bitcoin',
        'diff_real_estate','diff_bonds']
df = df[n_cols]
df.head()
```

This produces the next result, which shows us the relative changes in search trends:

geoName	diff_stocks	diff_bitcoin	diff_real_estate	diff_bonds
Argentina	-1.0	1.0	-1.0	1.0
Australia	0.0	-1.0	1.0	0.0
Belgium	1.0	1.0	-2.0	0.0
Brazil	0.0	0.0	0.0	0.0
Canada	1.0	2.0	-3.0	0.0

Figure 3.7: Relative differences between the last 3 and 12 months compared

4. Some countries have no changes, so we will filter them out by summing across the axis and comparing this result to zero to create a mask that we can use to filter out these cases:

```
# Create a mask for of the null results
mask = df.abs().sum(axis=1)!=0
df = df[mask]
df.head()
```

It's important to note that this comparison is made over absolute values only.

The preceding code shows us the results that have now been filtered.

geoName	diff_stocks	diff_bitcoin	diff_real_estate	diff_bonds
Argentina	-1.0	1.0	-1.0	1.0
Australia	0.0	-1.0	1.0	0.0
Belgium	1.0	1.0	-2.0	0.0
Canada	1.0	2.0	-3.0	0.0
Germany	0.0	0.0	1.0	-1.0

Figure 3.8: Filtered results of relative differences

5. Now, we can visualize the results obtained. We will first look at the regions where there has been a change in the searches of the term stock.

To do this, we will use the results in *Figure 3.8* to filter them by the column we want and filter out the rows where there was no change, sort in ascending order and then visualize the results using the plot method of the pandas DataFrame:

```
data = df['diff_stocks'][df['diff_stocks']!=0]
data = data.sort_values(ascending = False)
data.plot(figsize=(14, 8),y=data.index, kind ='bar')
```

This produces the next result:

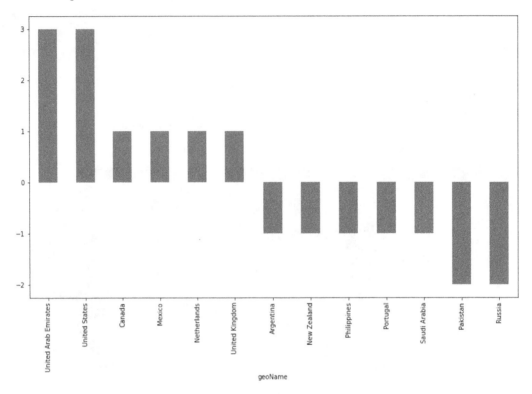

Figure 3.9: Countries where the search term stocks changed in popularity over the few 12 months

The results show us that in comparison, the popularity of stocks as a search trend has been consolidated in the UAE and the USA, while they have reduced in popularity in Pakistan and Russia. These results cannot be directly interpreted as an indication of a change of perception about the value of the asset itself, but rather as an indication of the amount of search traffic. An increase in traffic can be due because of both positive and negative reasons, so it's always important to dive in deeper.

6.   Now, we will look at the difference in changes in search trends for `bitcoin`:

```
df['diff_bitcoin'][df['diff_bitcoin']!=0
].sort_values(ascending = False).plot(figsize=(14, 8),
y=df['diff_bitcoin'][df['diff_bitcoin']!=0].index,kind
='bar')
```

The code generates the next graph:

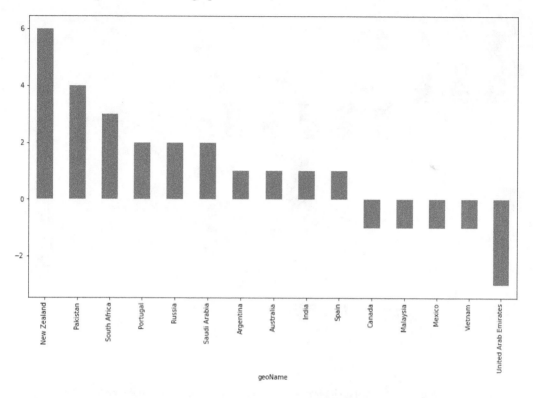

Figure 3.10: Countries where the search term bitcoin has changed in popularity over the last 12 months

One of the first things to note about this graph is that the majority of changes in recent months have been positive rather than negative. This could be an indication of a trend in even wider global adoption over the last few months.

The countries leading this chart in terms of growth are New Zealand, Pakistan, and South Africa, while the UAE is leading the decline.

7. The next block of code illustrates the same effect in the case of bonds:

```
df['diff_bonds'][df['diff_bonds']!=0
].sort_values(ascending = False).plot(figsize=(14, 8),y =
df['diff_bonds'][df['diff_bonds']!=0].index,kind ='bar')
```

The results are shown in the next graph:

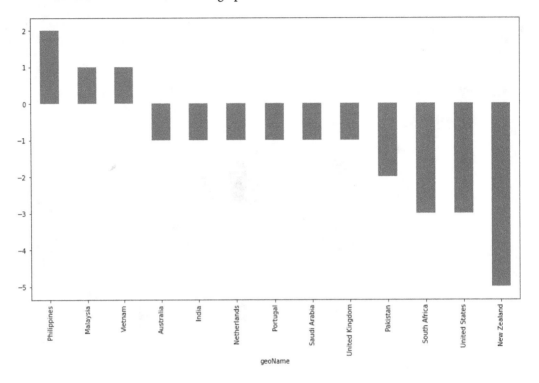

Figure 3.11: Countries where the search term bond has changed in popularity over the last 12 months

There can be seen an interesting change in trend in which now the vast majority of the countries have experienced a decline in the search term. This might be an indication of a consistent change in investment patterns globally, which affects some countries more than others. It is also noticeable that New Zealand now leads the countries with the largest decline in search trends over the analyzed period when in the case of bitcoin, it was leading the positive growth. This is also the case in the US, where there has a descending trend, but in the case of the search term stocks, it showed a positive change.

8. Finally, the next block of code shows the search variations in the search term real estate:

```
df['diff_real_estate'][df['diff_real_estate']!=0].
sort_values(ascending = False).plot(figsize=(14,
8),y=df['diff_real_estate'][df['diff_real_estate']!=0].
index,kind ='bar')
```

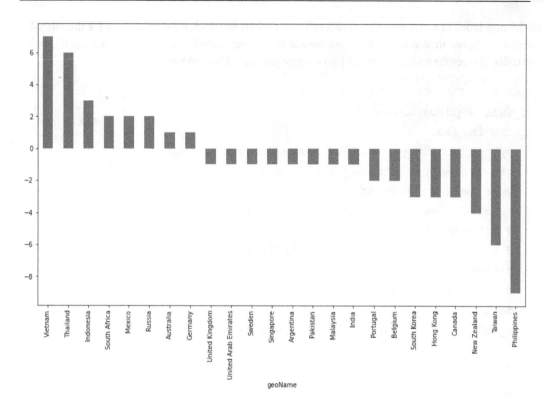

Figure 3.12: Countries where the search term real estate has changed in popularity over the last months

In this case, the change can also be seen as more globally negative than positive. Although some countries experienced a positive change, such as Vietnam and Thailand, more of the cases have seen a reduction in the search term. This can not only be caused by investment decisions but also by search patterns. Depending on the region, in most cases, real estate can be seen as an investment, and in other cases, it is only for living and commercial purposes.

In the next section, we will dive more into the countries that experienced significant changes and try to understand the cause in more detail.

Using related queries to get insights on new trends

If we want to find more information about the terms that are most associated with the search terms we are looking for, we can use the related queries to obtain queries that are similar to the ones we are searching for. This is useful because it provides not only contextual information but also information about trends that can be further analyzed.

In the next block of code, we will define a series of regions in which we want to look for the related queries for a given timeframe. In this case, we will be looking at the USA, Canada, New Zealand, and Australia. The results will be arranged into a single pandas DataFrame:

```python
geo = ['US','CA','NZ','AU']
d_full = pd.DataFrame()
for g in geo:
    pytrend.build_payload(kw_list=['bitcoin','stocks'],
    geo=g,timeframe='today 3-m')
    #get related queries
    related_queries = pytrend.related_queries()
    # Bitcoin top
    d = related_queries['bitcoin']['top']
    d['source_query'] = 'bitcoin'
    d['type'] = 'top'
    d['geo'] = g
    d_full = pd.concat([d_full,d],axis=0)
    # Bitcoin rising
    d = related_queries['bitcoin']['rising']
    d['source_query'] = 'bitcoin'
    d['type'] = 'rising'
    d['geo'] = g
    d_full = pd.concat([d_full,d],axis=0)


    # stocks top
    d = related_queries['stocks']['top']
    d['source_query'] = 'stocks'
    d['type'] = 'top'
    d['geo'] = g
    d_full = pd.concat([d_full,d],axis=0)
    # stocks rising
    d = related_queries['stocks']['rising']
    d['source_query'] = 'stocks'
    d['type'] = 'rising'
    d['geo'] = g
    d_full = pd.concat([d_full,d],axis=0)
```

This code will loop over the defined regions and concatenate the results of related queries that are the top results of the given timeframe, and also the ones that are rising in that given region.

Finally, we reset the index and display the first 10 rows:

```
d_full = d_full.reset_index(drop=True)
d_full.head(10)
```

This results in the following output:

	query	value	source_query	type	geo
0	bitcoin price	100	bitcoin	top	US
1	bitcoin stock	16	bitcoin	top	US
2	bitcoin stock price	13	bitcoin	top	US
3	bitcoin usd	10	bitcoin	top	US
4	ethereum	9	bitcoin	top	US
5	bitcoin today	8	bitcoin	top	US
6	bitcoin price usd	8	bitcoin	top	US
7	ethereum price	8	bitcoin	top	US
8	bitcoin price ethereum	8	bitcoin	top	US
9	bitcoin price today	7	bitcoin	top	US

Figure 3.13: Similar queries to bitcoin in the US region

We can use the information of related queries to run an analysis on the frequency and the terms associated with the original search term. This would give us a better context to understand the correlated factors for a given asset in a certain region. This means that in this case, we can see that the people searching for bitcoin are also searching for Ethereum, so we can expect a certain degree of correlation between them:

1. Let's use a simple method to show the most frequent terms in these queries by using a word cloud to show the most significant terms. We will use `wordcloud` and the `matplotlib` package:

    ```
    from wordcloud import WordCloud
    from wordcloud import ImageColorGenerator
    ```

```
from wordcloud import STOPWORDS
import matplotlib.pyplot as plt
```

2. We will use the results of top related queries in the US associated with the term `stocks` as the data:

```
data = d_full[(d_full['source_query']=='stocks')&(
        d_full['type']=='top')&(d_full['geo']=='US')]
```

3. After this, we will concatenate all the results for the result column, replacing the source query to avoid this redundancy and remove the stopwords. Finally, the last part of the code will generate the figure and display the results:

```
text = " ".join(i for i in data['query']).
replace('stock','')
stopwords = set(STOPWORDS)
wordcloud = WordCloud(stopwords=stopwords, background_
color="white").generate(text)
plt.figure( figsize=(12,8))
plt.imshow(wordcloud, interpolation='bilinear')
plt.axis("off")
plt.show()
```

This generates the next word cloud with the size adapted to the relative frequency of the term. Take into account that we always need to have at least one word to plot, otherwise we will get an error saying that we got 0 words.

Figure 3.14: Frequent top related queries to the search term stocks in the US

The results show that the term stocks a mostly related to terms such as the following:

- **penny**: Refers to the penny stock market
- **now**, **today**: There is a need for day-to-day frequency of information, and live updates
- **dividend**: A preference for stocks that pay dividends
- **amazon**, **tesla**: Stocks that are popular
- **reddit**, **news**: Sources of information
- **buy**, **invest**: The action of the user

This information can be really interesting when trying to gain information about the patterns that drive users.

4. Next is the same code used as before, but now it references the rising search term stocks in the US:

```
data = d_full[(d_full['source_query']=='stocks')&(
        d_full['type']=='rising')&(d_full['geo']=='US')]
text = " ".join(i for i in data['query']).
replace('stock','')
stopwords = set(STOPWORDS)
wordcloud = WordCloud(stopwords=stopwords,
        background_color="white").generate(text)
plt.figure( figsize=(12,8))
plt.imshow(wordcloud, interpolation='bilinear')
plt.axis("off")
plt.show()
```

The next figure will show us the terms found in the rising queries related to our original search terms. The size of the terms varies according to their frequency, providing us with information about their relative importance.

Figure 3.15: Frequent top queries related to the search term stocks in the US

It shows a different level of information as we can see events currently happening, such as the fear of a recession in the short term, indicating a bullish market, and some new stock names such as Twitter, Disney, and Haliburton.

5. We repeat the same exercise by looking at the top queries related to the `bitcoin` search term in New Zealand:

```
data = d_full[(d_full['source_query']=='bitcoin')&(
        d_full['type']=='top')&(d_full['geo']=='NZ')]
text = " ".join(i for i in data['query']).
replace('bitcoin','')
stopwords = set(STOPWORDS)
wordcloud = WordCloud(stopwords=stopwords,
        background_color="white").generate(text)
plt.figure( figsize=(12,8))
plt.imshow(wordcloud, interpolation='bilinear')
plt.axis("off")
plt.show()
```

This generates the next word cloud of terms.

Figure 3.16: Frequent top queries related to the search term bitcoin in New Zealand

Here, we can see that there is a relationship between Tesla and bitcoin, as well as Dow Jones. The latter can be an indication that the people looking to invest in bitcoin already have an investment in stocks, or are considering investing in one or the other.

6. The next one focuses on the rising related terms to `bitcoin` in New Zealand:

```
data = d_full[(d_full['source_query']=='bitcoin')&(
        d_full['type']=='rising')&(d_full['geo']=='NZ')]
```

```
text = " ".join(i for i in data['query']).
replace('bitcoin','')
stopwords = set(STOPWORDS)
wordcloud = WordCloud(stopwords=stopwords,
      background_color="white").generate(text)
plt.figure( figsize=(12,8))
plt.imshow(wordcloud, interpolation='bilinear')
plt.axis("off")
plt.show()
```

The results are shown in the next word cloud.

Figure 3.17: Frequent top queries related to the search term bitcoin in New Zealand

The results show the names of other cryptocurrencies such as Cardano and Luna, also we can see the term crash, possibly associated with the latter.

These visualizations are useful to be able to detect at a glance certain terms that are becoming more and more relevant by representing the trending popularity of each term using size. Humans are not very good at absorbing a lot of detailed information at once, so we need to think about the storytelling of the data in advance.

Analyzing the performance of related queries over time

After capturing more information about the context, we can track the evolution of these queries over time. This could provide us with valuable information about local trends that have been rising in importance under our radar. We will do so using the following steps:

1. We will select the rising queries related to bitcoin in the US:

    ```
    query_data = d_full[(d_full['source_query']=='bitcoin'
    )&(d_full['type']=='rising')&(d_full['geo']=='US')]
    ```

```
query_data.head()
```

This results in the following output:

	query	value	source_query	type	geo
0	dwac stock	8700	bitcoin	rising	US
1	solana price	4650	bitcoin	rising	US
2	rivian stock	3150	bitcoin	rising	US
3	shiba inu price	2200	bitcoin	rising	US
4	shiba inu coin price	2050	bitcoin	rising	US

Figure 3.18: Rising queries related to bitcoin in the US

2. We will use the top five resulting queries to track their performance in the last 12 months:

```
kw_list = query_data.head()['query'].tolist() # list of
keywords to get data
# build payload
pytrend.build_payload(kw_list, cat=0, timeframe='today
12-m')
# Interest over Time
data = pytrend.interest_over_time()
data = data.reset_index()
```

3. Finally, we will show the results using the Plotly library to be able to display the information more interactively:

```
import plotly.express as px
fig = px.line(data, x="date", y=kw_list, title='Keyword
Web Search Interest Over Time')
fig.show()
```

This shows us the following graph, where we can see the evolution of the rising trends over time:

Bitcoin related queries - Interest Over Time

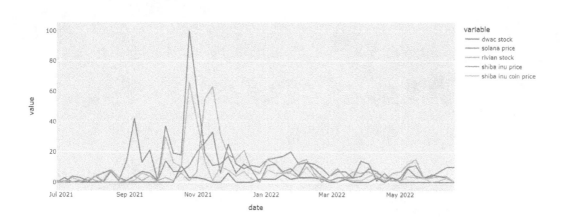

Figure 3.19: Rising query performance over time

We can see that the queries had a peak around November 2021, with a mixed performance.

Summary

Information about specific live trends in different markets can be expensive to obtain, but the use of web search engine traffic can provide us with valuable tools to analyze different regions. In this chapter, we have focused on the analysis of regions at the country level, but we can also use different regional geo codes, such as US-NY representing New York.

This information can be used also in combination with sales data to obtain valuable correlations that, with causal analysis, can produce a variable that can be used for predicting behavior, as we will see in the next chapters.

The following chapters will continue to focus on the understanding of underlying value, but this time, it will be at the level of product characteristics scoring with conjoint analysis.

4

Understanding Customer Preferences with Conjoint Analysis

Conjoint analysis is a well-known approach to product and pricing research that identifies customer preferences and makes use of that knowledge to choose product features, evaluate price sensitivity, anticipate market shares, and foretell consumer acceptance of new goods or services.

Conjoint analysis is often utilized for all sorts of items, including consumer goods, electrical goods, life insurance policies, retirement communities, luxury goods, and air travel, across several sectors. It may be used in a variety of situations that revolve around learning what kind of product customers are most likely to purchase and which features consumers value the most (and least) in a product. As a result, it is widely used in product management, marketing, and advertising.

Conjoint analysis is beneficial for businesses of all sizes, even small local eateries and grocery stores.

In this chapter, you will learn how to understand how conjoint analysis is used in market research and how experiments are performed. You will then perform a conjoint analysis using **ordinary least squares (OLS)** models and predict the performance of new product features using different **machine learning (ML)** models.

This chapter covers the following topics:

- Understanding conjoint analysis
- Designing a conjoint experiment
- Determining a product's relevant attributes
- OLS with Python and Statsmodels

- Working with more product features
- Predicting new feature combinations

Let's jump into the analysis using some simulation data for consumer retail products.

Technical requirements

In order to be able to follow the steps in this chapter, you will need to meet the next requirements:

- A Jupyter notebook instance running Python 3.7 and above. You can use a Google Colab notebook to run the steps as well if you have a Google Drive account.
- An understanding of basic math and statistical concepts.

Understanding conjoint analysis

Conjoint analysis is a research-based statistical method used in market research to determine how people evaluate the different attributes (characteristics, functions, and benefits) that make up a single product or service.

Conjoint analysis has its roots in mathematical psychology, the goal of which is to determine which combination of a limited number of attributes has the greatest impact on respondents' choices and decisions. Respondents are presented with a controlled set of potential products or services, and by analyzing how to choose from those products, an implicit assessment of each component of the product or service is made. You can decide. You can use these implicit ratings (utilities or fractions) to create market models that estimate market share, sales, and even the profitability of new designs.

There are different types of conjoint studies that may be designed:

- Ranking-based conjoint
- Rating-based conjoint
- Choice-based conjoint

Conjoint analysis is also utilized in a variety of social sciences and practical sciences, including operations research, product management, and marketing. It is commonly employed in service design, advertising appeal analysis, and consumer acceptability testing of new product designs. Although it has been applied to product placement, some object to this use of conjoint analysis.

Conjoint analysis approaches, which are a subset of a larger group of trade-off analysis tools used for systematic decision analysis, are also known as multi-attribute compositional modeling, discrete choice modeling, or expressed preference research. Conjoint analysis breaks down a product or service into its called attributes and tests different combinations of those components to determine consumer preferences.

In the next diagram, we see how products are a combination of different levels of features—for example, a bag of chips can be represented with levels such as brand, flavor, size, and price:

Figure 4.1: Different products as unique combinations of features

Here's how the combination of these attributes and levels may appear as options to a respondent in a conjoint choice task:

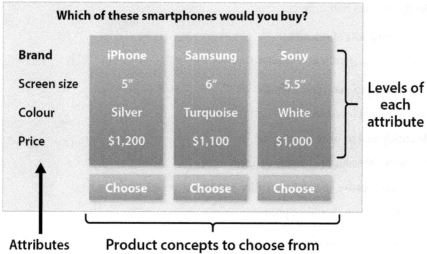

Figure 4.2: Conjoint choice task

The conjoint analysis takes a more realistic approach, rather than just asking what you like about the product or which features are most important.

During a survey, each person is asked to choose between products with the same level of attributes, but different combinations of them. This model is called choice-based conjoint, which in most cases is composed of 8 to 12 "battles" of products. This process looks to simulate the buying behavior, and the closer it gets to real-life conditions, the better. The selection of attributes and the battle setup are designed as an experiment that requires domain knowledge. The information is later used to weigh the influence of each one of the attributes on the buying patterns of the users.

Now that we know what conjoint analysis is and how it can be used to measure how customers ponder certain product characteristics, we will look into how each of these experiments can be designed.

Designing a conjoint experiment

A product or service area is described as a set of attributes. For example, a laptop may have characteristics such as screen size, screen size, brand, and price. Therefore, each attribute can be divided into several levels—for example, the screen size can be 13, 14, or 15 inches. Respondents are presented with a set of products, prototypes, mockups, or images created from a combination of all or some layers of configuration attributes to select, rank, or display products for evaluation. You will be asked to rank. Each example is similar enough for consumers to consider it a good alternative but different enough for respondents to clearly identify their preferences. Each example consists of a unique combination of product features. The data can consist of individual ratings, rankings, or a selection from alternative combinations.

Conjoint design involves four different steps:

1. Identifying the sort of research.

2. Determining the pertinent characteristics:

    - Be pertinent to managerial choices

    - Have different levels in reality

    - Be anticipated to sway preferences

    - Be comprehensible and clearly defined

    - Show no excessive correlations (price and brand are an exception)

    - At least two tiers should be present

3. Specifying the attributes' levels:

    - Unambiguous

    - Mutually exclusive

    - Realistic

4. **Design questionnaire**: The number of alternatives grows exponentially with the number of attribute and level combinations. One of the ways in which we deal with the exponential increase is by taking a fractional factorial design approach, which is frequently used to decrease the number of profiles to be examined while making sure that there is enough data available

for statistical analysis. This in turn produces a well-controlled collection of "profiles" for the respondent to consider.

Taking these points into account when designing a conjoint experiment will allow us to accurately model and replicate the consumer pattern we want to understand. We must always have in mind that the purpose of this analysis is to undercover hidden patterns by simulating the buying action as close to reality as possible.

Determining a product's relevant attributes

As mentioned before, we will perform a conjoint analysis to weigh the importance that a group of users gives to a given characteristic of a product or service. To achieve this, we will perform a multivariate analysis to determine the optimal product concept. By evaluating the entire product (overall utility value), it is possible to calculate the degree of influence on the purchase of individual elements (partial utility value). For example, when a user purchases a PC, it is possible to determine which factors affect this and how much (important). The same method can be scaled to include many more features.

The data to be used is in the form of different combinations of notebook features in terms of RAM, storage, and price. Different users ranked these combinations.

We will use the following Python modules in the next example:

- **Pandas**: Python package for data analysis and data manipulation.
- **NumPy**: Python package that allows the use of matrices and arrays, as well as the use of mathematical and statistical functions to operate in those matrices.
- **Statsmodels**: Python package that provides a complement to SciPy for statistical computations, including descriptive statistics and estimation and inference for statistical models. It provides classes and functions for the estimation of many different statistical models.
- **Seaborn and Matplotlib**: Python packages for effective data visualization.

1. The next block of code will import the necessary packages and functions, as well as create a sample DataFrame with simulated data:

```
import numpy as np
import pandas as pd
import seaborn as sns
import matplotlib.pyplot as plt
import statsmodels.api as sm

# data: Laptop spec data
data = pd.DataFrame([[6000, '4GB', '128GB', 3],
```

```
                       [6000, '8GB', '512GB', 9],
                       [8000, '4GB', '512GB', 5],
                       [8000, '8GB', '128GB', 7],
                       [6000, '4GB', '128GB', 4]],
                 columns=['price', 'memory',
                                   'storage', 'score'])
    data.head()
```

This results in the following output:

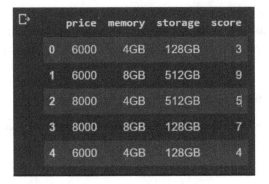

Figure 4.3: Product features along with the score

2. The next code will separate our data into predictor and target variables:

```
X = data[[col for col in data.columns if col != 'score']]
y = data['score']
X.head()
```

This results in the following output:

	price	memory	storage
0	6000	4GB	128GB
1	6000	8GB	512GB
2	8000	4GB	512GB
3	8000	8GB	128GB
4	6000	4GB	128GB

Figure 4.4: Product features

3. These next lines of code will create dummy variables using the encoded categorical variables:

```
X_dum = pd.get_dummies(X, columns=X.columns)
X_dum.head()
```

This results in the following output:

	price_6000	price_8000	memory_4GB	memory_8GB	storage_128GB	storage_512GB
0	1	0	1	0	1	0
1	1	0	0	1	0	1
2	0	1	1	0	0	1
3	0	1	0	1	1	0
4	1	0	1	0	1	0

Figure 4.5: Products and features in a one-hot representation

Now that the information has been properly encoded, we can use different predictor models to try to predict, based on the product characteristics, what would be the scoring of each product. In the next section, we can use an OLS regression model to determine the variable importance and infer which are the characteristics that users ponder most when selecting a product to buy.

OLS with Python and Statsmodels

OLS, a kind of linear least squares approach, is used in statistics to estimate unidentified parameters in a linear regression model. By minimizing the sum of squares of the differences between the observed values of the dependent variable and the values predicted by the linear function of the independent variable, OLS derives the parameters of a linear function from a set of explanatory variables in accordance with the least squares principle.

As a reminder, a linear regression model establishes the relationship between a dependent variable (y) and at least one independent variable (x), as follows:

$$\hat{Y} = B_1 * X + B_0$$

In the OLS method, we have to choose the values of B_1 and B_0, such that the total sum of squares of the difference between the calculated and observed values of Y is minimized.

OLS can be described in geometrical terms as the sum of all the squared distances between each point to the regression surface. This distance is measured parallel to the axis of the adjusted surface, and the lower the distances, the better the surface will adjust to the data. OLS is a method especially useful when the errors are homoscedastic and uncorrelated between themselves, yielding great results when the variables used in regression are exogenous.

When the errors have finite variances, the OLS method provides a minimum-variance mean-unbiased estimate. OLS is the maximum likelihood estimator under the additional presumption that the errors are normally distributed.

We will use Python's statsmodels module to implement the OLS method of linear regression:

```
model = sm.OLS(y, sm.add_constant(X_dum))
result = model.fit()
result.summary()
```

An OLS regression process is used to estimate the linear relationship on the multivariate data, achieving an R-squared value of **0.978**:

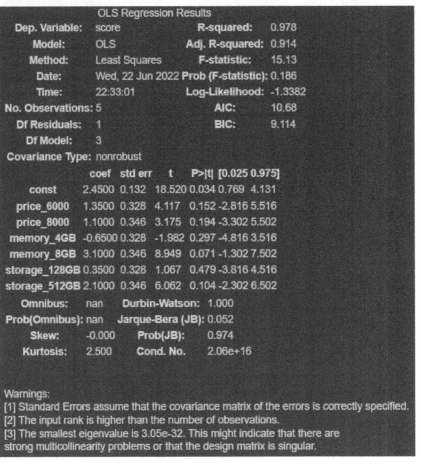

OLS Regression Results

Dep. Variable:	score	R-squared:	0.978
Model:	OLS	Adj. R-squared:	0.914
Method:	Least Squares	F-statistic:	15.13
Date:	Wed, 22 Jun 2022	Prob (F-statistic):	0.186
Time:	22:33:01	Log-Likelihood:	-1.3382
No. Observations:	5	AIC:	10.68
Df Residuals:	1	BIC:	9.114
Df Model:	3		
Covariance Type:	nonrobust		

	coef	std err	t	P>|t|	[0.025	0.975]
const	2.4500	0.132	18.520	0.034	0.769	4.131
price_6000	1.3500	0.328	4.117	0.152	-2.816	5.516
price_8000	1.1000	0.346	3.175	0.194	-3.302	5.502
memory_4GB	-0.6500	0.328	-1.982	0.297	-4.816	3.516
memory_8GB	3.1000	0.346	8.949	0.071	-1.302	7.502
storage_128GB	0.3500	0.328	1.067	0.479	-3.816	4.516
storage_512GB	2.1000	0.346	6.062	0.104	-2.302	6.502

Omnibus:	nan	Durbin-Watson:	1.000
Prob(Omnibus):	nan	Jarque-Bera (JB):	0.052
Skew:	-0.000	Prob(JB):	0.974
Kurtosis:	2.500	Cond. No.	2.06e+16

Warnings:
[1] Standard Errors assume that the covariance matrix of the errors is correctly specified.
[2] The input rank is higher than the number of observations.
[3] The smallest eigenvalue is 3.05e-32. This might indicate that there are strong multicollinearity problems or that the design matrix is singular.

Figure 4.6: OLS model summary

The resulting summary shows us some basic information, as well as relevant metrics. Some of these are the R-squared values, the number of observations used to train the model, the degrees of freedom in modality, the covariance, and other information.

Some of the most important aspects to interpret in this summary are the next values:

- **R-squared**: R-squared, which calculates how much of the independent variable is explained by changes in our dependent variables, is perhaps the most significant statistic this summary produces. 0.685, expressed as a percentage, indicates that our model accounts for 68.5% of the variation in our `'score'` variable. With the property that the R-squared value of your model will never decrease with additional variables, your model may appear more accurate with multiple variables, even if they only contribute a small amount. This property is significant for analyzing the effectiveness of multiple dependent variables on the model. A lower adjusted score can suggest that some variables are not adequately contributing to the model since adjusted R-squared penalizes the R-squared formula based on the number of variables.

- **F-statistic:** The F-statistic evaluates whether a set of variables is statistically significant by contrasting a linear model built for a variable with a model that eliminates the variable's impact on 0. To correctly interpret this number, you must make use of the F table and the chosen alpha value. This value is used by probability (F statistics) to assess the validity of the `null` hypothesis, or whether it is accurate to state that the effect of the variable is zero. You can see that this situation has a probability of 15.3%.

- **Intercept**: If all of the variables in our model were set to 0, the intercept would be the outcome. This is our b, a constant that is added to declare a starting value for our row in the classic linear equation "y = mx+b". These are the variables below the intersection. The coefficient is the first useful column in our table. It is the section's value for our section. It is a measurement of the impact of changing each variable on the independent variable. The "m" in "y = mx + b" is the culprit, with "m" being the rate of change value of the variable's coefficient in the independent variable, or the outcome of a unit change in the dependent variable. They have an inverse relationship if the coefficient is negative, meaning that if one rises, then the other declines.

- **std error**: The coefficient's standard deviation, or how much the coefficient varies among the data points, is estimated by the std error (or standard error) variable, which is a measurement of the accuracy with which the coefficient was measured and is connected. In cases where we have a high t statistic, which denotes a high significance for your coefficient, this is produced by a low standard error in comparison to a high coefficient.

- **P>|t|**: One of the most significant statistics in the summary is the p-value. The t statistic is used to generate the p-value, which expresses how likely it is that your coefficient was determined by chance in our model. A low p-value, such as 0.278, indicates that there is a 27.8% chance that the provided variable has no effect on the dependent variable and that our results are the result of chance. The p-value will be compared to an alpha value that has been predetermined, or a threshold, by which we can attach significance to our coefficient, in proper model analysis.

- **[0.025 and 0.975]**: Is the range of measurements of values of our coefficients within 95% of our data or within two standard deviations? Outside of these, values can generally be considered outliers. Is the data contained between two standard deviations, where data outside of this range can be regarded as outliers?

- **Omnibus**: Using skew and kurtosis as metrics, Omnibus describes the normality of the distribution of our residuals. 0 would represent complete normalcy. A statistical test called Prob (Omnibus) determines the likelihood that the residuals are normally distributed. 1 would represent a distribution that is exactly normal. Skew, which ranges from 0 to perfect symmetry, measures the degree of symmetry in our data. Kurtosis gauges how peaky our data is or how concentrated it is at 0 on a normal curve. Fewer outliers are implied by higher kurtosis.

- **Durbin-Watson**: The homoscedasticity, or uniform distribution of mistakes in our data, is measured by the Durbin-Watson statistic. Heteroscedasticity would indicate an unequal distribution, such as when the relative error grows as the number of data points grows. Homoscedasticity should be between 1 and 2. Alternative ways to measure the same value of Omnibus and Prob (Omnibus) using asymmetry and kurtosis are Jarque-Bera (JB) and Prob. These ideals help us validate one another. A measure of how sensitive our model is to changes in the data it is processing is the condition number. Many different conditions strongly imply multicollinearity, which is a term to describe two or more independent variables that are strongly related to each other and are falsely affecting our predicted variable by redundancy.

In our case, we will use the results of the data and store the variable names, their weights, and p-values in a DataFrame that later on we will use to plot the data:

```
data_res = pd.DataFrame({'name': result.params.keys(),
                         'weight': result.params.values,
                         'p_val': result.pvalues})
data_res = data_res[1:]
data_res
```

When looking at the p-value, if the significance level is below 5%, it can be an indication that the variable is not statistically significant:

```
data_res = data_res.sort_values(by='weight')
data_res
```

This results in the following output:

	name	weight	p_val
price_6000	price_6000	1.35	0.151678
price_8000	price_8000	1.10	0.194224
memory_4GB	memory_4GB	-0.65	0.297414
memory_8GB	memory_8GB	3.10	0.070845
storage_128GB	storage_128GB	0.35	0.479226
storage_512GB	storage_512GB	2.10	0.104078

Figure 4.7: Product features' weights and p-values

Although it's important to consider the p-value to establish a level of statistical certainty, the model should be used with all variables. Here, we can use the Prob (F-statistic), which in our case is higher than 0.05, thus we cannot reject the null hypothesis. By looking also at a very high R-squared value, we can see that the model is overfitting. We would need to have much more data in order to create a significant model, but I'll leave that challenge to you.

The next screenshot shows the characteristics of the product ordered by relative weight. In this case, users positively weigh the 8 GB memory, followed by the 128 GB storage:

```
sns.set()
xbar = np.arange(len(data_res['weight']))
plt.barh(xbar, data_res['weight'])
plt.yticks(xbar, labels=data_res['name'])
plt.xlabel('weight')
plt.show()
```

This results in the following output:

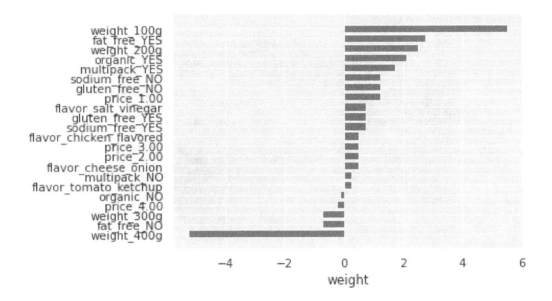

Figure 4.8: Product features' weights sorted

It can be seen that memory has the highest contribution to evaluation, followed by storage.

We have seen how OLS can be used as a mean to estimate the importance of each product feature. In this case, it has been modeled as a regression over a single variable, but we could include information about the type of respondent in order to discover how different customer segments react to product features.

In the next section, we evaluate a case of a consumer goods product with even more features.

Working with more product features

In the example, we will use a dataset that contains many more features than the previous example. In this case, we will simulate data obtained from a crisp retail vendor that has asked some of its customers to rank its products according to their level of preference:

1. The following block of code will read the dataset, which is a CSV file, and will prompt us with the result:

```
# Load data
conjoint_dat = pd.read_csv('/content/conjoint_data.csv')
conjoint_dat
```

This results in the following output:

	flavor	price	weight	fat_free	sodium_free	gluten_free	organic	multipack	ranking
1	cheese_onion	1.00	100g	NO	NO	NO	NO	NO	11
2	salt_vinegar	3.00	100g	NO	YES	YES	YES	NO	12
3	chicken_flavored	4.00	200g	NO	NO	NO	YES	NO	9
4	salt_vinegar	4.00	400g	YES	YES	NO	NO	NO	2
5	salt_vinegar	2.00	300g	NO	NO	NO	YES	YES	8
6	salt_vinegar	1.00	200g	YES	NO	YES	NO	YES	13
7	chicken_flavored	3.00	300g	YES	NO	YES	NO	NO	7
8	cheese_onion	4.00	300g	NO	YES	YES	NO	YES	4
9	cheese_onion	2.00	400g	YES	NO	YES	YES	NO	5
10	tomato_ketchup	4.00	100g	YES	NO	YES	YES	YES	16
11	chicken_flavored	1.00	400g	NO	YES	YES	YES	YES	3
12	tomato_ketchup	2.00	200g	NO	YES	YES	NO	NO	6
13	tomato_ketchup	1.00	300g	YES	YES	NO	YES	NO	10
14	chicken_flavored	2.00	100g	YES	YES	NO	NO	YES	15
15	tomato_ketchup	3.00	400g	NO	NO	NO	NO	YES	1
16	cheese_onion	3.00	200g	YES	YES	NO	YES	YES	14

Figure 4.9: Crisps data

2. We can see that the data contains only categorical values, so it will be necessary to transform this categorical data into a one-hot vector representation using the get_dummies pandas function, which is what we do in the next block of code:

```
conjoint_dat_dum = pd.get_dummies(conjoint_dat.iloc[:,:-
1], columns = conjoint_dat.iloc[:,:-1].columns)
conjoint_dat_dum
```

We can see that now we have created a set of columns that describe the product features using 1s and 0s:

	flavor_cheese_onion	flavor_chicken_flavored	flavor_salt_vinegar	flavor_tomato_ketchup	price_1.00	price_2.00
1	1	0	0	0	1	0
2	0	0	1	0	0	0
3	0	1	0	0	0	0
4	0	0	1	0	0	0
5	0	0	1	0	0	1

5 rows × 22 columns

Figure 4.10: Crisps data in a one-hot representation

3. We can now construct an OLS model using the one-hot vector representation of the product features and passing the ranking as the target variable:

```
main_effects_model_fit = sm.OLS(conjoint_dat['ranking'].
astype(int), sm.add_constant(conjoint_dat_dum))
result = main_effects_model_fit.fit()
result.summary()
```

This results in the following output:

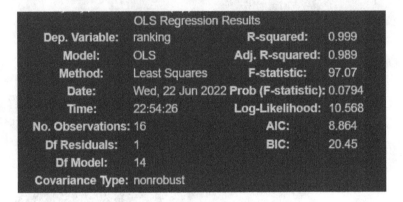

OLS Regression Results			
Dep. Variable:	ranking	R-squared:	0.999
Model:	OLS	Adj. R-squared:	0.989
Method:	Least Squares	F-statistic:	97.07
Date:	Wed, 22 Jun 2022	Prob (F-statistic):	0.0794
Time:	22:54:26	Log-Likelihood:	10.568
No. Observations:	16	AIC:	8.864
Df Residuals:	1	BIC:	20.45
Df Model:	14		
Covariance Type:	nonrobust		

Figure 4.11: OLS regression results

The terms **AIC** and **BIC** in the model summary, which stand for **Akaike's Information Criteria** and **Bayesian Information Criteria**, respectively, are frequently used in model selection criteria; however, they are not interchangeable. BIC is a type of model selection among a class of parametric models with variable numbers of parameters, whereas AIC may be thought of as a measure of the goodness of fit of an estimated statistical model. The penalty for additional parameters is greater in BIC than in AIC. BIC penalizes free parameters more severely than AIC.

AIC typically looks for undiscovered models with high-dimensional reality. This indicates that AIC models are not accurate models. BIC, on the other hand, only encounters `True` models. Additionally, BIC is consistent, although AIC is not, it might be said. BIC will indicate the risk that it would underfit, while AIC is more suited to examine whether the model has anger that it would outfit. Although BIC is more forgiving than AIC, it becomes less forgiving as the number increases. Cross-validation can be made asymptotically equal with the help of AIC. BIC, on the other hand, is useful for accurate estimation.

The penalty for additional parameters is higher in BIC than in AIC when comparing the two. AIC often looks for an unidentified model with a high-dimensional reality. BIC, on the other hand, exclusively finds `True` models. AIC is not consistent, whereas BIC is. Although BIC is more forgiving than AIC, it becomes less forgiving as the number increases. BIC penalizes free parameters more severely than AIC.

4. The next code will create a DataFrame where we can store the most important values from the analysis, which in this case are the weights and p-values:

```
data_res = pd.DataFrame({'name': result.params.keys(),
                         'weight': result.params.values,
                         'p_val': result.pvalues})
data_res = data_res[1:]
data_res
```

This results in the following output:

	name	weight	p_val
flavor_cheese_onion	flavor_cheese_onion	0.500	0.260281
flavor_chicken_flavored	flavor_chicken_flavored	0.500	0.260281
flavor_salt_vinegar	flavor_salt_vinegar	0.750	0.179010
flavor_tomato_ketchup	flavor_tomato_ketchup	0.250	0.454553
price_1.00	price_1.00	1.250	0.109244
price_2.00	price_2.00	0.500	0.260281
price_3.00	price_3.00	0.500	0.260281
price_4.00	price_4.00	-0.250	0.454553
weight_100g	weight_100g	5.500	0.025062
weight_200g	weight_200g	2.500	0.055027
weight_300g	weight_300g	-0.750	0.179010
weight_400g	weight_400g	-5.250	0.026254
fat_free_NO	fat_free_NO	-0.750	0.105849
fat_free_YES	fat_free_YES	2.750	0.029117
sodium_free_NO	sodium_free_NO	1.250	0.063886
sodium_free_YES	sodium_free_YES	0.750	0.105849
gluten_free_NO	gluten_free_NO	1.250	0.063886
gluten_free_YES	gluten_free_YES	0.750	0.105849
organic_NO	organic_NO	-0.125	0.502188

Figure 4.12: OLS variable weights and p-values

5. Now that we have the values arranged, we can check the significance of each one of the relationships to check the validity of the assumption and visualize the weights:

```
xbar = np.arange(len(data_res['weight']))
plt.barh(xbar, data_res['weight'])
plt.yticks(xbar, labels=data_res['name'])
plt.xlabel('weight')
plt.show()
```

This results in the following output

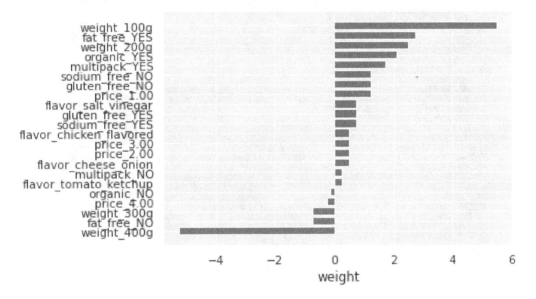

Figure 4.13: Variable weights sorted by importance

In this case, it can be seen that there are factors that are positively related, such as the weight of 100 grams, and the option for the product to be fat-free, while there are other factors that are negatively related, such as the weight of 400 grams, followed by that the product is not fat-free.

One of the questions that might arise is this: *If we have a regressor model to estimate the product score, can we use the same model to predict how customers will react to new product combinations?* In theory, we could, but in that case, we would have to use a scoring system instead of a ranking and have much, much more data. For demonstration purposes, we will continue regardless as this data is difficult to get and even more difficult to disclose.

Predicting new feature combinations

Now that we have properly trained our predictor, we can use it besides capturing information about the product features' importance to also provide us with information about how new product features will perform:

1. After going through the EDA, we will develop some predictive models and compare them. We will use the DataFrame where we had created dummy variables, scaling all the variables to a range of 0 to 1:

```
from sklearn.preprocessing import StandardScaler
X = conjoint_dat_dum
y = conjoint_dat['ranking'].astype(int)
# The target variable will be normalized from a ranking
to a 1 to 10 score
y = y.apply(lambda x: int(x/len(y)*10))


features = X.columns.values
scaler = StandardScaler()
scaler.fit(X)
X = pd.DataFrame(scaler.transform(X))
X.columns = features
```

This results in the following output:

	flavor_cheese_onion	flavor_chicken_flavored	flavor_salt_vinegar	flavor_tomato_ketchup	price_1.00	price_2.00	price_3.00	price_4.00	weight_100g	weight_200g	...
0	1.732051	-0.577350	-0.577350	0.57735	1.732051	-0.577350	0.577350	-0.577350	1.732051	-0.577350	
1	-0.577350	-0.577350	1.732051	-0.57735	-0.577350	-0.577350	1.732051	-0.577350	1.732051	-0.577350	
2	-0.577350	1.732051	-0.577350	-0.57735	-0.577350	-0.577350	0.577350	1.732051	-0.577350	1.732051	
3	-0.577350	-0.577350	1.732051	0.57735	-0.577350	-0.577350	-0.577350	1.732051	-0.577350	-0.577350	
4	-0.577350	-0.577350	1.732051	-0.57735	-0.577350	1.732051	0.577350	-0.577350	-0.577350	-0.577350	

5 rows × 22 columns

Figure 4.14: Scaled variables

One of the most popular ML models is Logistic Regression, which is an algorithm that uses independent variables to make predictions. This algorithm can be used in the context of classification and regression tasks. It's a supervised algorithm that requires the data to be labeled. This algorithm uses example answers to fit the model to the target variable, which in our case is the product ranking. In mathematical terms, the model seeks to predict Y given a set of independent X variables. Logistic Regression can be defined between binary and multinomial logistic regression. Namely, the characteristic of these two can be described as follows:

*   **Binary**: The most used of all the types of logistic regression, the algorithm seeks to differentiate between 0s and 1s, a task that is regarded as classification.

- **Multinomial**: When the target or independent variable has three or more potential values, multinomial logistic regression is used. For instance, using features of chest X-rays can indicate one of three probable outcomes (absence of disease, pneumonia, or fibrosis). The example, in this case, is ranked according to features into one of three possible outcomes using multinomial logistic regression. Of course, the target variable can have more than three possible values.

- **Ordinal logistic regression**: If the target variable is ordinal in nature, ordinal logistic regression is utilized. Each category has a quantitative meaning and is considerably ordered in this type. Additionally, the target variable contains more categories than just two. Exam results, for instance, are categorized and sorted according to quantitative criteria. Grades can be A, B, or C, to put it simply.

2. The primary distinction between linear and logistic regression is that whereas logistic regression is used to solve classification problems, linear regression is used to address regression difficulties. Target variables in regression issues might have continuous values, such as a product's price or a participant's age, while classification problems are concerned with predicting target variables that can only have discrete values, such as determining a person's gender or whether a tumor is malignant or benign:

```
# Logistic Regression
from sklearn.model_selection import train_test_split
from sklearn.linear_model import LogisticRegression
from sklearn import metrics

X_train, X_test, y_train, y_test = train_test_split(X, y,
test_size=0.5, random_state=101)

# Running logistic regression model
model = LogisticRegression()
result = model.fit(X_train, y_train)
```

By feeding the train set features and their matching target class values to the model, it can be trained. This will help the model learn how to categorize new cases. It is crucial to assess the model's performance on instances that have not yet been encountered because it will only be helpful if it can accurately classify examples that are not part of the training set.

The average of the error squares is measured by the **mean squared error** (**MSE**), which is the average of the sums of the squares of each discrepancy between the estimated value and the true value.

3. The MSE is always positive, although it can be 0 if the predictions are completely accurate. It includes the variance of the estimator (how widespread the estimates are) and the bias (how different the estimated values are from their actual values):

```
prediction_test = model.predict(X_test)
# Print the prediction accuracy
print(metrics.mean_squared_error(y_test, prediction_
test))
```

This results in the following output:

```
# Print the prediction accuracy
print(metrics.mean_squared_error(y_test, prediction_test))

10.125
```

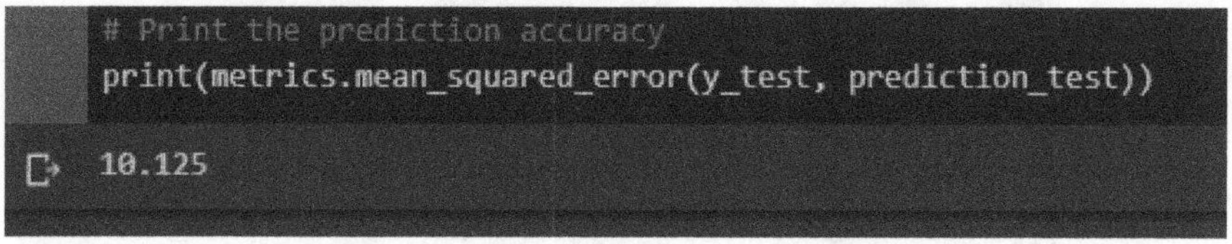

Figure 4.15: MSE of the simple regression

4. The MSE is always 0 or positive. If the MSE is large, this indicates that the linear regression model does not accurately predict the model. The important point is that MSE is sensitive to outliers. This is because the error at each data point is averaged. Therefore, if the outlier error is large, the MSE will be amplified. There is no "target" value for MSE. However, MSE is a good indicator of how well your model fits your data. You can also indicate whether you prefer one model to another:

```
# To get the weights of all the variables
weights = pd.Series(model.coef_[0],
                    index=X.columns.values)
print(weights.sort_values(ascending = False)[:10].
plot(kind='bar'))
```

This results in the following output:

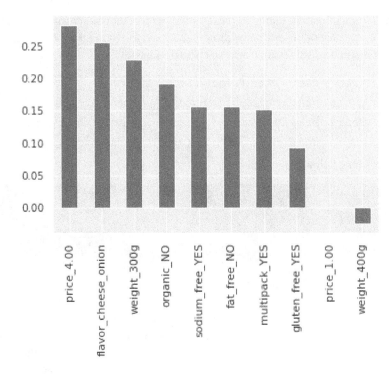

Figure 4.16: Linear regression top variable contribution

Here, we can see the first 10 variables that the model has identified as positively related to the score.

5. The next code will show us the ones that are more negatively related:

```
print(weights.sort_values(ascending = False)[-10:].
plot(kind='bar'))
```

This results in the following output:

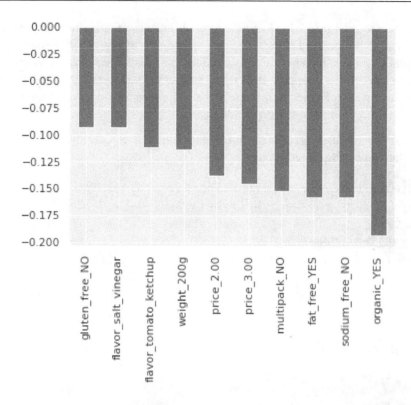

Figure 4.17: Linear regression negative variable contribution

Random Forest is a **supervised learning** (**SL**) algorithm. It can be used both for classification and regression. Additionally, it is the most adaptable and user-friendly algorithm. There are trees in a forest. A forest is supposed to be stronger the more trees it has. On randomly chosen data samples, random forests generate decision trees, obtain a prediction from each tree, and then vote for the best option. They also offer a fairly accurate indication of the significance of the feature.

Applications for random forests include feature selection, picture classification, and recommendation engines. They can be used to categorize dependable loan candidates, spot fraud, and forecast sickness.

A random forest is a meta-estimator that employs the mean to increase predicted accuracy and reduce overfitting. It fits a number of decision-tree classifications over various dataset subsamples. If `bootstrap = True` (the default), the size of the subsample is specified by the `max_samples` argument; otherwise, each tree is constructed using the complete dataset. In random forests, each tree in the ensemble is constructed using a sample taken from the training set using a substitution (that is, a bootstrap sample). Additionally, the optimal split of all input features or any subset of `max_features` size is discovered when splitting each node during tree construction.

These two random sources are used to lower the forest estimator's variance. In actuality, individual decision trees frequently overfit and have considerable variance. Decision trees with partially dissociated prediction errors are produced when randomness is added into forests. The average of these projections can help certain inaccuracies disappear. By merging various trees, random forests reduce variation, sometimes at the expense of a modest increase in distortion. The variance reduction is frequently large in practice, which leads to a stronger overall model.

Instead of having each classifier select a single class, the scikit-learn implementation combines classifiers by averaging their probabilistic predictions:

```
from sklearn.ensemble import RandomForestClassifier
model_rf = RandomForestClassifier(n_estimators=1000 , oob_
score = True, n_jobs = -1,random_state =50, max_features =
"auto",max_leaf_nodes = 30)
model_rf.fit(X_train, y_train)
# Make predictions
prediction_test = model_rf.predict(X_test)
print(metrics.mean_squared_error(y_test, prediction_test))
```

This results in the following output:

```
# Make predictions
prediction_test = model_rf.predict(X_test)
print(metrics.mean_squared_error(y_test, prediction_test))
```
```
10.125
```

Figure 4.18: Random Forest MSE

One of the available options in terms of ML models is the Random Forest algorithm, which is implemented in the scikit-learn package and includes the RandomForestRegressor and RandomForestClassifier classes. These classes can be fitted to data, yielding a model that can then be used to create new predictions or to obtain information about feature importance, a property that is at the core of the importance of conjoint analysis, as in the following example:

```
importances = model_rf.feature_importances_
weights = pd.Series(importances, index=X.columns.values)
weights.sort_values()[-10:].plot(kind = 'barh')
```

This results in the following output:

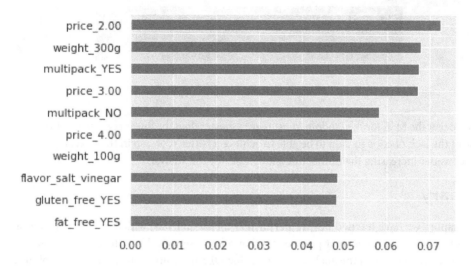

Figure 4.19: Random Forest variable importance

The XGBoost library is a highly effective, adaptable, and portable library for distributed gradient augmentation. It applies ML techniques within the Gradient Boosting framework and offers parallel tree amplification (also known as GBDT and GBM), which gives quick and accurate answers to a variety of data science issues. The same code can handle problems that involve more than a trillion examples and runs in massively distributed contexts.

It has been the primary impetus behind algorithms that have recently won significant ML competitions. It routinely surpasses all other algorithms for SL tasks due to its unrivaled speed and performance.

The primary algorithm can operate on clusters of GPUs or even on a network of PCs because the library is parallelizable. This makes it possible to train on hundreds of millions of training instances and solve ML tasks with great performance.

After winning a significant physics competition, it was rapidly embraced by the ML community despite being originally built in C++:

```
from xgboost import XGBClassifier
model = XGBClassifier()
model.fit(X_train, y_train)
preds = model.predict(X_test)
metrics.mean_squared_error(y_test, preds)
```

This results in the following output:

```
metrics.mean_squared_error(y_test, preds)
```
```
17.5
```

Figure 4.20: Random Forest MSE

We can see that the MSE for the random forest is even greater than the linear regression. This is possible because of the lack of enough data to be able to achieve a better score, so in the next steps, we would have to consider increasing the number of data points for the analysis.

Summary

In this chapter, we have learned how to perform conjoint analysis, which is a statistical tool that allows us to undercover consumer preferences that otherwise would be difficult to determine. The way in which we performed the analysis was by using OLS to estimate the performance of different combinations of features and try to isolate the impact of each one of the possible configurations in the overall perception of the client to undercover where the consumer perceives the value.

This has allowed us to create an overview of the factors that drive users to buy a product, and even be able to predict how a new combination of features will perform by using ML algorithms.

In the next chapter, we will learn how to adjust the price of items by studying the relationship between price variation and the number of quantities sold using price elasticity.

Selecting the Optimal Price with Price Demand Elasticity

Price elasticity of demand measures how much a product's consumption changes in response to price changes. A good is elastic if a price adjustment results in a significant shift in either supply or demand. If a price adjustment for the goods does not significantly affect demand or supply, it is inelastic. The elasticity of a product is impacted by the accessibility of an alternative. Demand won't change as the price increases if the product is necessary and there are no suitable alternatives, making it inelastic.

In this chapter, we will learn about the following:

- What is price elasticity and how it can be used to maximize revenue?
- Exploring the data to determine pricing patterns and consumer behavior around them
- Determining the demand curve for different products
- Optimizing the price to maximize revenue for all items

In this case, we will use food truck sales data to analyze the impact of different pricing strategies.

Technical requirements

In order to be able to follow the steps in this chapter, you will need to meet the next requirements:

- A Jupyter Notebook instance running Python 3.7 or above. You can also use the Google Colab notebook to run the steps if you have a Google Drive account.
- Understanding of basic math and statistical concepts.

Understanding price demand elasticity

The concept of price elasticity is used when trying to explain the responsiveness of the number of goods sold to proportional increases in price. This is valuable information for managers that need to anticipate how the finance of the company will be affected by price rises and cuts.

Mathematically, it is as follows:

$$e_p = (\Delta Q/Q)/(\Delta P/P)$$

Here, each term represents the following:

- e_p: Price elasticity
- Q: Quantity of the demanded good
- ΔQ: Variation in the quantity of the demanded good
- P: Price of the demanded good
- ΔP: Variation in the price of the demanded good

Price elasticity is a measure of how sensitive the quantity required is to price, with nearly all goods seeing a fall in demand when prices rise but some seeing a greater decline. Price elasticity determines, while holding all other factors constant, the percentage change in quantity demanded by a 1% rise in price. When the elasticity is -2, the amount demanded decreases by 2% for every 1% increase in price. Outside of certain circumstances, price elasticity is negative. When a good is described as having an elasticity of 2, it almost invariably indicates that the formal definition of that elasticity is -2.

The term **more elastic** means that the elasticity of a good is greater, regardless of the sign. Two uncommon exceptions to the rule of demand, the Veblen and Giffen goods are two groups of goods with positive elasticity. A good's demand is considered to be inelastic when its absolute value of elasticity is less than 1, meaning that price changes have a relatively minor impact on the amount demanded. If a good's demand is more elastic than 1, it is considered to be elastic. A good with an elastic demand of -2 has a drop-in quantity that is twice as great as its price rise, whereas a good with an inelastic demand of -0.5 has a decrease in the quantity that is only half as great as the price increase.

When the price is chosen so that the elasticity is exactly 1, revenue is maximized. The incidence (or "burden") of a tax on a good can be predicted using the elasticity of the good. To ascertain price elasticity, a variety of research techniques are employed, such as test markets, historical sales data analysis, and conjoint analysis.

Exploring the data

The experiment's initial data source is the sales of a food truck outside of office buildings. It's vital to review excessive prices because of the pressure on costs. The proprietor of a food truck must be aware of how a price increase affects the store's demand for hamburgers. In other words, to determine how much the price can be raised, it is critical to understand the price elasticity of demand for the burgers in the store. In actuality, price elasticity measures how much a product's price influences demand.

We will use the following Python modules in the next example:

- **Pandas**: A Python package for data analysis and data manipulation.
- **NumPy**: This is a library that adds support for large, multi-dimensional arrays and matrices, along with a large collection of high-level mathematical functions to operate on these arrays.
- **statsmodels**: A Python package that provides a complement to SciPy for statistical computations, including descriptive statistics and estimation and inference for statistical models. It provides classes and functions for the estimation of many different statistical models. It's a Python package that is used for statistical methods and descriptive statistics, as well as other models' statistical models.
- **Seaborn and Matplotlib**: Python packages for effective data visualization.

1. The following block of code will load all the required packages as well as load the data and show the first five rows of it:

```python
import pandas as pd
import numpy as np
import statsmodels.api as sm
from statsmodels.formula.api import ols
import matplotlib.pyplot as plt
import seaborn as sns; sns.set(style="ticks",
        color_codes=True)
data = pd.read_csv('foodcar_data.csv',
        parse_dates=['DATE'])
data.head()
```

This results in the next DataFrame, showing the data that contains the transactional data of items sold by a food truck, along with some other external variables:

	SELLER	CAT	ITEM_ID	ITEM_NAME	STORE	DATE	PRICE	QUANTITY	YEAR	HOLIDAY	WEEKEND	SCHOOLBREAK	AVG_TEMPERATURE
0	1070	0	2752	BURGER	1	2018-06-25	20.08	90	2012	New Year	1	0	24.8
1	2051	2	2752	BURGER	1	2018-06-25	16.54	42	2012	New Year	1	0	24.8
2	2051	2	4273	COKE	1	2018-06-25	16.54	42	2012	New Year	1	0	24.8
3	2052	2	2752	BURGER	1	2018-06-25	16.57	34	2012	New Year	1	0	24.8
4	2052	2	6249	WATER	1	2018-06-25	16.57	34	2012	New Year	1	0	24.8

Figure 5.1: Food truck sales data to be analyzed

The data consists of the following variables:

- **SELLER**: Identifier of who sold the item
- **CAT**: Variable indicating whether the product was sold by itself (**0**) or as part of a combo (**2**)
- **ITEM_ID**: Identifier of the item sold
- **ITEM_NAME**: Full name of the item
- **DATE**: When the item was sold
- **YEAR**: Year extracted from the date
- **HOLIDAY**: Boolean variable that indicates whether that day was a holiday
- **WEEKEND**: Boolean variable indicating whether it was a weekend
- **SCHOOLBREAK**: Boolean variable indicating whether it was a school break
- **AVG_TEMPERATURE**: Temperature that day in degrees Fahrenheit

2.   In the next command, we will run a descriptive statistical analysis, previously removing the **ITEM_ID** column, because although this is understood as a numeric variable, it represents a categorical dimension.

```
data.drop(['ITEM_ID'],axis=1).describe()
```

This results in the following output:

	SELLER	CAT	STORE	PRICE	QUANTITY	YEAR	WEEKEND	SCHOOLBREAK	AVG_TEMPERATURE
count	10840.000000	10840.000000	10840.0	10840.000000	10840.000000	10840.000000	10840.000000	10840.00000	10840.000000
mean	1929.375000	1.750000	1.0	16.210829	77.856089	2013.373432	0.284133	0.20369	56.234244
std	324.829137	0.661468	0.0	1.698700	41.874907	1.070637	0.451021	0.40276	20.224510
min	1070.000000	0.000000	1.0	13.220000	14.000000	2012.000000	0.000000	0.00000	14.000000
25%	2051.000000	2.000000	1.0	14.950000	46.000000	2012.000000	0.000000	0.00000	35.600000
50%	2052.000000	2.000000	1.0	16.200000	66.000000	2013.000000	0.000000	0.00000	60.800000
75%	2053.000000	2.000000	1.0	16.700000	98.000000	2014.000000	1.000000	0.00000	75.200000
max	2053.000000	2.000000	1.0	21.350000	246.000000	2015.000000	1.000000	1.00000	87.800000

Figure 5.2: Statistical description summary of the data

3.   One of the things we are interested to know is the different types of products that we will find in the data. In this case, we will just pick the **SELLER**, **ITEM_ID**, and **ITEM_NAME** data and remove the duplicates:

```
d = data[['SELLER','ITEM_ID','ITEM_NAME']].drop_duplicates()
print(d)
```

This results in the following output:

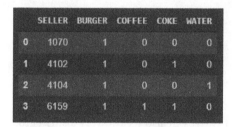

	SELLER	ITEM_ID	ITEM_NAME
0	1070	2752	BURGER
1	2051	2752	BURGER
2	2051	4273	COKE
3	2052	2752	BURGER
4	2052	6249	WATER
5	2053	2752	BURGER
6	2053	4273	COKE
7	2053	3052	COFFEE

Figure 5.3: Products that are being sold

4. By transforming this data into dummies, we can see that the seller column actually shows different combinations of products, some of them being sold alone and some of them being sold as combos, such as **4104**, which is a burger and a bottle of water:

```
pd.concat([d.SELLER, pd.get_dummies(d.ITEM_NAME)],
axis=1).groupby(d.SELLER).sum().reset_index(drop=True)
```

This results in the following output:

	SELLER	BURGER	COFFEE	COKE	WATER
0	1070	1	0	0	0
1	4102	1	0	1	0
2	4104	1	0	0	1
3	6159	1	1	1	0

Figure 5.4: Combination of products sold

5. One of the ways that we can use to start exploring the data is by running a pair plot. This Seaborn plot allows us to see the distribution of the values, as well as the relationship between the variables. It's really useful if we want to be able to see any possible relationship between them at first glance:

```
sns.
pairplot(data[['PRICE','QUANTITY']],height=5,aspect=1.2)
```

This results in the following output:

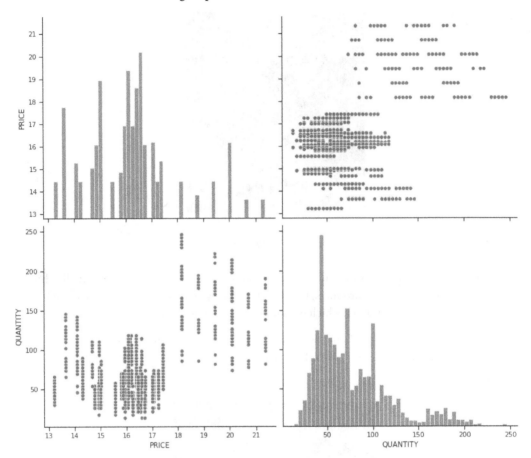

Figure 5.5: Pair plot of price and quantity

At a simple glance, we can see that there are many superimposed trends in the relationship between price and quantity. We can also see two very distinct groups, one placed in the lower-left quadrant and the other in the upper-right quadrant.

6.   We can explore the relationship between price and the CAT variable to dive into these differences using the Seaborn histogram plot and using the CAT variable as the hue. The next block of code does exactly this, first by creating a matplotlib figure, which is then populated with the defined histogram. This is useful for certain kinds of Seaborn plots that require this setup to define the figure size properly:

```
f, ax = plt.subplots(figsize=(10, 6))
fig = sns.histplot(x='PRICE',data=data,hue='CAT',
palette=['red','blue'])
```

This results in the following output:

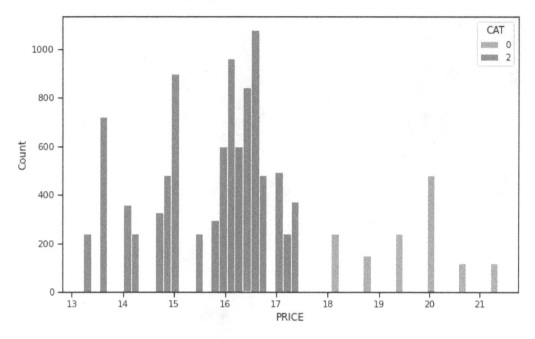

Figure 5.6: Price histogram differentiated by CAT

We can see in the preceding plot that the products that have a CAT value of **2** are more highly priced than the other ones.

7. These are the product sold in combos, so this is a reasonable outcome. We can keep exploring these price differences by running a new pair plot – this time, looking for the relationship between PRICE, QUANTITY, and ITEM_NAME:

```
sns.pairplot(data[['PRICE','QUANTITY','ITEM_NAME']], hue
= 'ITEM_NAME', plot_kws={'alpha':0.1},height=5,aspect=1.2)
```

This results in the following output:

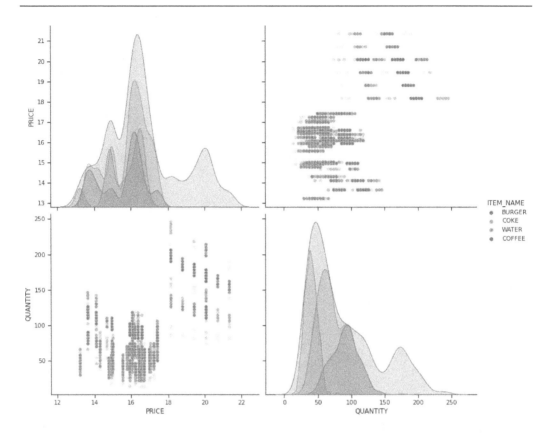

Figure 5.7: Price, quantity, and item name pair plot

We can see now the differences between the prices of each item in a bit more detail. In this case, the burgers have the highest price, and water is the cheapest (again, reasonable). What is interesting to see is that for the same items, we have different prices, and differences in the number of units being sold.

We can conclude then that is necessary to analyze the price difference by having a clear distinction per item, as we will most likely have different elasticities and optimal prices for each one of them.

8. The next block of code will create a Matplotlib figure of 10 x 6 inches and fill it up with a Seaborn histogram plot that will show us the distribution of item names per category:

```
f, ax = plt.subplots(figsize=(10, 6))
fig = sns.histplot(x='ITEM_NAME',data=data,hue='CAT',
palette=['red','blue'])
```

This results in the following output:

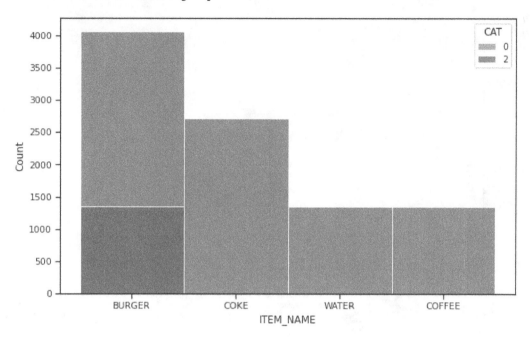

Figure 5.8: Histogram of item names per category

From this histogram, we can see that the burger is the only item that belongs to category **0**, so that is sold alone. This means that Coke, water, and coffee are all sold in a bundle along with a burger. This is useful information, as it shows us the way the food truck owner sells their products, thus allowing us to think of better ways to price or combine products to be offered to customers.

9. The next block of code will filter the data to only contain items that fall into CAT = 2 and will create a Seaborn relation plot to explain the relationship between price and quantity:

```
d = data[data['CAT']==2]
sns.
relplot(x=d['PRICE'],y=d['QUANTITY'],height=7,aspect=1.2)
```

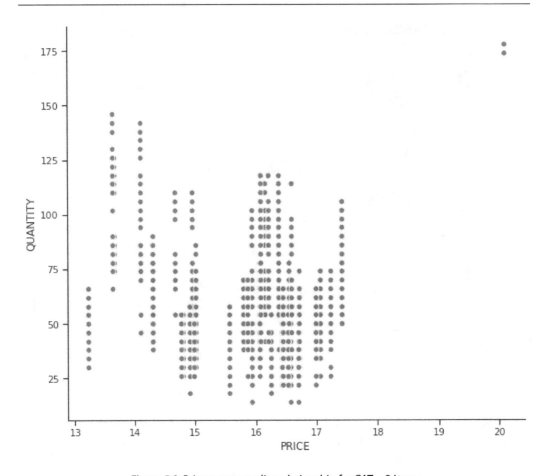

Figure 5.9: Price versus quality relationship for CAT = 2 items

In the relationship plot shown here, we can see the relationship between price and quality in items that belong to the second category, meaning that all of them were sold as part of a combo. Besides the outliers, which were priced much higher than the rest of the data points, most of the items are within a certain range. Although we are looking at several items at the same time, we can see a certain relationship by realizing that items that were priced lower were sold in greater quantities. Our job will now be to dive into the specifics of these relationships at the item level in order to be able to determine the price that will maximize the revenue.

10. In the next block of code, we will try to capture the changes in price and the quantities being sold over time. We will create a new set of data in which we will look at the prices and quantities in a normalized way by subtracting the mean and dividing it by the range:

```
d = data[['DATE','PRICE','QUANTITY']].sort_values(
['DATE'], ascending=True)
d['PRICE'] = (d['PRICE'] - d['PRICE'].mean())/
```

```
((d['PRICE'].max() - d['PRICE'].min()))
d['QUANTITY'] = (d['QUANTITY'] - d['QUANTITY'].mean())/
((d['QUANTITY'].max() - d['QUANTITY'].min()))
```

11. Once we have normalized the price and quantities on a scale that ranges from -1 to 1, we will set d['DATE'] as the index, and finally, apply a rolling average to soften the curves, and use the plot method of the pandas DataFrame object:

```
d.index = d['DATE']
d = d.drop(['DATE'],axis=1)
d.rolling(window=60).mean().plot(figsize=(20,8))
```

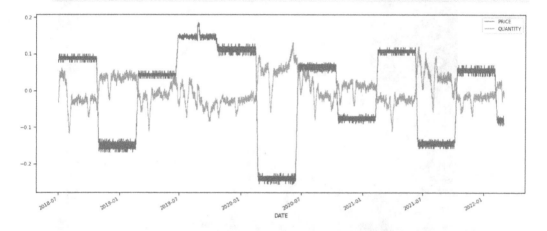

Figure 5.10: Price versus quality relationship over time

It is interesting to see that price reductions have always led to increases in the quantities being sold. In this case, we can see that the biggest price drop was in the first half of 2020, which led to an increase in the quantities being sold. The question that we need to ask is whether the amount of revenue that was lost by this price reduction has been compensated for by an increase in the number of products sold.

12. In the next block of code, we will try to dive into the correlation between the different variables and price. To do this, we will use both the corr() method of the pandas Dataframe, and the NumPy library to create a mask to "cover" the repeated values above the diagonal, as well as the matplotlib library to create a 12 x 12-inch figure to populate with a Seaborn heat map:

```
import numpy as np
df_corr = data.drop(['DATE','SELLER','STORE'],axis=1).
corr()
mask = np.triu(np.ones_like(df_corr, dtype=bool))
```

```
df_corr = df_corr.mask(mask).round(3)
fig, ax = plt.subplots(figsize=(12,12))
sns.heatmap(df_corr, annot=True,ax=ax)
```

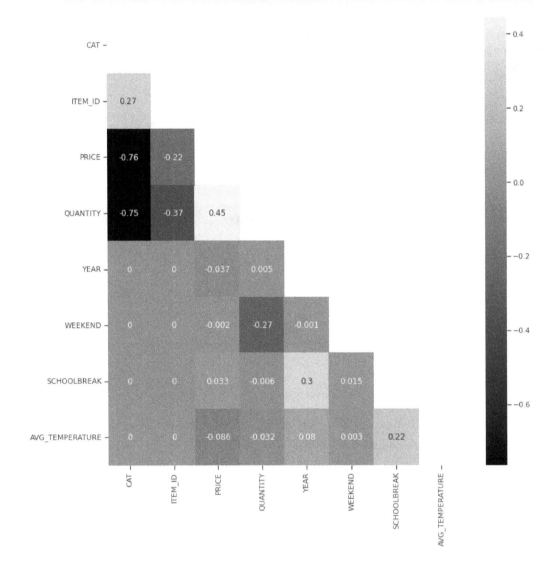

Figure 5.11: Correlation between variables

The data shown here gives us an idea of how the variables are correlated. We can see that there is a negative correlation between price versus temperature (people do not fancy a coffee and a burger combo when it is too hot perhaps), positive with a school break (maybe kids also buy products on these days), and a negative relationship with the weekend, which might indicate that the location of the food truck has less traffic during the weekends.

Please take these conclusions with a grain of salt, as we would need to go through a case-by-case analysis by item to corroborate these assumptions, and always remember the maxima that correlation does not imply causation.

Now that we have explored the data to understand the price differences for what would otherwise have seemed like the same items, as well as to understand how this distribution looks, we can try to estimate the demand curve. Knowing the demand curve allows us to establish the relationship between price and quantity sold, and it's what we will do in the next section.

Finding the demand curve

A demand curve in economics is a graph that depicts the relationship between the price of a specific good and the amount of that good needed at that price. Individual demand curves are used for price-volume interactions between individual consumers, while market-wide demand curves are utilized for all consumers (a market demand curve).

It is generally accepted that the demand curve declines because of the law of demand. For the majority of things, demand declines as price rises. This law does not apply in several peculiar circumstances. These include speculative bubbles, Veblen goods, and Giffen goods, and when prices rise, purchasers are drawn to the products.

Demand curves are used in combination with supply curves to establish an equilibrium price. At this ideal point, both sellers and buyers have achieved a mutual understanding of how valuable a good or service really is, which allows us to produce just enough to satisfy the demand without shortages or excess.

Exploring the demand curve in code

In order to find the demand curve for each one of the items, first, we will isolate the data for each item into a separate data frame:

1. In the next block of code, we create a DataFrame for `burger_2752` to dive into the specifics of the price versus demand relationship of this specific item, as we suspect that each item has its own specific demand curve:

```
burger_2752 = data[data['ITEM_ID']==2752].drop(['
        ITEM_ID','ITEM_NAME'],axis=1)
burger_2752.head()
```

	SELLER	CAT	STORE	DATE	PRICE	QUANTITY	YEAR	HOLIDAY	WEEKEND	SCHOOLBREAK	AVG_TEMPERATURE
0	1070	0	1	2018-06-25	20.08	90	2012	New Year	1	0	24.8
1	2051	2	1	2018-06-25	16.54	42	2012	New Year	1	0	24.8
3	2052	2	1	2018-06-25	16.57	34	2012	New Year	1	0	24.8
5	2053	2	1	2018-06-25	16.38	58	2012	New Year	1	0	24.8
8	1070	0	1	2018-06-26	20.08	138	2012	New Year	0	0	24.8

Figure 5.12: Burger data

2. Once we have isolated the data, we can start to determine the relationship between price versus data. To do this, we will use the `statsmodels` package, specifically the **Ordinary Least Squares (OLS)** module. We will analyze the relationship by passing the expected relationship as `"QUANTITY ~ PRICE"` as a parameter to the OLS function. This way, the OLS function will interpret `Quantity` as a dependent variable and `Price` as the independent variable. We could also pass other variables as dependent but for now, we will just focus on `Price`:

```
model = ols("QUANTITY ~ PRICE", burger_2752).fit()
```

3. Once the model is properly fitted to the data, we can print the slope of the relationship as the given item, `price_elasticity`, as well as the other parameters on the OLS model:

```
price_elasticity = model.params[1]
print("Price elasticity of the product: " + str(
        price_elasticity))
print(model.summary())
```

```
Price elasticity of the product: 16.11147227224823
                         OLS Regression Results
==============================================================================
Dep. Variable:               QUANTITY   R-squared:                      0.396
Model:                            OLS   Adj. R-squared:                 0.396
Method:                 Least Squares   F-statistic:                    3559.
Date:                Mon, 04 Jul 2022   Prob (F-statistic):              0.00
Time:                        00:50:43   Log-Likelihood:               -27634.
No. Observations:                5420   AIC:                        5.527e+04
Df Residuals:                    5418   BIC:                        5.529e+04
Df Model:                           1
Covariance Type:            nonrobust
==============================================================================
                 coef    std err          t      P>|t|      [0.025      0.975]
------------------------------------------------------------------------------
Intercept    -182.7699      4.549    -40.180      0.000    -191.687    -173.853
PRICE          16.1115      0.270     59.653      0.000      15.582      16.641
==============================================================================
Omnibus:                      374.179   Durbin-Watson:                  1.222
Prob(Omnibus):                  0.000   Jarque-Bera (JB):             456.318
Skew:                           0.710   Prob(JB):                   8.16e-100
Kurtosis:                       2.951   Cond. No.                        143.
==============================================================================
```

Figure 5.13: Burger OLS model summary

One of the ways in which we can analyze the model performance is by looking at the regression plots of the intercept and error. These are scatter plots that provide us with a sense of the relationship between dependent and independent variables in linear regression.

4. The next block of code will create a Matplotlib figure of 12 x 8 inches, and use statsmodels to create the partial regression plot for the model:

```
fig = plt.figure(figsize=(12,8))
fig = sm.graphics.plot_partregress_grid(model, fig=fig)
```

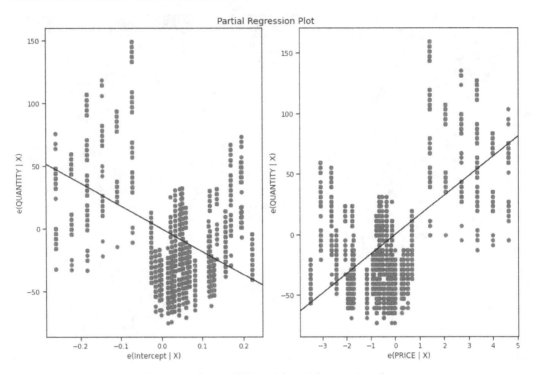

Figure 5.14: Burger OLS model partial regression plot

5. The next step in our analysis will be to create a function to pack the creation of the models, determine the price elasticity, and return the price elasticity and the model itself. This function takes the data for each item as a parameter:

```
def create_model_and_find_elasticity(data):
    model = ols("QUANTITY ~ PRICE", data).fit()
    price_elasticity = model.params[1]
    print("Price elasticity of the product: " +
str(price_elasticity))
    print(model.summary())
    fig = plt.figure(figsize=(12,8))
    fig = sm.graphics.plot_partregress_grid(model,
fig=fig)
    return price_elasticity, model
```

6. Now that we have defined the function, we will create two dictionaries to store the results: one for the elasticities, and the other for the models themselves. After this, we will loop over all the unique items in the data, apply the function to the subset of data, and finally, store the results for each one of the items:

```
elasticities = {}
models = {}
for item_id in data['ITEM_ID'].unique():
  print('item_id',item_id)
  price_elasticity, item_model =
    create_model_and_find_elasticity(data[data[
    'ITEM_ID']==item_id])
  elasticities[item_id] = price_elasticity
  models[item_id]= item_model
```

7. After running through all the unique items, we can print the results of the elasticities for each item.

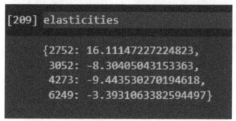

```
[209] elasticities

     {2752: 16.11147227224823,
      3052: -8.30405043153363,
      4273: -9.443530270194618,
      6249: -3.3931063382594497}
```

Figure 5.15: Product items elasticities

Now that we have determined the price elasticities for each item, we can simulate the different possible prices and find the point which maximizes revenue.

Optimizing revenue using the demand curve

Once we have established the relationship between the price and the quantity, we can simulate the revenue for each one of the possible prices. To do this, we will find the minimum and maximum price for each item, establish a threshold, create a range of possible prices, and use the stored model to predict the quantity sold. The next step is to determine the total revenue by multiplying the price by quantity. It is important to note that in this kind of analysis, it is always better to look at the revenue rather than the profit because most of the time, we don't have the data for the cost of each item. We will explore how to do so using the following steps:

1. The next block of code will take the data for `burger_2752`, determine the upper and lower price boundaries, create a range using a NumPy range, and finally, use the trained model to predict the quantity sold and therefore the revenue:

```
start_price = burger_2752.PRICE.min() - 1
end_price = burger_2752.PRICE.max() + 10
test = pd.DataFrame(columns = ["PRICE", "QUANTITY"])
test['PRICE'] = np.arange(start_price, end_price, 0.01)
test['QUANTITY'] = models[2752].predict(test['PRICE'])
test['REVENUE'] = test["PRICE"]  * test["QUANTITY"]
test.head()
```

	PRICE	QUANTITY	REVENUE
0	12.22	14.112284	172.452110
1	12.23	14.273399	174.563666
2	12.24	14.434513	176.678444
3	12.25	14.595628	178.796445
4	12.26	14.756743	180.917667

Figure 5.16: First rows of the predicted revenue for each price

2. To be able to visualize the relationship between the variables, regardless of the unit of measure, we will normalize the data variables by subtracting the mean and diving by the range. Finally, we will use the plot method to visualize the data:

```
test['PRICE'] = (test['PRICE']-test['PRICE'].mean())/
(test['PRICE'].max()-test['PRICE'].min())
test['QUANTITY'] = (test['QUANTITY']-test['QUANTITY'].
mean())/(test['QUANTITY'].max()-test['QUANTITY'].min())
test['REVENUE'] = (test['REVENUE']-test['REVENUE'].
mean())/(test['REVENUE'].max()-test['REVENUE'].min())
test.plot(figsize=(12,8),title='Price Elasticity - Item
2752)
```

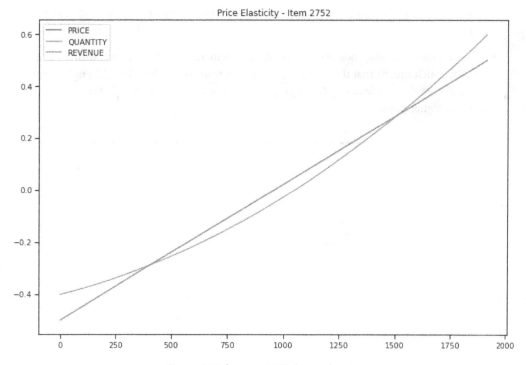

Figure 5.17: burger_2752 demand curve

We can see from the demand curve that this item is inelastic, meaning that even if the price goes up, more of this kind of product will continue to sell. To get a better picture, we will repeat the same exercise for a different item.

3. We will use the `coffee` data and repeat the same exercise to visualize the demand curve:

```
coffee_3052 = data[data['ITEM_ID']==3052]
start_price = coffee_3052.PRICE.min() - 1
end_price = coffee_3052.PRICE.max() + 10
test = pd.DataFrame(columns = ["PRICE", "QUANTITY"])
test['PRICE'] = np.arange(start_price, end_price,0.01)
test['QUANTITY'] = models[3052].predict(test['PRICE'])
test['REVENUE'] = test["PRICE"]  * test["QUANTITY"]
test['PRICE'] = (test['PRICE']-test['PRICE'].mean())/
(test['PRICE'].max()-test['PRICE'].min())
test['QUANTITY'] = (test['QUANTITY']-test['QUANTITY'].
mean())/(test['QUANTITY'].max()-test['QUANTITY'].min())
test['REVENUE'] = (test['REVENUE']-test['REVENUE'].
mean())/(test['REVENUE'].max()-test['REVENUE'].min())
```

```
test.plot(figsize=(12,8),title='Price Elasticity - Item
3052')
```

By running the preceding code, we can see that the demand curve is concave, with a negative elasticity, which means that if the price goes up, fewer units will be sold. Although this will create a decrease in revenue due to fewer units being sold, it also means that it will increase due to the higher price.

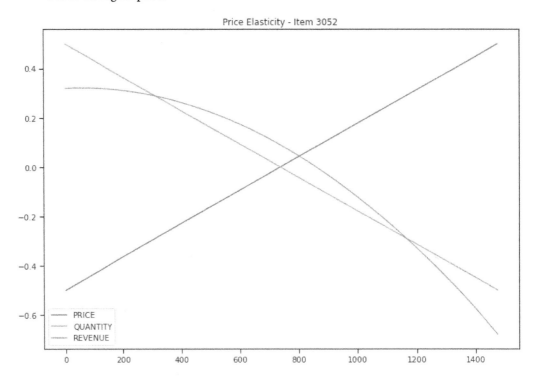

Figure 5.18: coffee_3052 demand curve

4. Now, we can take this procedure and transform it into a function that can be applied to each item's data to obtain the demand curve, and also determine the optimal price.

    The way in which we can determine the optimal price is quite simple. We just need to find the maximum value in the **REVENUE** column and find the optimal set of values. We can do this simply by using the NumPy package and the `where` clause, which will return the values at which the revenue is highest:

```
def find_optimal_price(data, model,item_id):
    start_price = data.PRICE.min() - 1
    end_price = data.PRICE.max() + 10
    test = pd.DataFrame(columns = ["PRICE", "QUANTITY"])
```

```
   test['PRICE'] = np.arange(start_price, end_price,0.01)
   test['QUANTITY'] = model.predict(test['PRICE'])
   test['REVENUE'] = test["PRICE"] * test["QUANTITY"]
   test['P'] = (test['PRICE']-test['PRICE'].mean())/
(test['PRICE'].max()-test['PRICE'].min())
   test['Q'] = (test['QUANTITY']-test['QUANTITY'].mean())/
(test['QUANTITY'].max()-test['QUANTITY'].min())
   test['R'] = (test['REVENUE']-test['REVENUE'].mean())/
(test['REVENUE'].max()-test['REVENUE'].min())
   test[['P','Q','R']].plot(figsize=(12,8),title='Price
Elasticity - Item'+str(item_id))
   ind = np.where(test['REVENUE'] == test['REVENUE'].
max())[0][0]
   values_at_max_profit = test.drop(['P','Q','R'],axis=1).
iloc[[ind]]
   values_at_max_profit = {'PRICE':values_at_max_
profit['PRICE'].values[0],'QUANTITY':values_at_max_
profit['QUANTITY'].values[0],'REVENUE':values_at_max_
profit['REVENUE'].values[0]}
   return values_at_max_profit
```

5. Now that we have the function to determine the maximum profit, we can calculate the optimal price for all items and store them in a dictionary:

```
optimal_price = {}
for item_id in data['ITEM_ID'].unique():
  print('item_id',item_id)
  optimal_price[item_id] =
    find_optimal_price(data[data['ITEM_ID']==item_id],
  models[item_id],item_id)
```

After running this for all of the items in the data, we can determine the parameters that will maximize the revenue for the food truck.

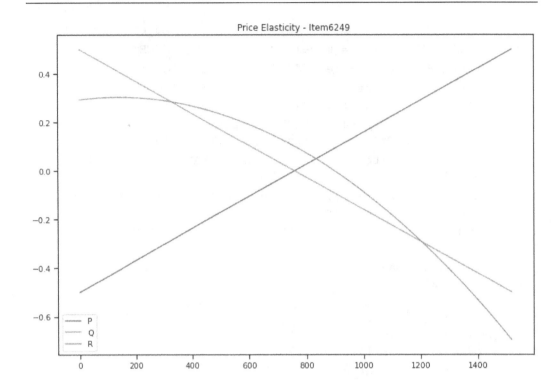

Figure 5.19: item_6249 demand curve

We can see for the other two items left to be analyzed that their elasticity is also negative, implicating that the higher the price, the lower the number of units sold is.

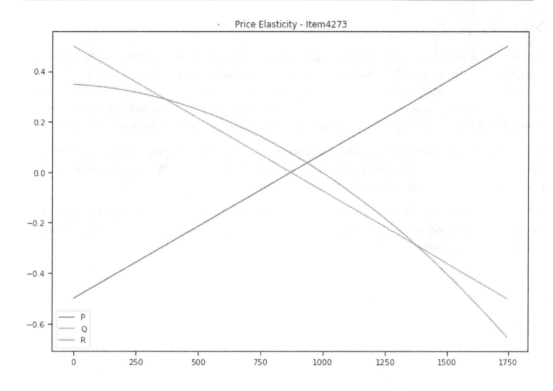

Figure 5.20: item_4273 demand curve

6. Now that we have the optimal prices, we can print the parameters that lead to a maximization of the revenue. The next block of code iterates over the optimal_price dictionary:

```
for item_id in optimal_price:
    print(item_id,optimal_price[item_id])
```

2752 {'PRICE': 31.34999999999959, 'QUANTITY': 322.3247485303399, 'REVENUE': 10104.880866426023}
4273 {'PRICE': 12.64, 'QUANTITY': 103.35978051094523, 'REVENUE': 1306.4676256583477}
6249 {'PRICE': 13.61999999999997, 'QUANTITY': 46.184112609833626, 'REVENUE': 629.0276137459326}
3052 {'PRICE': 13.199999999999989, 'QUANTITY': 109.59320508662924, 'REVENUE': 1446.6303071435048}

Figure 5.21: Optimal parameters for each item

In this way, we can determine the optimal price, regardless of the item's characteristics, and how much the customers are willing to pay for each item.

Summary

In this chapter, we dived into the relationship between the price of an item and the number of items being sold. We studied that different items have different demand curves, which means that in most cases, a higher price leads to the least items being sold, but this is not always the case. The relationship between price and quantity being sold can be modeled using price elasticity, which gives us an idea of how much the number of products being sold will be reduced by a given increase in the price.

We looked into the food truck sales data in order to determine the best price for each one of their items and we discovered that these items have different elasticities and that for each item, we can determine the price, which will maximize the revenue.

In the next chapter, we will focus on improving the way we bundle and recommend products by looking at how to perform a Market Basket analysis to recommend meaningful products that are frequently bought together.

6

Product Recommendation

Product recommendation is essentially a filtering system that aims to anticipate and present the goods that a user would be interested in buying. It is used to generate recommendations that keep users engaged with your product and service and provides relevant suggestions to them. In this chapter, we will learn how to do the following:

- Detect clients who are reducing their sales
- Target clients with personalized product suggestions for products that they are not yet buying
- Create specific product recommendations based on already bought products using market basket analysis and the Apriori algorithm

Let's determine what will be the requirements to understand the steps and follow the chapter.

This chapter covers the following topics:

- Targeting decreasing returning buyers
- Understanding product recommendation systems
- Using the Apriori algorithm for product bundling

Technical requirements

In order to be able to follow the steps in this chapter, you will need to meet the next requirements:

- Have a Jupyter notebook instance running Python 3.7 and above. You can also use the Google Colab notebook to run the steps if you have a Google Drive account.
- Have an understanding of basic math and statistical concepts.

Targeting decreasing returning buyers

One important aspect of businesses is that recurring customers always buy more than new ones, so it's important to keep an eye on them and act if we see that they are changing their behavior. One of the things that we can do is identify the clients with decreasing buying patterns and offer them new products that they are not yet buying. In this case, we will look at consumer goods distribution center data to identify these customers with decreasing purchases:

1. First, we will import the necessary libraries, which are the following: pandas for data manipulation, NumPy for masking and NaNs handling, and scikit-surprise for collaborative filtering product recommendation.

2. We will explore the data to determine the right strategy to normalize the data into the right format.

3. Once the data is structured, we will set up a linear regression to determine the clients with a negative slope to identify the ones with decreasing consumption patterns. This information will allow us to create specific actions for these clients and avoid customer churn.

Let's get started with the following steps:

1. Our first stage will be to load these packages and install the `scikit-surprise` package for collaborative filtering, which is a method to filter out items that a user might like based on the ratings of similar users. It works by linking the behaviors of a smaller set of users with tastes similar to a particular user product recommendations:

```
!pip install --upgrade openpyxl scikit-surprise
import pandas as pd
import numpy as np
```

2. For readability purposes, we will limit the maximum number of rows to be shown to 20, set the limit of maximum columns to 50, and show the floats with 2 digits of precision:

```
pd.options.display.max_rows = 20
pd.options.display.max_columns = 50
pd.options.display.precision = 2
```

3. Now we can load the data to be analyzed:

```
df = pd.read_csv('/content/distributed_products.csv')
df.head()
```

In the next figure, we show the historical sales of sold goods by period, details of both the client and product, and the quantity sold:

period	sub_market	client_class	division	brand	cat	product	client_code	client_name	kgs_sold
0	201807	CTAS.ESPECIALES	VTA	AGUA	AQUAFINA	DESCARTABLE	AQF C/GAS 2L	10034	LA TROYA	6
1	201807	CTAS.ESPECIALES	VTA	AGUA	AQUAFINA	DESCARTABLE	AQF C/GAS 2L	10137	PACHECO	7
2	201807	CTAS.ESPECIALES	VTA	AGUA	AQUAFINA	DESCARTABLE	AQF C/GAS 2L	10208	BOGGIANI	4
3	201807	CTAS.ESPECIALES	VTA	AGUA	AQUAFINA	DESCARTABLE	AQF C/GAS 2L	10226	BAHIA S.A.	0
4	201807	CTAS.ESPECIALES	VTA	AGUA	AQUAFINA	DESCARTABLE	AQF C/GAS 2L	10229	PAR PARIRI	0

Figure 6.1: Data of consumer goods transactions

The data consists of buy orders from different clients, for different products and different periods. The data has a period column with information about both the year and the month when the buy was made.

4. We can keep exploring the data by taking a look at the columns list:

```
df.columns.tolist()
>>> ['period', 'sub_market', 'client_class', 'division',
'brand','cat', 'product', 'client_code', 'client_name',
'kgs_sold']
```

5. Now, let's look at the total number of clients to analyze:

```
len(df.client_name.unique())
>>> 11493
```

In this case, we have almost 12,000 clients. For the demonstration purposes of this chapter, we will focus on the most important clients, based on the criteria of who are the ones that consume the most.

6. Now, we will find the clients that have been reducing sales. We will gauge the information to get the list of clients that have the highest total number of kilograms of products purchased to determine the best customers. We will use the groupby method with the sum by period to get the kilograms bought per client and period:

```
kgs_by_period = df[['period','client_name','kgs_sold']]
kgs_by_period = kgs_by_period.groupby(['
        period','client_name']).sum().reset_index()
kgs_by_period.head()
```

In the next figure, we can see the total kilograms of goods sold by client and `period`:

	period	client_name	kgs_sold
0	201807	DE SOTERO VI	2
1	201807	LUIS GIMENEZ	0
2	201807	DE LIZ PEREZ	8
3	201807	E ALCIBIADES	9
4	201807	NILDA SANCH	8

Figure 6.2: Aggregate sum of goods in kg by client and period

7. Now that we have the list of total clients, we will characterize them by the number of purchases per period:

```
unique_clients = kgs_by_period.client_name.value_
counts().reset_index()
unique_clients.columns = ['client_name','purchases']
unique_clients.head()
```

In the next DataFrame, we can see the count of purchases by client:

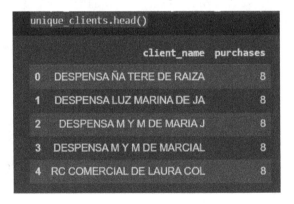

	client_name	purchases
0	DESPENSA ÑA TERE DE RAIZA	8
1	DESPENSA LUZ MARINA DE JA	8
2	DESPENSA M Y M DE MARIA J	8
3	DESPENSA M Y M DE MARCIAL	8
4	RC COMERCIAL DE LAURA COL	8

Figure 6.3: Data of users per number of purchases

8. Now we will filter top clients by the number of purchases, keeping the ones with at least five purchases of the total 8 periods we have. This limit is arbitrary in this case to find the clients that are mostly regular clients:

```
unique_clients = unique_clients[unique_clients.purchases>5]
```

9. Now, we can check the total number of clients again:

```
unique_clients.shape
>>> (7550, 2)
```

As we can see, most of the clients have more than 5 periods of purchases, so we have reduced around 30% of the total users.

10. Now, we will list the total kgs of goods sold in all of the periods, filtering the clients that have less than 5 periods of buys:

```
kgs_by_client = df[['client_name','kgs_sold']]
kgs_by_client = kgs_by_client[kgs_by_client.client_name.
isin(unique_clients.client_name)]
```

11. Now, to get the total number of kgs sold in all of the periods, we will use the groupby method and sort the values in ascending order:

```
kgs_by_client = kgs_by_client.groupby(['client_name']).
sum().reset_index()
kgs_by_client.columns = ['client','total_kgs']
kgs_by_client = kgs_by_client.sort_values([
        'total_kgs'],ascending= False)
```

12. As the next step and only for visualization and demonstration, we will limit the clients to the top 25 clients:

```
kgs_by_client = kgs_by_client.head(25)
kgs_by_client.head()
```

We can then see the top 25 clients by total kgs:

	client	total_kgs
759	BCDSA	34318
5797	GROUP SA	20235
763	LAMBARE	19074
775	SHOPPING LUQ	17702
6250	KAJA DISTRIBUIDORA	17262

(Output shown under command `kgs_by_client.head()`)

Figure 6.4: Clients with the highest kgs bought

13. Now that we have the information about the top clients in terms of kgs sold, we can create a histogram to understand their consumption patterns. We will be using the plot method to create a bar chart for the pandas Dataframe:

```
kgs_by_client.plot(kind='bar',x='client',y='total_
kgs',figsize=(14,6),rot=90)
```

This results in the following output:

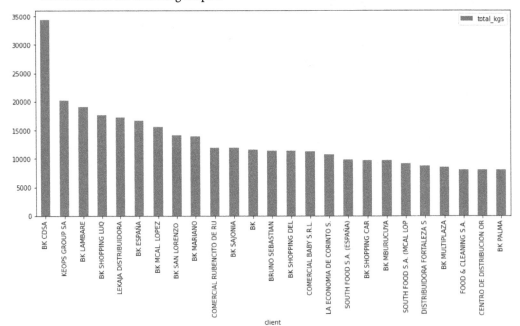

Figure 6.5: Chart of clients with the highest amount of kgs sold

14. To capture the clients that have been decreasing their level of expenditure, we will create a mask that filters all but the top clients, to visualize the kgs bought per client and period:

```
mask = kgs_by_period.client_name.isin(kgs_by_client.
client)
kgs_by_period = kgs_by_period[mask]
kgs_by_period = kgs_by_period.sort_values([
        'kgs_sold'],ascending=False)
kgs_by_period
```

This is the filtered data after filtering the top clients by weight:

	period	client_name	kgs_sold
49614	201812	LEKAJA DISTRIBUIDORA	3973
61384	201902	CENTRO DE DISTRIBUCION OR	92
44531	201812	CENTRO DE DISTRIBUCION OR	17
36060	201811	CENTRO DE DISTRIBUCION OR	17
53066	201901	COMERCIAL BABY S.R.L.	-1

199 rows × 3 columns

Figure 6.6: Kgs sold by period and client

15. Finally, we will pivot the DataFrame for visualization, and we will fill the NaN values with 0 as this is an indication that the client did not buy anything for this period:

```
dfx = kgs_by_period.pivot(index='period',columns=
        'client_name',values='kgs_sold').reset_index()
dfx.columns.name = ''
dfx = dfx.fillna(0)
dfx
```

The next DataFrame has the data pivoted and is better encoded for working with machine learning models:

	period	BK	BK CDSA	BK ESPAÑA	BK LAMBARE	BK MARIANO	BK MBURUCUYA	BK MCAL. LOPEZ	BK MULTIPLAZA	BK PALMA	...
0	201807	1245.0	4867.0	1664.0	2416.0	3264.0	838.0	2137.0	1092.0	803.0	...
1	201808	1442.0	3063.0	2654.0	2142.0	1319.0	1452.0	2292.0	979.0	1027.0	...
2	201809	1214.0	3790.0	2376.0	2273.0	1624.0	1466.0	2190.0	908.0	1011.0	...
3	201810	1342.0	3516.0	2366.0	2392.0	1699.0	1080.0	1788.0	904.0	797.0	...
4	201811	1043.0	5035.0	1193.0	2996.0	1364.0	1358.0	2403.0	1274.0	931.0	...
5	201812	1772.0	6542.0	3068.0	2381.0	1641.0	1320.0	2223.0	1336.0	1348.0	...
6	201901	2209.0	4552.0	1559.0	3063.0	1434.0	1011.0	1614.0	1171.0	728.0	...
7	201902	1340.0	2953.0	1831.0	1411.0	1550.0	1129.0	898.0	770.0	1351.0	...

8 rows × 26 columns

Figure 6.7: Pivoted data

16. Now, we can visualize the consumption throughout the periods:

```
import seaborn as sns
import matplotlib.pyplot as plt # visualization
f, ax = plt.subplots(figsize=(20, 6))
# Load the long-form example gammas dataset
g = sns.lineplot(data=dfx.drop(['period'],axis=1))
# Put the legend out of the figure
g.legend(loc='center left', bbox_to_anchor=(1, 0.5))
```

The line plot allows us to see at first glance the clients with the biggest sales:

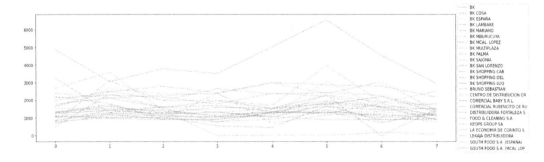

Figure 6.8: Line plot of kgs sold by client and period

17. To identify the curves with a decreasing trend, we will determine the slope and the standard deviation in terms of sales per month. This will allow us to identify the clients with decreasing consumer behavior by looking at the slope as well as to identify users with high consumption variability:

```
from scipy import stats
results = []
for i in range(1,dfx.shape[1]):
  client = dfx.columns[i]
  slope, intercept, r_value, p_value, std_err = stats.
linregress(dfx.index,dfx.iloc[0:,i])
  results.append([client,slope,std_err])
  print('Client Name:',client,'; Buy Tendency
(Slope):',round(slope,3),'; Common Standard
deviation:',round(std_err,3))
```

We can see in the prints that some of the clients have a negative slope, which indicates that their consumer patterns show a decline in monthly purchases:

```
Client Name:    PALMA ; Buy Tendency (Slope): 41.5 ; Common Standard deviation: 36.274
Client Name:    SAJONIA ; Buy Tendency (Slope): -23.381 ; Common Standard deviation: 32.367
Client Name:    SAN LORENZO  ; Buy Tendency (Slope): -44.488 ; Common Standard deviation: 33.777
Client Name:    SHOPPING CAR ; Buy Tendency (Slope): 28.488 ; Common Standard deviation: 23.601
Client Name:    SHOPPING DEL ; Buy Tendency (Slope): 13.238 ; Common Standard deviation: 40.739
Client Name:    SHOPPING LUQ ; Buy Tendency (Slope): -44.238 ; Common Standard deviation: 60.457
Client Name: BRUNO SEBASTIAN ; Buy Tendency (Slope): -151.929 ; Common Standard deviation: 86.955
Client Name: CENTRO DE DISTRIBUCION OR ; Buy Tendency (Slope): -469.202 ; Common Standard deviation: 139.437
Client Name: COMERCIAL BABY S.R.L. ; Buy Tendency (Slope): -47.333 ; Common Standard deviation: 105.873
```

Figure 6.9: Slope of clients buying trends

In this case, the values are shown in absolutes, but it would be even better to show it as a percentage of the median purchase of each client to keep the consistency. You can apply this change and evaluate the difference.

18. Next, we will store the results in a DataFrame and use it to visualize the results:

```
results_df = pd.DataFrame(results).dropna()
results_df.columns = ['client','slope','std']
results_df.index = results_df.client
results_df = results_df.drop(['client'],axis=1)
results_df.head()
```

The DataFrame shows us the clients, along with the parameter estimated by the regression model:

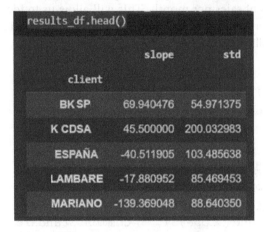

Figure 6.10: Final slope and standard deviation

19. Now that our information is neatly structured, we can create a seaborn heatmap to visualize the resulting data more graphically:

```
f, ax = plt.subplots(figsize=(12, 12))
sns.heatmap(results_df, annot=True)
```

This results in the following output:

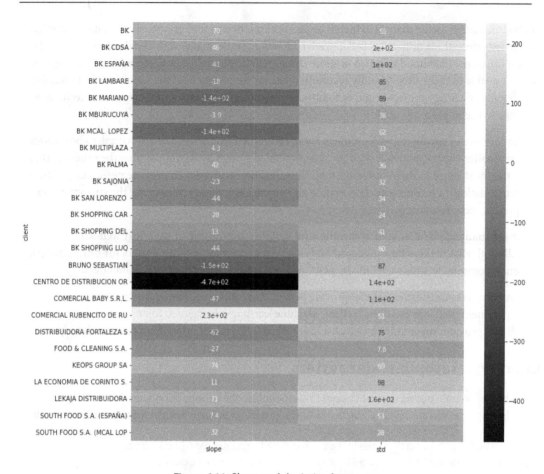

Figure 6.11: Slope and deviation heatmap

From the data, we can see some clients that show a marked decline in their monthly purchases, and some of them have been increasingly buying more. It is also helpful to look at the standard deviation to find how varying the purchases that this client does are.

Now that we understand the performance of each one of the clients, we can act on the clients with a pattern of declining sales by offering them tailor-made recommendations. In the next section, we will train recommender systems based on the purchase pattern of the clients.

Understanding product recommendation systems

Now that we have identified the customers with decreasing consumption, we can create specific product recommendations for them. How do you recommend products? In most cases, we can do this with a recommender system, which is a filtering system that attempts to forecast and display the products that a user would like to purchase as what makes up a product suggestion. The k-nearest neighbor method and latent factor analysis, which is a statistical method to find groups of correlated variables, are the two algorithms utilized in collaborative filtering. Additionally, with collaborative filters, the system learns the likelihood that two or more things will be purchased collectively. A recommender system's goal is to make user-friendly recommendations for products in the same way that you like. Collaborative filtering approaches and content-based methods are the two main categories of techniques available to accomplish this goal.

The importance of having relevant products being recommended to the clients is critical, as businesses can personalize client experience with the recommended system by recommending the products that make the most sense to them based on their consumption patterns. To provide pertinent product recommendations, a recommendation engine also enables companies to examine the customer's past and present website activity.

There are many applications for recommender systems, with some of the most well-known ones including playlist makers for video and audio services, product recommenders for online shops, content recommenders for social media platforms, and open web content recommenders.

In summary, recommendation engines provide personalized, direct recommendations that are based on the requirements and interests of each client. Machine learning is being used to improve online searches as well as it provides suggestions based on a user's visual preferences rather than product descriptions.

Creating a recommender system

Our first step to train our recommender system is to capture the consumption patterns of the clients. In the following example, we will focus on the products that the customers bought throughout the periods:

```
dfs = df[['client_name','product']].groupby(['client_
name','product']).size().reset_index(name='counts')
dfs =  dfs.sort_values(['counts'],ascending=False)
dfs.head()
```

This results in the following output:

	client_name	product	counts
157102	DESPENSA SAN CAYETANO	SPLIT GUA 3LTS	189
157240	DESPENSA SAN CAYETANO DE	PEPSI 300 CC	163
157257	DESPENSA SAN CAYETANO DE	SPLIT GUA 3LTS	163
157204	DESPENSA SAN CAYETANO DE	LS CLA 17G	162
157076	DESPENSA SAN CAYETANO	PASO T. POM 2LT	152

Figure 6.12: Products bought by client

We will train the recommender with a rating scale between 0 and 1 so we need to scale these values. Now we can see that some clients have consistently bought some products, so we will use the `sklearn` min max scaler to adjust the scale.

In machine learning, we normalize the data by generating new values, maintaining the general distribution, and adjusting the ratio in the data; normalization prevents the use of raw data and numerous dataset issues. Utilizing a variety of methods and algorithms also enhances the efficiency and accuracy of machine learning models.

The `MinMaxScaler` from scikit-learn can be applied to scale the variables within a range. It's important to note that the distribution of the variables should be normal. The original distribution's shape is preserved by `MinMaxScaler` making sure that the information present in the original data is not materially altered. Keep in mind that `MinMaxScaler` does not lessen the significance of outliers and that the resulting feature has a default range of 0 to 1.

Which scaler—`MinMaxScaler` or `StandardScaler`—is superior? For features that follow a normal distribution, `StandardScaler` is helpful. When the upper and lower boundaries are well defined from domain knowledge, `MinMaxScaler` may be employed (pixel intensities that go from 0 to 255 in the RGB color range).

```
from sklearn.preprocessing import MinMaxScaler
scaler = MinMaxScaler()
dfs['count_sc'] = scaler.fit_transform(dfs[['counts']])
dfs = dfs.drop(['counts'],axis=1)
```

Now that we have standardized the values, we can start working on the recommender system. Here, we will be using the SVDpp algorithm, which is an extension of SVD that takes into account implicit ratings. SVD is employed as a collaborative filtering mechanism in the recommender system. Each row in the matrix symbolizes a user, and each column is a piece of merchandise. The ratings that users provide for items make up the matrix's elements.

The general formula of SVD is:

$M=U\Sigma V^{t}$

where:

- M is the original matrix we want to decompose, which is the dense matrix of users and products they bought
- U is the left singular matrix (columns are left singular vectors)
- Σ is a diagonal matrix containing singular eigenvalues
- V is the right singular matrix (columns are right singular vectors)

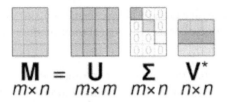

$$\underset{m\times n}{\mathbf{M}} = \underset{m\times m}{\mathbf{U}} \quad \underset{m\times n}{\mathbf{\Sigma}} \quad \underset{n\times n}{\mathbf{V}^*}$$

Figure 6.13: Collaborative filtering factorization matrix

The `scikit-surprise` package efficiently implements the SVD algorithm. Without having to reinvent the wheel, we can quickly construct rating-based recommender systems using the simple-to-use Python module called `SurpriseSVD`. When utilizing models such as SVD, `SurpriseSVD` also gives us access to the matrix factors, which enables us to visually see how related the objects in our dataset are:

1. We will start by importing the libraries:

    ```
    from surprise import SVDpp
    from surprise.model_selection import cross_validate
    from surprise import Reader, Dataset
    ```

2. Now, we will initiate the reader for which we will set the scale between 0 and 1:

    ```
    reader = Reader(rating_scale=(0,1))
    ```

3. Then, we can load the data with the `Dataset` method from the DataFrame with standardized value counts of products:

    ```
    data = Dataset.load_from_df(dfs, reader)
    ```

4. Finally, we can instantiate the SVD algorithm and train it on the data:

    ```
    algo = SVDpp()
    algo.fit(data.build_full_trainset())
    ```

    The training process should take a couple of minutes depending on the hardware specs that you have, but once it is finished, we can start using it to make predictions.

5. We will start by taking a particular user and filtering up all the products that they are still not buying to offer them the ones that are more recommended:

    ```
    usr = 'LA TROYA'
    # Filter the products that the client is already buying
    user_prods = dfs[dfs.client_name==usr]['product'].
    unique().tolist()
    ```

```
prods = dfs[dfs.client_name!=usr]['product'].unique().
tolist()
prods = [p for p in prods if p not in user_prods]
```

6. Now that we have determined the products that the user is not buying, let's see how the algorithm rates them to this specific user:

```
my_recs = []
for iid in prods:
    my_recs.append((iid, algo.predict(uid=usr,iid=iid).
est))
```

7. The preceding code will iterate over the products in the following data and create a DataFrame with the products that have the highest recommendation value:

```
dk = pd.DataFrame(my_recs)
dk.columns = ['product', 'rating']
dk = dk.sort_values('rating',ascending= False).reset_
index(drop=True)
dk.head()
```

The next DataFrame shows us the recommended products for the client:

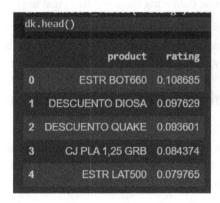

	product	rating
0	ESTR BOT660	0.108685
1	DESCUENTO DIOSA	0.097629
2	DESCUENTO QUAKE	0.093601
3	CJ PLA 1,25 GRB	0.084374
4	ESTR LAT500	0.079765

Figure 6.14: Client-recommended products

8. Now that we have determined this for a single user, we can extrapolate this to the rest of the clients. We will keep only the first 20 recommendations, as the number of products is too extensive:

```
dki_full = pd.DataFrame()
# For top 25 clients
users = kgs_by_period.client_name.unique()
```

```
for usr in users:
  print(usr)
  user_prods = dfs[dfs.client_name==usr]['product'].
unique().tolist()
  prods = dfs[dfs.client_name!=usr]['product'].unique().
tolist()
  prods = [p for p in prods if p not in user_prods]
  my_recs = []
  for iid in prods:
      my_recs.append((iid, algo.
predict(uid=usr,iid=iid).est))
  dk = pd.DataFrame(my_recs)
  dk.columns = ['product', 'rating']
  dk = dk.sort_values('rating',ascending= False).reset_
index(drop=True)
  dk['client'] = usr
  dki_full = pd.concat([dki_full, dk.head(20)])
```

This script will allow us to loop through our clients and generate a list of recommendations for each one of them. In this case, we are looking into a specific analysis, but this could be implemented into a pipeline delivering these results in real time.

Now we have data that allows us to target each one of our clients with tailor-made product recommendations for products that they are not buying yet. We can also offer products that are complementary to the ones they are already buying, and this is what we will do in the next section.

Using the Apriori algorithm for product bundling

For now, we have focused on clients that are decreasing their purchases to create specific offers for them for products that they are not buying, but we can also improve the results for those that are already loyal customers. We can improve the number of products that they are buying by doing a market basket analysis and offering products that relate to their patterns of consumption. For this, we can use several algorithms.

One of the most popular methods for association rule learning is the Apriori algorithm. It recognizes the things in a data collection and expands them to ever-larger groupings of items. Apriori is employed in association rule mining in datasets to search for several often-occurring sets of things. It expands on the itemsets' connections and linkages. This is the implementation of the "You may also like" suggestions that you frequently see on recommendation sites are the result of an algorithm.

Apriori is an algorithm for association rule learning and frequent item set mining in relational databases. As long as such item sets exist in the database frequently enough, it moves forward by detecting the frequent individual items and extending them to larger and larger item sets. The Apriori algorithm is generally used with transactional databases that are mined for frequent item sets and association rules using the Apriori method. "Support", "Lift", and "confidence" are utilized as parameters, where support is the likelihood that an item will occur, and confidence is a conditional probability. An item set is made up of the items in a transaction. This algorithm uses two steps, "join" and "prune," to reduce the search space. It is an iterative approach to discovering the most frequent itemsets. In association rule learning, the items in a dataset are identified, and the dataset is expanded to include ever-larger groupings of things.

The Apriori method is a common algorithm used in market basket analysis and is a well-known and widely used association rule algorithm. It aids in the discovery of frequent itemsets in transactions and pinpoints the laws of association between these items.

Performing market basket analysis with Apriori

For this analysis, we will use separate data found in the UCI ML repository (http://archive.ics.uci.edu/ml/datasets/Online+Retail):

1. We begin the analysis by importing the packages and loading the data. Remember to install the mlxtend module prior to running this block of code, otherwise, we will have a **Module Not Found** error:

```
from mlxtend.frequent_patterns import apriori,
association_rules
data = pd.read_csv('/content/Online Retail.
csv',encoding='iso-8859-1')
data.head()
```

	InvoiceNo	StockCode	Description	Quantity	InvoiceDate	UnitPrice	CustomerID	Country
0	536365	85123A	WHITE HANGING HEART T-LIGHT HOLDER	6	01/12/2010 08:26	2.55	17850.0	United Kingdom
1	536365	71053	WHITE METAL LANTERN	6	01/12/2010 08:26	3.39	17850.0	United Kingdom
2	536365	84406B	CREAM CUPID HEARTS COAT HANGER	8	01/12/2010 08:26	2.75	17850.0	United Kingdom
3	536365	84029G	KNITTED UNION FLAG HOT WATER BOTTLE	6	01/12/2010 08:26	3.39	17850.0	United Kingdom
4	536365	84029E	RED WOOLLY HOTTIE WHITE HEART.	6	01/12/2010 08:26	3.39	17850.0	United Kingdom

Figure 6.15: Online retail data

This international data collection includes every transaction made by a UK-based, registered non-store internet retailer between December 1, 2010, and December 9, 2011. The company primarily offers one-of-a-kind gifts for every occasion. The company has a large number of wholesalers as clients.

2. We begin exploring the columns of the data:

```
data.columns
>>> Index(['InvoiceNo', 'StockCode', 'Description',
'Quantity', 'InvoiceDate','UnitPrice', 'CustomerID',
'Country'],dtype='object')
```

The data contains transactional sales data with information about codes and dates that we will not use now. Instead, we will focus on the description, quantity, and price.

3. We can look at the statistical summary of the data:

```
data.describe()
```

	Quantity	UnitPrice	CustomerID
count	541909.000000	541909.000000	406829.000000
mean	9.552250	4.611114	15287.690570
std	218.081158	96.759853	1713.600303
min	-80995.000000	-11062.060000	12346.000000
25%	1.000000	1.250000	13953.000000
50%	3.000000	2.080000	15152.000000
75%	10.000000	4.130000	16791.000000
max	80995.000000	38970.000000	18287.000000

Figure 6.16: Descriptive statistical summary

4. In order to assess the categorical variables, we use the `describe` method focused on object columns in the DataFrame:

```
data.describe(include='O')
```

	InvoiceNo	StockCode	Description	InvoiceDate	Country
count	541909	541909	540455	541909	541909
unique	25900	4070	4223	23260	38
top	573585	85123A	WHITE HANGING HEART T-LIGHT HOLDER	31/10/2011 14:41	United Kingdom
freq	1114	2313	2369	1114	495478

Figure 6.17: Descriptive categorical summary

This information shows us some of the counts for each object column and shows us that the most common country is the UK, as expected.

5. We will also explore the different regions of transactions to gain some understanding of the data:

```
data['Country'].value_counts().head(10).
plot(kind='bar',figsize=(12,6))
```

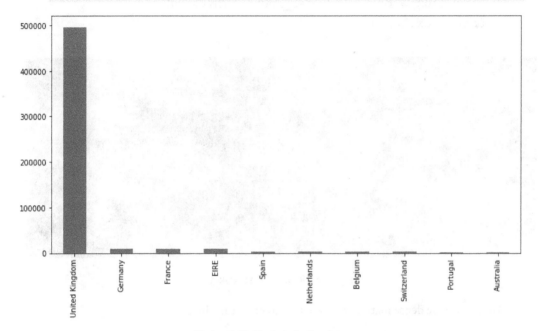

Figure 6.18: Markets in the data

We can confirm that the vast majority of transactions are in the UK, followed by Germany and France.

6. For readability, we will be stripping extra spaces in the description:

```
data['Description'] = data['Description'].str.strip()
```

7. Now, we will drop rows with NaNs in the invoice number and convert them into strings for categorical treatment:

```
data = data[~data['InvoiceNo'].isna()]
data['InvoiceNo'] = data['InvoiceNo'].astype('str')
```

8. For now, we will focus on noncredit transactions, so we will be dropping all transactions that were done on credit:

```
data = data[~data['InvoiceNo'].str.contains('C')]
```

9. We will begin the analysis by looking at the UK association rules:

```
data_uk = data[data['Country'] =="United Kingdom"]
basket_uk = data_uk.groupby(['InvoiceNo', 'Description'])
['Quantity'].sum()
basket_uk = basket_uk.unstack().reset_index().fillna(0)
basket_uk = basket_uk.set_index('InvoiceNo')
basket_uk.head()
```

Description	*Boombox Ipod Classic	*USB Office Mirror Ball	10 COLOUR SPACEBOY PEN	12 COLOURED PARTY BALLOONS	12 DAISY PEGS IN WOOD BOX	12 EGG HOUSE PAINTED WOOD	12 HANGING EGGS HAND PAINTED	12 IVORY ROSE PEG PLACE SETTINGS	12 MESSAGE CARDS WITH ENVELOPES	12 PENCIL SMALL TUBE WOODLAND	...
InvoiceNo											
536365	0.0	0.0	0.0	0.0	0.0	0.0	0.0	0.0	0.0	0.0	...
536366	0.0	0.0	0.0	0.0	0.0	0.0	0.0	0.0	0.0	0.0	...
536367	0.0	0.0	0.0	0.0	0.0	0.0	0.0	0.0	0.0	0.0	...
536368	0.0	0.0	0.0	0.0	0.0	0.0	0.0	0.0	0.0	0.0	...
536369	0.0	0.0	0.0	0.0	0.0	0.0	0.0	0.0	0.0	0.0	...

5 rows × 4176 columns

Figure 6.19: UK market basket

We can see the dense matrix of products bought on each invoice.

10. We will do the same with the transactions done in France:

```
basket_fr = data[data['Country'] =="France"]
basket_fr = basket_fr.groupby(['InvoiceNo',
'Description'])['Quantity'].sum()
basket_fr = basket_fr.unstack().reset_index().fillna(0)
basket_fr = basket_fr.set_index('InvoiceNo')
```

11. Finally, we will do the same for the data for Germany:

```
basket_de = data[data['Country'] =="Germany"]
basket_de = basket_de.groupby(['InvoiceNo',
'Description'])['Quantity'].sum()
basket_de = basket_de.unstack().reset_index().fillna(0)
basket_de = basket_de.set_index('InvoiceNo')
```

12. Now, we will be defining the hot encoding function to make the data suitable for the concerned libraries as they need discrete values (either 0 or 1):

```
basket_uk = (basket_uk>0).astype(int)
basket_fr = (basket_fr>0).astype(int)
basket_de = (basket_de>0).astype(int)
```

13. Once we have encoded the results into a one hot encoder, we can start to build the models for each market:

```
frq_items_uk = apriori(basket_uk, min_support = 0.01,
use_colnames = True)
```

14. Once the model is built, we can look at the found association rules for the UK market:

```
# Collecting the inferred rules in a dataframe
rules_uk = association_rules(frq_items_uk, metric
="lift", min_threshold = 1)
# rules_uk = rules_uk.sort_values(['confidence', 'lift'],
ascending =[False, False])
rules_uk.head()
```

	antecedents	consequents	antecedent support	consequent support	support	confidence	lift	leverage	conviction
0	(6 RIBBONS RUSTIC CHARM)	(DOTCOM POSTAGE)	0.045800	0.037926	0.010821	0.236257	6.229451	0.009084	1.259684
1	(DOTCOM POSTAGE)	(6 RIBBONS RUSTIC CHARM)	0.037926	0.045800	0.010821	0.285311	6.229451	0.009084	1.335125
2	(6 RIBBONS RUSTIC CHARM)	(JAM MAKING SET PRINTED)	0.045800	0.053996	0.011571	0.252632	4.678697	0.009098	1.265780
3	(JAM MAKING SET PRINTED)	(6 RIBBONS RUSTIC CHARM)	0.053996	0.045800	0.011571	0.214286	4.678697	0.009098	1.214436
4	(6 RIBBONS RUSTIC CHARM)	(JAM MAKING SET WITH JARS)	0.045800	0.053514	0.010339	0.225731	4.218164	0.007888	1.222425

Figure 6.20: UK association rules

If the rules for the UK transactions are examined in more detail, it becomes clear that the British bought variously colored tea plates collectively. This may be due to the fact that the British often enjoy tea very much and frequently collect various colored tea dishes for various occasions.

15. We will now do the same for the data for France:

```
frq_items_fr = apriori(basket_fr, min_support = 0.05,
use_colnames = True)
# Collecting the inferred rules in a dataframe
rules_fr = association_rules(frq_items_fr, metric
```

```
="lift", min_threshold = 1)
rules_fr = rules_fr.sort_values(['confidence', 'lift'],
ascending =[False, False])
rules_fr.head()
```

	antecedents	consequents	antecedent support	consequent support	support	confidence	lift	leverage	conviction
44	(JUMBO BAG WOODLAND ANIMALS)	(POSTAGE)	0.076531	0.765306	0.076531	1.000	1.306667	0.017961	inf
260	(PLASTERS IN TIN CIRCUS PARADE, RED TOADSTOOL ...	(POSTAGE)	0.051020	0.765306	0.051020	1.000	1.306667	0.011974	inf
272	(RED TOADSTOOL LED NIGHT LIGHT, PLASTERS IN TI...	(POSTAGE)	0.053571	0.765306	0.053571	1.000	1.306667	0.012573	inf
301	(SET/6 RED SPOTTY PAPER CUPS, SET/20 RED RETRO...	(SET/6 RED SPOTTY PAPER PLATES)	0.102041	0.127551	0.099490	0.975	7.644000	0.086474	34.897959
302	(SET/6 RED SPOTTY PAPER PLATES, SET/20 RED RET...	(SET/6 RED SPOTTY PAPER CUPS)	0.102041	0.137755	0.099490	0.975	7.077778	0.085433	34.489796

Figure 6.21: France association rules

It is clear from this data that paper plates, glasses, and napkins are frequently purchased together in France. This is due to the French habit of gathering with friends and family at least once every week. Additionally, since the French government has outlawed the use of plastic in the nation, citizens must purchase replacements made of paper.

16. Finally, we will build the model for the German data:

```
frq_items_de = apriori(basket_de, min_support = 0.05,
use_colnames = True)
# Collecting the inferred rules in a dataframe
rules_de = association_rules(frq_items_de, metric
="lift", min_threshold = 1)
rules_de = rules_de.sort_values(['confidence', 'lift'],
ascending =[False, False])
rules_de.head()
```

	antecedents	consequents	antecedent support	consequent support	support	confidence	lift	leverage	conviction
35	(PLASTERS IN TIN STRONGMAN)	(POSTAGE)	0.070022	0.818361	0.067834	0.968750	1.183740	0.010529	5.811816
50	(RETROSPOT TEA SET CERAMIC 11 PC)	(POSTAGE)	0.056893	0.818361	0.054705	0.961538	1.174928	0.008145	4.722101
53	(ROUND SNACK BOXES SET OF 4 FRUITS)	(POSTAGE)	0.157549	0.818361	0.150985	0.958333	1.171012	0.022049	4.358862
104	(ROUND SNACK BOXES SET OF 4 WOODLAND, ROUND SNA...	(POSTAGE)	0.131291	0.818361	0.124726	0.950000	1.160829	0.017280	3.632385
33	(PLASTERS IN TIN SPACEBOY)	(POSTAGE)	0.107221	0.818361	0.100656	0.938776	1.147113	0.012909	2.966448

Figure 6.22: Germany association rules

The preceding data shows us that most of the items are associated with costs of delivery, so it might be an indication that German transactions are mostly made of single items.

Summary

In this chapter, we have learned to identify the clients that have a decreasing number of sales in order to offer them specific product recommendations based on their consumption patterns. We have identified the decreasing sales by looking at the slope in the historical sales in the given set of periods, and we used the SVD collaborative filtering algorithm to create personalized recommendations for products that customers are not buying.

As the next step and to improve the loyalty of existing customers, we have explored the use of the Apriori algorithm to run a market basket analysis and to be able to offer product recommendations based on specific products being bought.

In the next chapter, we will dive into how we identify the common traits of customers that churn in order to complement these approaches with a deeper understanding of our customer churn.

Part 3:
Operation and Pricing
Optimization

The final part of the book will cover how to optimize business operations. We will move away from understanding the market and customers, and dive into how we can adjust the operations to improve the revenue margin. This will be done by improving the pricing strategies, optimizing the use of promotions, and finally, improving the digital marketing strategies to reach more possible customers.

This part covers the following chapters:

- *Chapter 7, Predicting Customer Churn*
- *Chapter 8, Grouping Users with Customer Segmentation*
- *Chapter 9, Using Historical Markdown Data to Predict Sales*
- *Chapter 10, Web Analytics Optimization*
- *Chapter 11, Creating a Data-Driven Culture in Business*

7

Predicting Customer Churn

The churn rate is a metric used to determine how many clients or staff leave a business in a certain time frame. It might also refer to the sum of money that was lost because of the departures. Changes in a company's churn rate might offer insightful information about the firm. Understanding the amount or proportion of consumers who don't buy more goods or services is possible through customer churn analysis.

In this chapter, we will understand the concept of churn and why it is important in the context of business. We will then prepare the data for further analysis and create an analysis to determine the most important factors to take into account to understand the churn patterns. Finally, we will learn how to create machine learning models to predict customers that will churn.

This chapter covers the following topics:

- Understanding customer churn
- Exploring customer data
- Exploring variable relationships
- Predicting users who will churn

Technical requirements

In order to be able to follow the steps in this chapter, you will need to meet the next requirements:

- A Jupyter Notebook instance running Python 3.7 and above. You can also use the Google Colab notebook to run the steps if you have a Google Drive account.
- An understanding of basic math and statistical concepts.

Understanding customer churn

In business, the number of paying customers that fail to become repeat customers for a given product or service is known as customer churn, also known as customer attrition. Churn in this sense refers to a measurable rate of change that happens over a predetermined period of time.

Analyzing the causes of churn, engaging with customers, educating them, knowing who is at risk, identifying your most valuable customers, offering incentives, selecting the correct audience to target, and providing better service are a few strategies to reduce customer turnover.

It's crucial to lower churn because it increases **Customer Acquisition Cost** (**CAC**) and lowers revenue. In actuality, maintaining and improving current client relationships is much less expensive than gaining new consumers. The more clients you lose, the more money you'll need to spend on acquiring new ones in order to make up for the lost revenue. You can use the following formula to determine CAC: CAC is calculated by dividing the cost of sales and marketing by the number of new customers attracted. The proportion of consumers who come back to your firm is known as the retention rate.

$$CAC = \frac{Cost\ of\ Sales + Cost\ of\ Marketing}{New\ Customers\ Aquired}$$

This is different from the churn rate, which measures how many clients you've lost over time. By default, a business with a high churn rate will have a lower retention rate.

Now that we have an idea of the business value that we get by identifying the patterns that make our clients churn, in the next section, we will start to explore the data and its variables.

Exploring customer data

Our goal is to create a model to estimate the likelihood of abandonment using data pertaining to Telecom customers. This is to answer the question of how likely it is that a consumer will discontinue utilizing the service.

Initially, the data is subjected to exploratory analysis. Knowing the data types of each column is the first step in the process, after which any necessary adjustments to the variables are made.

To explore the data, we will plot the relationships between the churn variable and the other important factors that make up the dataset. Prior to suggesting a model, this work is carried out to get a preliminary understanding of the underlying relationships between the variables.

A thorough approach is taken while performing descriptive statistics, which focus on client differences based on one or more attributes. The primary variable of interest, churn, is now the focus, and a new set of interesting graphs is produced for this reason.

To examine the variables, we have to handle unstructured data and adjust data types; the first step is to explore the data. In essence, we will be learning about data distribution and arranging the data for the clustering analysis.

For the analysis we will use in the next example, the following Python modules were used:

- **Pandas**: Python package for data analysis and data manipulation.

- **NumPy**: This is a library that adds support for large, multi-dimensional arrays and matrices, along with an extensive collection of high-level mathematical functions to operate on these arrays.

- **statsmodels**: A Python package that provides a complement to SciPy for statistical computations, including descriptive statistics and estimation and inference for statistical models. It provides classes and functions for the estimation of many different statistical models.

- **Seaborn, mpl_toolkits, and Matplotlib**: Python packages for effective data visualization.

We'll now get started with the analysis as follows:

1. The first step is in the following block of code, we will load all the required packages just mentioned, including the functions that we will be using, such as `LabelEncoder`, `StandardScaler`, and `KMeans`:

```
import numpy as np
import pandas as pd
import seaborn as sns
import matplotlib.pyplot as plt
import os
```

2. For readability purposes, we will limit the maximum rows to 20, set the maximum columns to 50, and show the floats with 2 digits of precision:

```
pd.options.display.max_rows = 20
pd.options.display.max_columns = 50
pd.options.display.precision = 2
path = 'customer_churn.csv'
data = pd.read_csv(path)
data.head()
```

This block of code will load the data and show the first rows of it:

gender	SeniorCitizen	Partner	Dependents	tenure	PhoneService	MultipleLines	InternetService	OnlineSecurity	OnlineBackup	DeviceProtection
Female	0	Yes	No	1	No	No phone service	DSL	No	Yes	No
Male	0	No	No	34	Yes	No	DSL	Yes	No	Yes
Male	0	No	No	2	Yes	No	DSL	Yes	Yes	No
Male	0	No	No	45	No	No phone service	DSL	Yes	No	Yes
Female	0	No	No	2	Yes	No	Fiber optic	No	No	No

Figure 7.1: Customer data

3. Now, we can now look at the columns that the DataFrame has:

```
data.columns
```

In order to obtain information about the type of each column and the number of missing values, we can use the `info` method:

```
data.info()
```

```
<class 'pandas.core.frame.DataFrame'>
RangeIndex: 7043 entries, 0 to 7042
Data columns (total 21 columns):
 #   Column            Non-Null Count  Dtype
---  ------            --------------  -----
 0   customerID        7043 non-null   object
 1   gender            7043 non-null   object
 2   SeniorCitizen     7043 non-null   int64
 3   Partner           7043 non-null   object
 4   Dependents        7043 non-null   object
 5   tenure            7043 non-null   int64
 6   PhoneService      7043 non-null   object
 7   MultipleLines     7043 non-null   object
 8   InternetService   7043 non-null   object
 9   OnlineSecurity    7043 non-null   object
 10  OnlineBackup      7043 non-null   object
 11  DeviceProtection  7043 non-null   object
 12  TechSupport       7043 non-null   object
 13  StreamingTV       7043 non-null   object
 14  StreamingMovies   7043 non-null   object
 15  Contract          7043 non-null   object
 16  PaperlessBilling  7043 non-null   object
 17  PaymentMethod     7043 non-null   object
 18  MonthlyCharges    7043 non-null   float64
 19  TotalCharges      7043 non-null   object
 20  Churn             7043 non-null   object
dtypes: float64(1), int64(2), object(18)
memory usage: 1.1+ MB
```

Figure 7.2: Pandas column data types

4. We can see that although we don't have `null` values to impute, most of the variables are categorical – meaning that we need to cast them into `boolean` numerical columns before using machine learning models or clustering methods. The first step is converting `TotalCharges` into a numerical data type:

```
data.TotalCharges = pd.to_numeric(data.TotalCharges,
errors='coerce')
```

The preceding code casts the variable to a numeric variable, coercing any errors instead of failing.

We can see the results of the transformation using `info` again:

```
data.info()
```

```
<class 'pandas.core.frame.DataFrame'>
RangeIndex: 7043 entries, 0 to 7042
Data columns (total 21 columns):
 #   Column            Non-Null Count   Dtype
---  ------            --------------   -----
 0   customerID        7043 non-null    object
 1   gender            7043 non-null    object
 2   SeniorCitizen     7043 non-null    int64
 3   Partner           7043 non-null    object
 4   Dependents        7043 non-null    object
 5   tenure            7043 non-null    int64
 6   PhoneService      7043 non-null    object
 7   MultipleLines     7043 non-null    object
 8   InternetService   7043 non-null    object
 9   OnlineSecurity    7043 non-null    object
 10  OnlineBackup      7043 non-null    object
 11  DeviceProtection  7043 non-null    object
 12  TechSupport       7043 non-null    object
 13  StreamingTV       7043 non-null    object
 14  StreamingMovies   7043 non-null    object
 15  Contract          7043 non-null    object
 16  PaperlessBilling  7043 non-null    object
 17  PaymentMethod     7043 non-null    object
 18  MonthlyCharges    7043 non-null    float64
 19  TotalCharges      7032 non-null    float64
 20  Churn             7043 non-null    object
dtypes: float64(2), int64(2), object(17)
memory usage: 1.1+ MB
```

Figure 7.3: Corrected data types

The resulting transformation has been successful but has generated 10 `null` values that we can later drop.

5. Now, we will determine the total list of categorical columns that we need to cast to dummies for better analysis:

```
object_cols = [c for c in data.
drop(['customerID'],axis=1).columns if data[c].
dtype=='O']
object_cols
```

6. There are several columns that could be easily represented by ones and zeros given that there are Yes or No values; we will determine which of these variables has only these two options and then map these values to their numerical counterparts:

```
yn_cols = []
# Iterate over the column names
For c in object_cols:
    # count the unique values by accessing the column
    val_counts = data[c].value_counts()
    # If the count of unique values is equal to two, we
assume that it's a Yes/No column
    if len(val_counts.index)==2 and all(val_counts.index.
isin(['No', 'Yes'])):
        print(c)
        print(data[c].value_counts().to_string())
        yn_cols.append(c)
```

7. The preceding code will generate a list of categorical Yes/No columns to which we can map the data into ones and zeros:

```
# Iterate over the yes/no column names
for c in yn_cols:
    # Normalize the column values by lowering them and
mapping them to new values.
    data[c] = data[c].str.lower().map({'yes': 1, 'no': 0})
```

We can now re-evaluate the results of these replacements:

```
data.head()
```

gender	SeniorCitizen	Partner	Dependents	tenure	PhoneService	MultipleLines	InternetService	Onli
Female	0	1	0	1	0	No phone service	DSL	
Male	0	0	0	34	1	No	DSL	
Male	0	0	0	2	1	No	DSL	
Male	0	0	0	45	0	No phone service	DSL	
Female	0	0	0	2	1	No	Fiber optic	

Figure 7.4: Column transformed into a normalized Boolean column

We can now look at the numerical variable distribution to get a better understanding of the data using the describe method:

```
data.describe()
```

	SeniorCitizen	Partner	Dependents	tenure	PhoneService	PaperlessBilling	MonthlyCharges	TotalCharges	Churn
count	7043.00	7043.00	7043.00	7043.00	7043.0	7043.00	7043.00	7032.00	7043.00
mean	0.16	0.48	0.30	32.37	0.9	0.59	64.76	2283.30	0.27
std	0.37	0.50	0.46	24.56	0.3	0.49	30.09	2266.77	0.44
min	0.00	0.00	0.00	0.00	0.0	0.00	18.25	18.80	0.00
25%	0.00	0.00	0.00	9.00	1.0	0.00	35.50	401.45	0.00
50%	0.00	0.00	0.00	29.00	1.0	1.00	70.35	1397.47	0.00
75%	0.00	1.00	1.00	55.00	1.0	1.00	89.85	3794.74	1.00
max	1.00	1.00	1.00	72.00	1.0	1.00	118.75	8684.80	1.00

Figure 7.5: Statistical description of the data

It is interesting to see that here, 27% of clients churn, which is a very large proportion. In other contexts, these values tend to be much lower, making the dataset highly imbalanced and imposing the need to adapt the analysis to handle these imbalances. Thankfully, this is not the case, as the number of occurrences of churn is representative enough. Nevertheless, an imbalanced dataset requires us to take into consideration that we need to inspect the metrics used to evaluate the model in more depth. If we would just look into the precision, in our case, a model that just outputs the most common variable (the customer doesn't churn) will have an accuracy of 73%. That is why we need to add more performance metrics, precision, recall, and a combination of both, such as the F1 score, and especially look at the confusion matrix to find the proportion of correctly predicted cases for each type of class.

8. We can now visualize the distribution of some of these categorical variables accounting for the cases in which the users have churn. We can do this using Seaborn's `countplot`:

```
import seaborn as sns
import matplotlib.pyplot as plt
f, ax = plt.subplots(figsize=(10, 6))
pl = sns.
countplot(x=data["InternetService"],hue=data["Churn"])
pl.set_title("InternetService vs Churn")
pl.set_xlabel("InternetService")
pl.set_ylabel("Count")
```

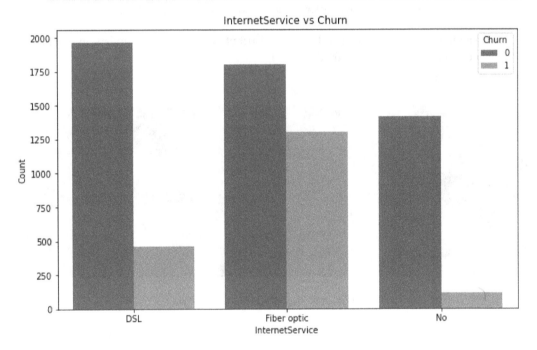

Figure 7.6: Customer internet contract versus churn

We can see that there is a big difference between the relative percentage of churn for the users that opted for the fiber optic service, compared to the ones who don't have internet service or have DSL.

9. This information can be useful for diving into the reasons or developing new promotions to address this situation:

```
f, ax = plt.subplots(figsize=(10, 6))
pl = sns.
countplot(x=data["MultipleLines"],hue=data["Churn"])
pl.set_title("MultipleLines vs Churn")
pl.set_xlabel("MultipleLines")
pl.set_ylabel("Count")
```

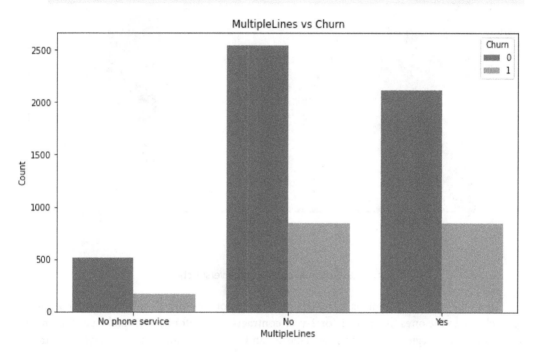

Figure 7.7: Customer phone contracts versus churn

We can see some relative differences, again, for clients that have multiple lines, whereas the ones that don't have multiple lines seem to churn more. These differences need to be validated with a t-test or other hypothesis testing methods to determine actual differences between the means of the groups.

10. The next step is to visualize the relationship between the contract and churn:

```
f, ax = plt.subplots(figsize=(10, 6))
pl = sns.countplot(x=data["Contract"],hue=data["Churn"])
pl.set_title("Contract vs Churn")
```

```
pl.set_xlabel("Contract")
pl.set_ylabel("Count")
```

The code here will show us a bar plot of contract type method versus churn:

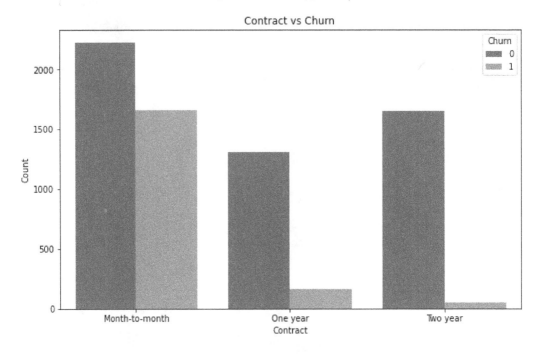

Figure 7.8: Customer contract type versus churn

Here, the client churn rate is extremely high for customers with month-to-month contracts relative to the ones that have 1- or 2-year contracts. This information can be used to create marketing strategies that seek to convert the month-to-month contracts into 1- or 2-year contracts.

11. Finally, our last variable exploration focuses on the type of payment method. The next plot will show us the relationship of churn to the type of payment used:

```
f, ax = plt.subplots(figsize=(10, 6))
pl = sns.
countplot(x=data["PaymentMethod"],hue=data["Churn"])
pl.set_title("PaymentMethod vs Churn")
pl.set_xlabel("PaymentMethod")
pl.set_ylabel("Count")
```

The code here will show us a bar plot of payment method versus churn:

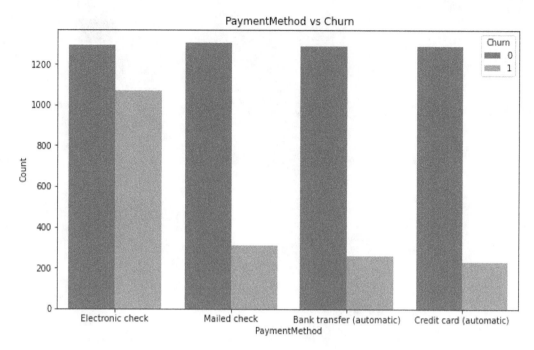

Figure 7.9: Customer payment method versus churn

Here, the difference is clear between the ones using electronic checks rather than other kinds of payment methods.

Up next, we will explore the variable relationships between the different variables using Seaborn's `pairplot` and with the use of correlation analysis.

Exploring variable relationships

Exploring the way in which variables move together can help us to determine the hidden patterns that govern the behaviors of our clients:

1. Our first step here will be using the Seaborn method to plot some of the relationships, mostly between numerical continuous variables such as tenure, monthly charges, and total charges, using the churn as the `hue` parameter:

    ```
    g = sns.pairplot(data[['tenure','MonthlyCharges',
    'TotalCharges','Churn']], hue= "Churn",palette=
    (["red","blue"]),height=6)
    ```

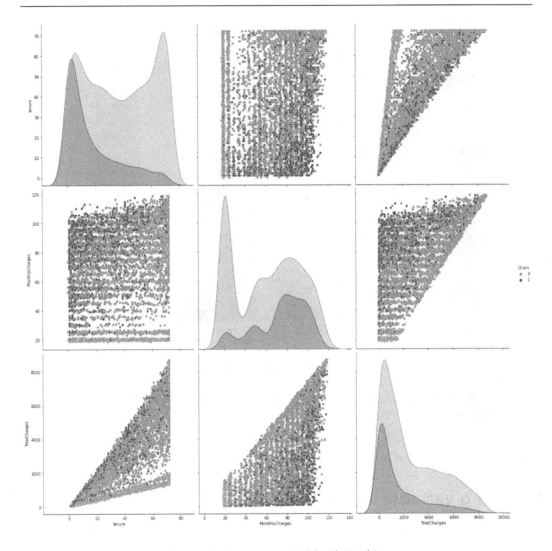

Figure 7.10: Continuous variable relationships

We can observe from the distributions that the customers who churn tend to have a low tenure number, generally having low amounts of monthly charges, as well as having much lower total charges on average.

2. Now, we can finally transform and determine the object columns that we will convert into dummies:

```
object_cols = [c for c in data.
drop(['customerID'],axis=1).columns if data[c].
dtype=='O']
object_cols
```

3. Once these columns are determined, we can use the `get_dummies` function and create a new DataFrame only with numeric variables:

```
df_dummies = pd.get_dummies(data[object_cols])
data = pd.concat([data.drop(object_
cols+['Churn'],axis=1),df_dummies,data[['Churn']]],axis=1)
data.head()
```

The preceding code will show us the data restructured:

	customerID	SeniorCitizen	Partner	Dependents	tenure	PhoneService	PaperlessBilling	MonthlyCharges	TotalCharges	gender_Female	gender_Male	MultipleLines_No	MultipleLines_No phone service	MultipleLines_Yes
0	7590-VHVEG	0	1	0	1	0	1	29.85	29.85	1	0	0	1	0
1	5575-GNVDE	0	0	0	34	1	0	56.95	1889.50	0	1	1	0	0
2	3668-QPYBK	0	0	0	2	1	1	53.85	108.15	0	1	1	0	0
3	7795-CFOCW	0	0	0	45	0	0	42.30	1840.75	0	1	0	1	0
4	9237-HQITU	0	0	0	2	1	1	70.70	151.65	1	0	1	0	0
...														
7038	6840-RESVB	0	1	1	24	1	1	84.80	1990.50	0	1	0	0	1
7039	2234-XADUH	0	1	1	72	1	1	103.20	7362.90	1	0	0	0	1
7040	4801-JZAZL	0	1	1	11	0	1	29.60	346.45	1	0	0	1	0
7041	8361-LTMKD	1	1	0	4	1	1	74.40	306.60	0	1	0	0	1
7042	3186-AJIEK	0	0	0	66	1	1	105.65	6844.50	0	1	1	0	0

7043 rows × 43 columns

Figure 7.11: Restructured data

Here, the data can effectively describe each one of the customers' descriptive levels so that the information is represented numerically rather than categorically. These factors consist of tenure, subscription type, cost, call history, and demographics, among other things. The fact that the dimensions need to be represented numerically is because most machine learning algorithms require the data to be this way.

4. As the next step, we will be studying the relationship of variables to determine the most important correlations between them:

```
import numpy as np
from matplotlib import colors
df_corr = data.corr()
mask = np.triu(np.ones_like(df_corr, dtype=bool))
df_corr = df_corr.mask(mask).round(2)
fig, ax = plt.subplots(figsize=(25,25))
sns.heatmap(df_corr, annot=True,ax=ax)
```

The code determines these correlations and constructs a triangular dataset that we can plot as a heat map to clearly visualize the relationship between the variables.

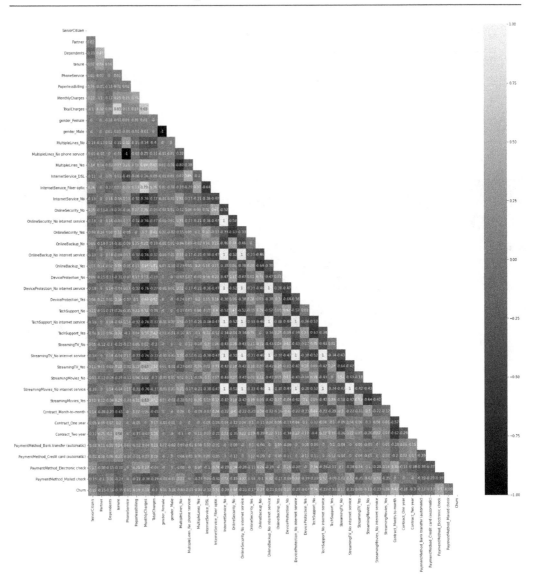

Figure 7.12: Variable correlations

Here, we can visualize the entire set of variable correlations, but we may just look at the ones that are related to our target variable. We can see that some variables that depend on others will have a correlation of 1 to this variable – for example, in the case of `internet contract = no`, which has a correlation equal to 1 with `streaming service = no`. This is because if there is no internet contract, it is obvious that you won't be able to access a streaming service that requires an internet contract.

5. We can do this just by looking at the correlations related to this variable:

```
churn_corr = data.corr()['Churn'].sort_values(ascending =
False)
churn_corr.plot(kind='bar',figsize=(20,8))
```

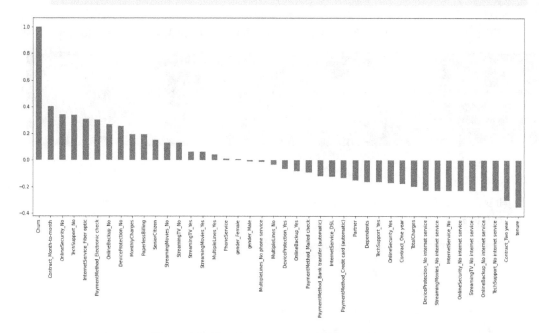

Figure 7.13: Most important correlations to churn

This information is really useful, as it not only determines the variables associated with a higher degree of churn but also the ones that lead to a lower churn rate, such as the tenure time and having a 2-year contract. It would be a good practice to remove the churn variable here as the correlation of the variable with itself is 1 and distorts the graphic.

After going through this EDA, we will develop some predictive models and compare them.

Predicting users who will churn

In this example, we will train logistic regression, random forest, and SVM machine learning models to predict the users that will churn based on the observed variables. We will need to scale the variables first and we will use the sklearn `MinMaxScaler` functionality to do so:

1. We will start with logistic regression and scale all the variables to a range of 0 to 1:

```
from sklearn.preprocessing import MinMaxScaler
y = data['Churn'].values
```

```
x = data.drop(columns = ['customerID','Churn']).fillna(0)
scaler = MinMaxScaler(feature_range = (0,1))
x_scaled = scaler.fit_transform(x)
x_scaled = pd.DataFrame(x_scaled,columns=x.columns)
x_scaled.head()
```

The preceding code will create the x and y variables, out of which we only need to scale x.

	SeniorCitizen	Partner	Dependents	tenure	PhoneService	PaperlessBilling	MonthlyCharges	TotalCharges	gender_Female	gender_Male	MultipleLines_No	MultipleLines_No phone service
0	0.0	1.0	0.0	0.01	0.0	1.0	0.12	3.44e-03	1.0	0.0	0.0	1.0
1	0.0	0.0	0.0	0.47	1.0	0.0	0.39	2.18e-01	0.0	1.0	1.0	0.0
2	0.0	0.0	0.0	0.03	1.0	1.0	0.35	1.25e-02	0.0	1.0	1.0	0.0
3	0.0	0.0	0.0	0.62	0.0	0.0	0.24	2.12e-01	0.0	1.0	0.0	1.0
4	0.0	0.0	0.0	0.03	1.0	1.0	0.52	1.75e-02	1.0	0.0	1.0	0.0

Figure 7.14: Model input features

It is important to scale the variables in logistic regression so that all of them are within a range of 0 to 1.

2. Next, we can train the logistic regression model by splitting the data to get a validation set first:

```
from sklearn.model_selection import train_test_split
from sklearn.linear_model import LogisticRegression
from sklearn import metrics
x_train, x_test, y_train, y_test = train_test_split(
    x_scaled, y, test_size=0.3, random_state=101)
model = LogisticRegression()
result = model.fit(x_train, y_train)
preds_lr = model.predict(x_test)
```

Finally, we can print the prediction accuracy:

```
print(metrics.accuracy_score(y_test, preds_lr))
```

```
print(metrics.accuracy_score(y_test, preds_lr))
0.8059630856601988
```

Figure7.15: Logistic regression model accuracy

We have obtained good accuracy in the model.

3. We can also get the weights of all the variables to weigh their importance in the predictive model:

```
weights = pd.Series(model.coef_[0],index=x_scaled.
columns)
pd.concat([weights.head(10),weights.tail(10)]).sort_
values(ascending = False).plot(kind='bar',figsize=(16,6))
```

The preceding code will create a data frame of the weights of the 10 most positive and 10 most negative weighted variables.

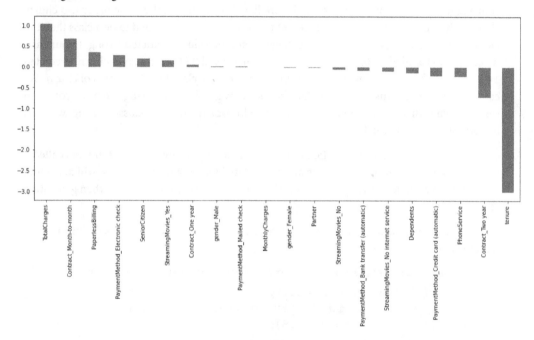

Figure 7.16: Model feature importance

It is interesting to see how the total charges and the tenure, especially the latter, have great importance in the regression. The importance of these variables is also validated by looking at the variable correlation. An important next step would be to do a deeper analysis of the relationship of this variable to the churn variable to understand the mechanism behind this relationship.

4. We can create the confusion matrix to visualize the performance of predicting each class:

```
from sklearn.metrics import classification_report,
confusion_matrix
print(confusion_matrix(y_test,preds_lr))
```

```
print(confusion_matrix(y_test,preds_lr))

[[1401  145]
 [ 265  302]]
```

Figure 7.17: Model confusion matrix

In the confusion matrix, the information shown in the columns are the distinct classes (no churn and churn) and in the rows are the predicted outcomes in the same order (no churn, churn). The values in the diagonal represent the true positives, predicted to be a class that it in fact was. The values that are outside the diagonal are the values predicted wrong. In our case, we correctly classified 1401 cases of no churn, mislabeled 265 no churn as churn, predicted 145 cases to churn when in fact they didn't, and correctly classified 302 cases of churn. We can see from the confusion matrix that the model is good at predicting the most common cases, which is that there is no churn, but it got almost a third of the classes wrong, which is important for us to predict.

5. Our next step is to create a classification system made up of several decision trees called a random forest. It attempts to produce an uncorrelated forest of decision trees, which is more accurate than a single individual tree, using bagging and feature randomness when generating each individual tree.

    In the next code, we will use the RandomForestClassifier class from sklearn and train it on the data:

    ```
    from sklearn.ensemble import RandomForestClassifier
    model_rf = RandomForestClassifier(n_estimators=750 ,
    oob_score = True, random_state =50, max_features =
    "auto",max_leaf_nodes = 15)
    model_rf.fit(x_train, y_train)
    ```

6. Finally, we have trained the model and we can make predictions:

    ```
    preds_rfc = model_rf.predict(x_test)
    print(metrics.accuracy_score(y_test, preds_rfc))
    ```

    ```
    print(metrics.accuracy_score(y_test, preds_rfc))

    0.8035967818267865
    ```

    Figure 7.18: Random forest model accuracy

We have obtained an accuracy very similar to the regression model.

7. Let's see the variable importance of the model as the next step:

```
importances = model_rf.feature_importances_
weights_rf = pd.Series(importances,index=x_scaled.
columns)
pd.concat([weights_rf.head(10),weights.tail(10)]).sort_
values(ascending = False).plot(kind='bar',figsize=(16,6))
```

The preceding code will show us the 10 most positive and 10 most negative weights of the model.

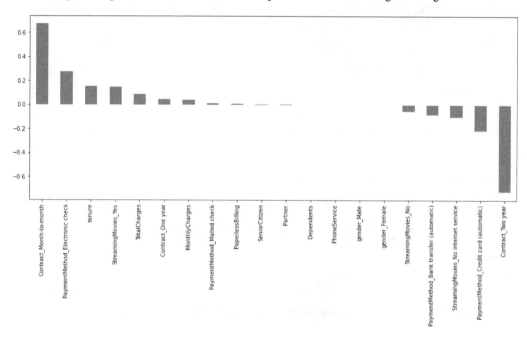

Figure 7.19: Model feature importance

This model has a different ranking, having, in the extremes, the month-to-month contract and the 2-year contract:

```
print(confusion_matrix(y_test,preds_rfc))
```

```
print(confusion_matrix(y_test,preds_rfc))

[[1447    99]
 [ 316   251]]
```

Figure 7.20: Model confusion matrix

This model predicts our target variable better, which makes it suitable for our needs.

8. Next, we will train a supervised machine learning technique known as a **Support Vector Classifier** (**SVC**), which is frequently used for classification problems. An SVC separates the data into two classes by mapping the data points to a high-dimensional space and then locating the best hyperplane:

```
from sklearn.svm import SVC
model_svm = SVC(kernel='linear')
model_svm.fit(x_train,y_train)
preds_svm = model_svm.predict(x_test)
metrics.accuracy_score(y_test, preds_svm)
```

The code here will fit the model to the data and print the accuracy score.

```
metrics.accuracy_score(y_test, preds_svm)

0.8021769995267393
```

Figure 7.21: Model accuracy score

9. The accuracy score is still in the same range as the other models, so let's look at the absolute weight importance of the model:

```
pd.Series(abs(model_svm.coef_[0]), index=x_scaled.
columns).nlargest(10).plot(kind='barh',figsize=(10,8))
```

The code here will prompt the 10 most important variables for the model.

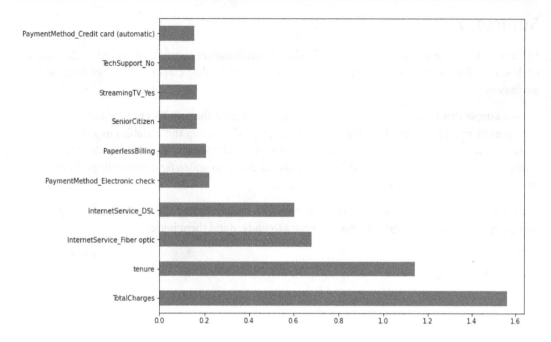

Figure 7.22: Model feature importance

We can see that tenure and total charges are variables of importance for the model, which is something that we saw in the other models as well. The drawback of this kind of visualization is that we cannot see the orientation of this importance.

10. Let's look at the performance of predicting our target variable:

```
print(confusion_matrix(y_test,preds_svm))
```

The next step is the confusion matrix, which will allow us to determine with more certainty which labels we are correctly predicting.

```
print(confusion_matrix(y_test,preds_svm))

[[1400  146]
 [ 272  295]]
```

Figure 7.23: Model confusion matrix

The model is less accurate than the random forest for predicting whether the clients will churn or not.

It is always good to combine the various perspectives of the confusion matrix, as the accuracy will not work as a performance metric alone if the set is imbalanced.

Summary

In this chapter, we analyzed a very common business case: customer churn. Understanding the causes of this, as well as being able to take preventive actions to avoid this, can create a lot of revenue for a company.

In the example that we have analyzed, we have seen how to clean the variables in a dataset to properly represent them and prepare them for machine learning. Visualizing the variables in a relationship against the target variable that we are analyzing allows us to understand the problem better. Finally, we trained several machine learning models that we later analyzed to understand how their performances were when predicting the target variable.

In the next chapter, we will focus more of our attention on understanding how variables affect segments and group users with homogenous characteristics to understand them better.

8

Grouping Users with Customer Segmentation

To better understand consumer needs, we need to understand that our customers have distinct consumer patterns. Each mass of consumers of a given product or service can be divided into segments, described in terms of age, marital status, purchasing power, and so on. In this chapter, we will be performing an exploratory analysis of consumer data from a grocery store and then applying clustering techniques to separate them into segments with homogenous consumer patterns. This knowledge will enable us to better understand their needs, create unique offers, and target them more effectively. In this chapter, we will learn about the following topics:

- Understanding customer segmentation

- Exploring data about a customer's database

- Applying feature engineering to standardize variables

- Creating users' segments with K-means clustering

- Describing the common characteristics of these clusters

Let us see the requirements to understand the steps and follow the chapter.

Technical requirements

To be able to follow the steps in this chapter, you will need to meet the following requirements:

- A Jupyter notebook instance running Python 3.7 and above. You can also use the Google Colab notebook to run the steps if you have a Google Drive account.

- An understanding of basic math and statistical concepts.

- A Kaggle account—you must agree to the terms and conditions of the competition from where we will get the data, which you can find here: `https://www.kaggle.com/datasets/imakash3011/customer-personality-analysis`.

Understanding customer segmentation

Customer segmentation is the practice of classifying customers into groups based on shared traits so that businesses may effectively and appropriately market to each group. In **business-to-business (B2B)** marketing, a firm may divide its clientele into several groups based on a variety of criteria, such as location, industry, the number of employees, and previous purchases of the company's goods.

Businesses frequently divide their clientele into segments based on demographics such as age, gender, marital status, location (urban, suburban, or rural), and life stage (single, married, divorced, empty nester, retired). Customer segmentation calls for a business to collect data about its customers, evaluate it, and look for trends that may be utilized to establish segments.

Job title, location, and products purchased—for example—are some of the details that can be learned from purchasing data to help businesses to learn about their customers. Some of this information might be discovered by looking at the customer's system entry. An online marketer using an opt-in email list may divide marketing communications into various categories based on the opt-in offer that drew the client, for instance. However, other data—for example, consumer demographics such as age and marital status—will have to be gathered through different methods.

Other typical information-gathering methods in consumer goods include:

- Face-to-face interviews with customers
- Online surveys
- Online marketing and web traffic information
- Focus groups

All organizations, regardless of size, industry, and whether they sell online or in person, can use customer segmentation. It starts with obtaining and evaluating data and concludes with taking suitable and efficient action on the information acquired.

We will execute an unsupervised clustering of data on the customer records from a grocery store's database in this chapter. To maximize the value of each customer to the firm, we will segment our customer base to alter products in response to specific needs and consumer behavior. The ability to address the needs of various clientele also benefits the firm.

Exploring the data

The first stage to understanding customer segments is to understand the data that we will be using. The first stage is, then, an exploration of the data to check the variables we must work with, handle non-structured data, and adjust data types. We will be structuring the data for the clustering analysis and gaining knowledge about the data distribution.

For the analysis we will use in the next example, the following Python modules are used:

- **Pandas**: Python package for data analysis and data manipulation.

- **NumPy**: This is a library that adds support for large, multi-dimensional arrays and matrices, along with an ample collection of high-level mathematical functions to operate on these arrays.

- **Statsmodels**: Python package that provides a complement to `scipy` for statistical computations, including descriptive statistics and estimation and inference for statistical models. It provides classes and functions for the estimation of many different statistical models.

- **Yellowbrick**: A Python package of visual analysis and diagnostic tools designed to facilitate **machine learning** (ML) with scikit-learn.

- **Seaborn, mpl_toolkits, and Matplotlib**: Python packages for effective data visualization.

We'll now get started with the analysis, using the following steps:

1. The following block of code will load all the required packages mentioned earlier, including the functions that we will be using, such as `LabelEncoder`, `StandardScaler`, and `Kmeans`:

```python
import numpy as np
import pandas as pd
import datetime
import seaborn as sns
import matplotlib.pyplot as plt
from matplotlib import colors
from matplotlib.colors import ListedColormap
from sklearn.preprocessing import LabelEncoder
from sklearn.preprocessing import StandardScaler
from sklearn.decomposition import PCA
from yellowbrick.cluster import KElbowVisualizer
from sklearn.cluster import KMeans
from mpl_toolkits.mplot3d import Axes3D
from sklearn.cluster import AgglomerativeClustering
```

2. For readability purposes, we will limit the maximum rows to be shown to 20, set the limit of maximum columns to 50, and show the floats with 2 digits of precision:

```
pd.options.display.max_rows = 20
pd.options.display.max_columns = 50
pd.options.display.precision = 2
```

3. Next, we will load the data, which is stored in the local data folder. The file is in CSV format with a tab delimiter. We will read the data into a Pandas DataFrame and print the data shape as well as show the first rows:

```
path = "data/marketing_campaign.csv"
data = pd.read_csv(path, sep="\t")
print("Data Shape", data.shape)
data.head()
```

This results in the following output:

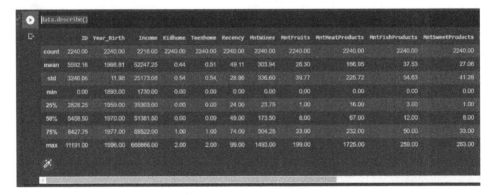

Figure 8.1: User data

4. In order to get a full picture of the steps that we will be taking to clean the dataset, let us have a look at the statistical summary of the data with the `describe` method:

```
data.describe()
```

This results in the following output:

	ID	Year_Birth	Income	Kidhome	Teenhome	Recency	MntWines	MntFruits	MntMeatProducts	MntFishProducts	MntSweetProducts
count	2240.00	2240.00	2216.00	2240.00	2240.00	2240.00	2240.00	2240.00	2240.00	2240.00	2240.00
mean	5592.16	1968.81	52247.25	0.44	0.51	49.11	303.94	26.30	166.95	37.53	27.06
std	3246.66	11.98	25173.08	0.54	0.54	28.96	336.60	39.77	225.72	54.63	41.28
min	0.00	1893.00	1730.00	0.00	0.00	0.00	0.00	0.00	0.00	0.00	0.00
25%	2828.25	1959.00	35303.00	0.00	0.00	24.00	23.75	1.00	16.00	3.00	1.00
50%	5458.50	1970.00	51381.50	0.00	0.00	49.00	173.50	8.00	67.00	12.00	8.00
75%	8427.75	1977.00	68522.00	1.00	1.00	74.00	504.25	33.00	232.00	50.00	33.00
max	11191.00	1996.00	666666.00	2.00	2.00	99.00	1493.00	199.00	1725.00	259.00	263.00

Figure 8.2: Descriptive statistical summary

5. To get more information on features, we can use the `info` method to display the number of `null` values and data types:

```
data.info()
```

This results in the following output:

```
<class 'pandas.core.frame.DataFrame'>
RangeIndex: 2240 entries, 0 to 2239
Data columns (total 29 columns):
 #   Column               Non-Null Count  Dtype
---  ------               --------------  -----
 0   ID                   2240 non-null   int64
 1   Year_Birth           2240 non-null   int64
 2   Education            2240 non-null   object
 3   Marital_Status       2240 non-null   object
 4   Income               2216 non-null   float64
 5   Kidhome              2240 non-null   int64
 6   Teenhome             2240 non-null   int64
 7   Dt_Customer          2240 non-null   object
 8   Recency              2240 non-null   int64
 9   MntWines             2240 non-null   int64
 10  MntFruits            2240 non-null   int64
 11  MntMeatProducts      2240 non-null   int64
 12  MntFishProducts      2240 non-null   int64
 13  MntSweetProducts     2240 non-null   int64
 14  MntGoldProds         2240 non-null   int64
 15  NumDealsPurchases    2240 non-null   int64
 16  NumWebPurchases      2240 non-null   int64
 17  NumCatalogPurchases  2240 non-null   int64
 18  NumStorePurchases    2240 non-null   int64
 19  NumWebVisitsMonth    2240 non-null   int64
 20  AcceptedCmp3         2240 non-null   int64
 21  AcceptedCmp4         2240 non-null   int64
 22  AcceptedCmp5         2240 non-null   int64
 23  AcceptedCmp1         2240 non-null   int64
 24  AcceptedCmp2         2240 non-null   int64
 25  Complain             2240 non-null   int64
 26  Z_CostContact        2240 non-null   int64
 27  Z_Revenue            2240 non-null   int64
 28  Response             2240 non-null   int64
dtypes: float64(1), int64(25), object(3)
memory usage: 507.6+ KB
```

Figure 8.3: Column data types and null values

From the preceding output shown with the `describe` and `info` methods of Pandas DataFrames, we can see the following:

- There are 26 missing values in the `Income` column

- The date variable named `Dt_Customer`, indicating the date a customer joined the database, is not parsed as `DateTime`

- There are categorical features in our DataFrame of the `dtype` object that we will need to encode into numerical features later to be able to apply the clustering method

6. To address the missing values, we will drop the rows that have missing income values, as it is an important variable to describe to customers:

```
data = data.dropna()
print("Data Shape", data.shape)
```

7. We will parse the date column using the pd.to_datetime Pandas method. Take into account that the method will infer the format of the date, but we can otherwise specify it if it is necessary:

```
data["Dt_Customer"] = pd.to_datetime(data["Dt_Customer"])
```

8. After parsing the dates, we can look at the values of the newest and oldest recorded customer:

```
str(data["Dt_Customer"].min()),str(data["Dt_Customer"].
max())
>>>> ('2012-01-08 00:00:00', '2014-12-06 00:00:00')
```

9. In the next step, we will create a feature out of Dt_Customer that indicates the number of days a customer is registered in the firm's database, relative to the first user that was registered in the database, although we could use today's date. We do this because we are analyzing historical records and not up-to-date data. The Customer_For feature is, then, the date of when the customer was registered minus the minimum value in the date column and can be interpreted as the number of days since customers started to shop in the store relative to the last recorded date:

```
data["Customer_For"] = data["Dt_Customer"]-data["Dt_
Customer"].min()
data["Customer_For"] = data["Customer_For"].dt.days
```

10. Now, we will explore the unique values in the categorical features to get a clear idea of the data:

```
data["Marital_Status"].value_counts().plot.
bar(figsize=(12,6),title = 'Categories in the feature
Marital_Status:')
```

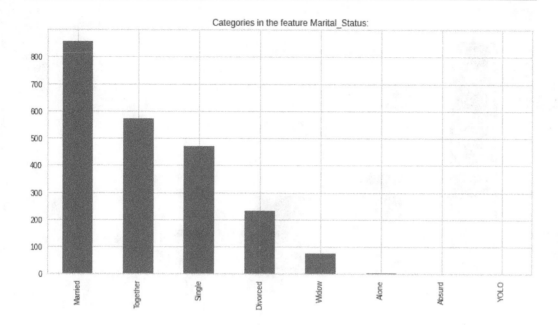

Figure 8.4: Marital status

Here, we can see that there are several types of marital status, which may have been caused by free text entry during the data capturing. We will have to standardize these values.

11. Next, we will look at the values in the Education feature using the value_counts method to create a bar chart using the Pandas plot method:

```
data["Education"].value_counts().plot.
bar(figsize=(12,6),title = 'Categories in the feature
Education:')
```

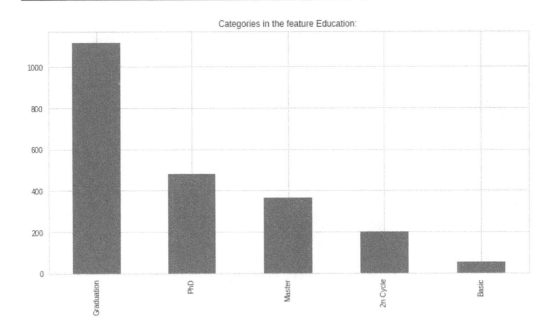

Figure 8.5: Education values

Again, we can see the effects of free text entry as there are several values that have the same underlying meaning; thus, we will need to standardize them as well.

In the next section, we will apply feature engineering to structure the data for better understanding and treatment of the data.

Feature engineering

To be able to properly analyze the data as well as to model the clusters, we will need to clean and structure the data—a step that is commonly referred to as feature engineering—as we need to restructure some of the variables according to our plan of analysis.

In this section, we will be performing the next steps to clean and structure some of the dataset features, with the goal of simplifying the existing variables and creating features that are easier to understand and describe the data properly:

1. Create an Age variable for a customer by using the Year_Birth feature, indicating the birth year of the respective person.

2. Create a Living_With feature to simplify the marital status, to describe the living situation of couples.

3. Create a Children feature to indicate the total number of children in a household—that is, kids and teenagers.

4.   Aggregate spending by product type to better capture consumer behaviors.

5.   Indicate parenthood status with a feature named `Is_Parent`.

So, let's apply the steps mentioned here to structure the data:

1.   First, let us start with the age of the customer as of today, using the `pd.to_datetime` method to get the current year and the year of birth of the customers:

```
data["Age"] = pd.to_datetime('today').year -
       data["Year_Birth"]
```

2.   Now, we will model the spending on distinct items by using the `sum` method on selected columns and summing along the column axis:

```
prod_cols = ["MntWines","MntFruits","MntMeatProducts",
"MntFishProducts","MntSweetProducts","MntGoldProds"]
data["Spent"] = data[prod_cols].sum(axis=1)
```

3.   As the next step, we will map the marital status values into a different encoding to simplify terms with close meaning. For this, we define a mapping dictionary and use it to replace the values in the `marital_status` column to create a new feature:

```
marital_status_dict= {"Married":"Partner",
                      "Together":"Partner",
                      "Absurd":"Alone",
                      "Widow":"Alone",
                      "YOLO":"Alone",
                      "Divorced":"Alone",
                      "Single":"Alone",}
data["Living_With"] = data["Marital_Status"].
replace(marital_status_dict)
```

4.   Next, we create a `Children` feature by summing up the total number of children living in the household plus teens living at home:

```
data["Children"]=data["Kidhome"]+data["Teenhome"]
```

5.   Now, we model the total members in the household using the relationship and children data:

```
data["Family_Size"] = data["Living_With"].
replace({"Alone": 1, "Partner":2})+ data["Children"]
```

6. Finally, we capture the parenthood status in a new variable:

```
data["Is_Parent"] = (data.Children> 0).astype(int)
```

7. Now, we will segment education levels into three groups for simplification:

```
edu_dict = {"Basic":"Undergraduate","2n
Cycle":"Undergraduate", "Graduation":"Graduate",
"Master":"Postgraduate", "PhD":"Postgraduate"}
data["Ed_level"]=data["Education"].replace(edu_dict)
```

8. Now, to simplify, we rename columns into more understandable terms using a mapping dictionary:

```
col_rename_dict = {"MntWines": "Wines",
                   "MntFruits":"Fruits",
                   "MntMeatProducts":"Meat",
                   "MntFishProducts":"Fish",
                   "MntSweetProducts":"Sweets",
                   "MntGoldProds":"Gold"}
data = data.rename(columns=col_rename_dict)
```

9. Now, we will drop some of the redundant features to focus on the clearest features, including the ones we just created. Finally, we will look at the statistical descriptive analysis using the `describe` method:

```
to_drop = ["Marital_Status", "Dt_Customer",
        "Z_CostContact", "Z_Revenue", "Year_Birth", "ID"]
data = data.drop(to_drop, axis=1)
data.describe()
```

10. The stats show us that there are some discrepancies in the `Income` and `Age` features, which we will visualize to better understand these inconsistencies. We will start with a histogram of `Age`:

```
data["Age"].plot.hist(figsize=(12,6))
```

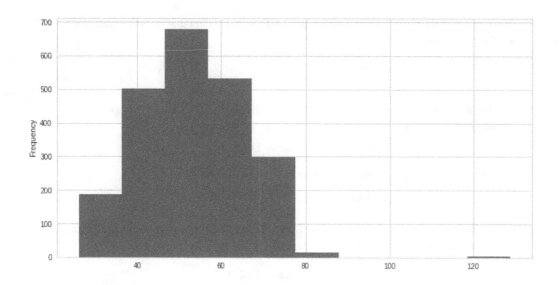

Figure 8.6: Age data

We can see that there are some outliers, more than 120 years old, so we will be removing those.

11. Next, we look at the income distribution:

```
data["Income"].plot.hist(figsize=(12,6))
```

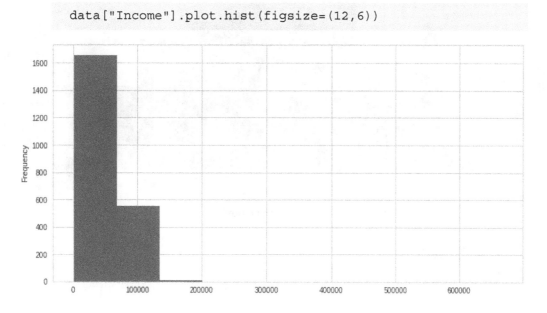

Figure 8.7: Income data

Again, we can see that most incomes are below 20,000, so we will be limiting the spending level.

12. Next, we drop the outliers by setting a cap on Age to avoid data that doesn't reflect reality, and the income to include 99% of the cases:

```
prev_len = len(data)
data = data[(data["Age"]<99)]
data = data[(data["Income"]<150000)]
new_len = prev_len - len(data)
print('Removed outliers:',new_len)
```

The preceding code prints the next output:

```
>>> Removed outliers: 11
```

13. Now, we can look back at the Age and Spend data distribution to better understand our customers. We start by creating a histogram plot of the Age feature:

```
data["Age"].plot.hist(figsize=(12,6))
```

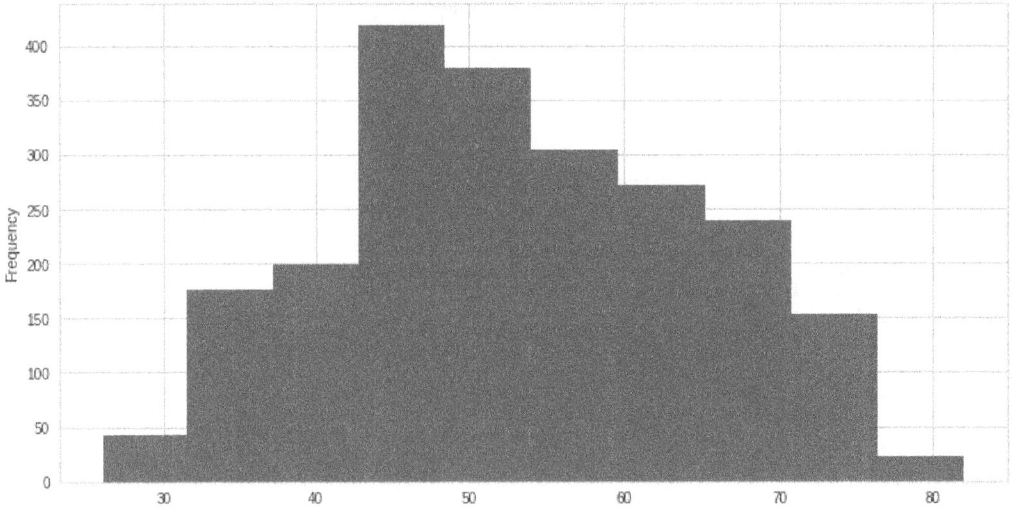

Figure 8.8: Age with no outliers

The age is centered on the 50s, with a skew to the right, meaning that the average age of our customers is above 45 years.

```
data["Income"].plot.hist(figsize=(12,6))
```

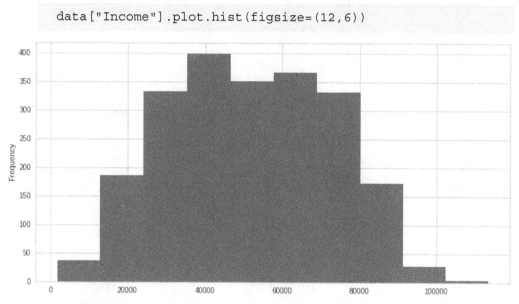

Figure 8.9: Income with no outliers

Looking at the spend distribution, it has a normal distribution, centered on 4,000 and slightly skewed to the left.

14. Up next, we will create a Seaborn pair plot to show the relationships between the different variables, with color labeling according to the parental status:

```
sns.pairplot(data[["Income", "Recency", "Customer_For",
"Age", "Spent", "Is_Parent"]], hue= "Is_Parent",palette=
(["red","blue"]))
```

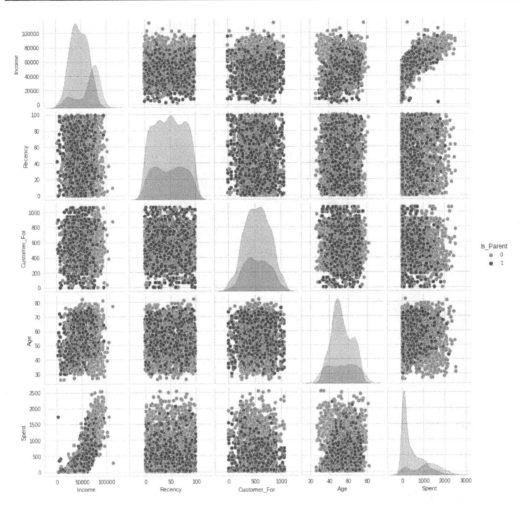

Figure 8.10: Relationship plot

These graphics allow us to quickly observe relationships between the different variables, as well as their distribution. One of the clearest is the relationship between spend and income, in which we can see that the higher the income, the higher the expenditure, as well as observing that single parents spend more than people who are not. We can also see that the consumers with higher recency are parents, while single consumers have lower recency values. Next, let us look at the correlation among the features (excluding the categorical attributes at this point).

15. We will create a correlation matrix using the `corr` method, and show only the lower triangle of data using a `numpy` mask. Finally, we will use a Seaborn method to display the values:

```
df_corr = data.corr()
mask = np.triu(np.ones_like(df_corr, dtype=bool))
```

```
df_corr = df_corr.mask(mask).round(3)
fig, ax = plt.subplots(figsize=(16,16))
cmap = colors.ListedColormap(["#682F2F", "#9E726F",
"#D6B2B1", "#B9C0C9", "#9F8A78", "#F3AB60"])
sns.heatmap(df_corr, cmap=cmap,annot=True,ax=ax)
```

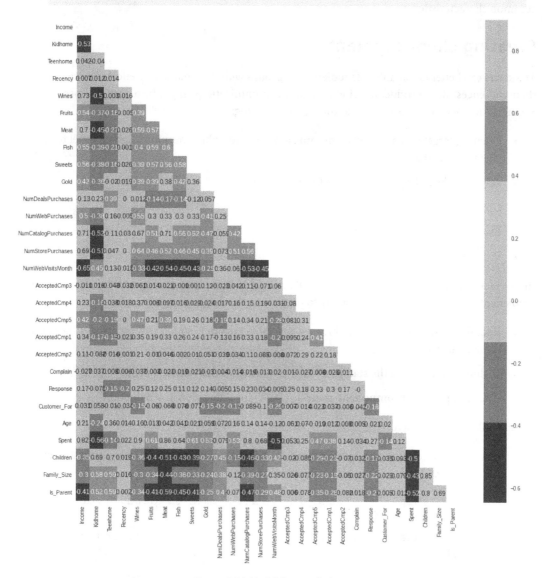

Figure 8.11: Variable correlation

The correlations allow us to explore the variable relationships in more detail. We can see negative correlations between children and expenditure in the mean, while there are positive relationships between children and recency. These correlations allow us to better understand consumption patterns.

In the next section, we will use the concept of clustering to segment the clients into groups that share common characteristics.

Creating client segments

Marketers can better target different audience subgroups with their marketing efforts by segmenting their audiences. Both product development and communications might be a part of those efforts. Segmentation benefits a business by allowing the following:

- Creating targeted marketing communication on the right communication channel for each client or user segment
- Applying the right pricing options to the right clients
- Concentrating on the most lucrative clients
- Providing better client service
- Promoting and cross-promoting other goods and services

In this section, we will be preprocessing the data to be able to apply clustering methods for customer segmentation. The steps that we will apply to preprocess the data are set out here:

- Encoding the categorical variables using a label encoder, which will transform them into numerical columns
- Scaling features using the standard scaler to normalize the values
- Applying **principal component analysis** (**PCA**) for dimensionality reduction

So, let's follow the steps here:

1. First, we need to list the categorical variables. Here, we will use the column names and check the column dtype to get only the object columns:

    ```
    object_cols = [c for c in data.columns if data[c].dtypes
    == 'object']
    print("Categorical variables in the dataset:", object_
    cols)
    ```

2. Next, we will encode the `dtypes` object using the `sklearn` `LabelEncoder` function:

```
LE = LabelEncoder()
for i in object_cols:
    data[i]=data[[i]].apply(LE.fit_transform)
```

3. We subset the data and apply scaling to the numerical variables by dropping the features on deals accepted and promotions:

```
scaled_ds = data.copy()
cols_del = ['AcceptedCmp3', 'AcceptedCmp4',
'AcceptedCmp5', 'AcceptedCmp1','AcceptedCmp2',
'Complain', 'Response']
scaled_ds = scaled_ds.drop(cols_del, axis=1)
```

4. Finally, we can apply the scaling:

```
scaler = StandardScaler()
scaler.fit(scaled_ds)
scaled_ds = pd.DataFrame(scaler.transform(
        scaled_ds),columns= scaled_ds.columns )
```

There are numerous attributes in this dataset that describe the data. The more features there are, the more difficult it is to correctly analyze them in a business environment. Many of these characteristics are redundant since they are connected. Therefore, before running the features through a classifier, we will conduct dimensionality reduction on the chosen features.

Dimensionality reduction is the process of reducing the number of random variables considered. To reduce the dimensionality of huge datasets, a technique known as PCA is frequently utilized. PCA works by condensing an ample collection of variables into a smaller set that still retains much of the data in the larger set.

Accuracy naturally suffers as a dataset's variables are reduced, but the answer to dimensionality reduction is to trade a little accuracy for simplicity since ML algorithms can analyze data much more quickly and easily with smaller datasets because there are fewer unnecessary factors to process. In conclusion, the basic principle of PCA is to keep as much information as possible while reducing the number of variables in the data collected.

The steps that we will be applying in this section are the following:

- Dimensionality reduction with PCA

- Plotting the reduced DataFrame in a 3D plot

- Dimensionality reduction with PCA, again

This will allow us to have a way to visualize the segments projected into three dimensions. In an ideal setup, we will use the weights of each component to understand what each component represents and make sense of the information we are visualizing in a better way. For reasons of simplicity, we will focus on the visualization of the components. Here are the steps:

1. First, we will initiate PCA to reduce dimensions or features to three in order to reduce complexity:

```
pca = PCA(n_components=3)
PCA_ds = pca.fit_transform(scaled_ds)
PCA_ds = pd.DataFrame(PCA_ds, columns=([
        "component_one","component_two", "component_three"]))
```

2. The amount of variation in a dataset that can be attributed to each of the main components (eigenvectors) produced by a PCA is measured statistically as "explained variance". This simply refers to how much of a dataset's variability may be attributed to each unique primary component.

```
print(pca.explained_variance_ratio_)
>>>>[0.35092717 0.12336458 0.06470715]
```

For this project, we will reduce the dimensions to three, which manages to explain the 54% total variance in the observed variables:

```
print('Total explained variance',sum(pca.explained_
variance_ratio_))
>>>> Total explained variance 0.5389989029179605
```

3. Now we can project the data into a 3D plot to see the points' distribution:

```
x,y,z=PCA_ds["component_one"],PCA_ds[
        "component_two"],PCA_ds["component_three"]
fig = plt.figure(figsize=(10,8))
ax = fig.add_subplot(111, projection="3d")
ax.scatter(x,y,z, c="maroon", marker="o" )
ax.set_title("A 3D Projection Of Data In The Reduced
Dimension")
plt.show()
```

The preceding code will show us the dimensions projected in three dimensions:

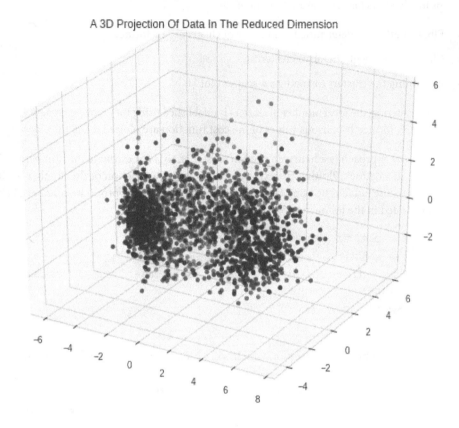

Figure 8.12: PCA variables in 3D

Since the attributes are now only three dimensions, agglomerative clustering will be used to perform the clustering. A hierarchical clustering technique is agglomerative clustering. Up until the appropriate number of clusters is reached, examples are merged.

The process of clustering involves grouping the population or data points into a number of groups so that the data points within each group are more like one another than the data points within other groups. Simply put, the goal is to sort into clusters any groups of people who share similar characteristics. Finding unique groups, or "clusters", within a data collection is the aim of clustering. The tool uses an ML algorithm to construct groups, where members of a group would typically share similar traits.

Two methods of pattern recognition used in ML are classification and clustering. Although there are some parallels between the two processes, clustering discovers similarities between things and groups them according to those features that set them apart from other groups of objects, whereas classification employs predetermined classes to which objects are assigned. "Clusters" is the name for these collections.

The steps involved in clustering are set out here:

- Elbow method to determine the number of clusters to be formed
- Clustering via agglomerative clustering
- Examining the clusters formed via a scatter plot

In K-means clustering, the ideal number of clusters is established using the elbow approach. The number of clusters, or K, formed by various values of the cost function are plotted using the elbow approac:.

1. The elbow approach is a heuristic used in cluster analysis to estimate the number of clusters present in a dataset. Plotting the explained variation as a function of the number of clusters, the procedure entails choosing the elbow of the curve as the appropriate number of clusters, as illustrated in the following code snippet:

```
fig = plt.figure(figsize=(12,8))
elbow = KElbowVisualizer(KMeans(), k=(2,12),
metric='distortion') # distortion: mean sum of squared
distances to centers
elbow.fit(PCA_ds)
elbow.show()
```

This code will plot an elbow plot, which will be a good estimation of the required number of clusters:

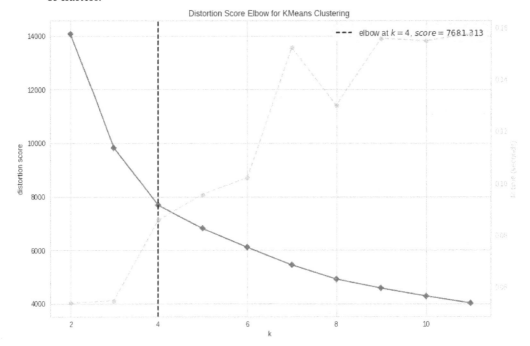

Figure 8.13: Elbow method

2. According to the preceding cell, four clusters will be the best choice for this set of data. To obtain the final clusters, we will then fit the agglomerative clustering model, like so:

```
AC = AgglomerativeClustering(n_clusters=4)
# fit model and predict clusters
yhat_AC = AC.fit_predict(PCA_ds)
PCA_ds["Clusters"] = yhat_AC
```

3. Finally, we will add a `Clusters` feature to the original DataFrame for visualization:

```
data["Clusters"]= yhat_AC
```

4. Now, we can visualize the clusters in three dimensions using the color codes of each cluster:

```
classes = [0,1,2,3]
values = PCA_ds["Clusters"]
colors = ListedColormap(['red','blue','green','orange'])
fig = plt.figure(figsize=(10,8))
ax = plt.subplot(projection='3d')
scatter = ax.scatter(x, y,z, c=values, cmap=colors)
plt.legend(handles=scatter.legend_elements()[0],
labels=classes)
```

The preceding code will show a three-dimensional visualization of the PCA components colored according to the clusters:

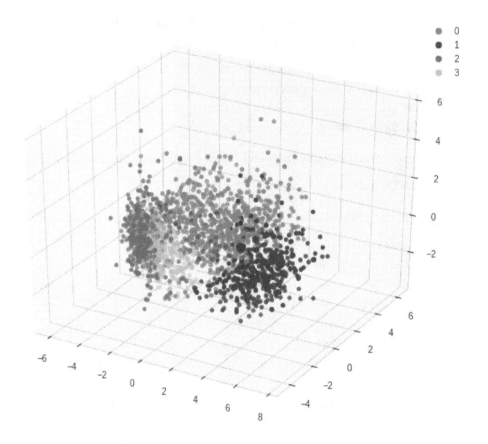

Figure 8.14: PCA variables with cluster labeling

From this, we can see that each cluster occupies a specific space in the visualization. We will now dive into a description of each cluster to better understand these segments.

Understanding clusters as customer segments

To rigorously evaluate the output obtained, we need to evaluate the depicted clusters. This is because clustering is an unsupervised method and the patterns extracted should always reflect reality, otherwise; we might just as well be analyzing noise.

Common traits among consumer groups can help a business choose which items or services to advertise to which segments and how to market to each one.

To do that, we will use **exploratory data analysis (EDA)** to look at the data in the context of clusters and make judgments. Here are the steps:

1. Let us first examine the clustering group distribution:

```
cluster_count = PCA_ds["Clusters"].value_counts().reset_
index()
cluster_count.columns  = ['cluster','count']
f, ax = plt.subplots(figsize=(10, 6))
fig = sns.barplot(x="cluster", y="count",
palette=['red','blue','green','orange'],data=cluster_
count)
```

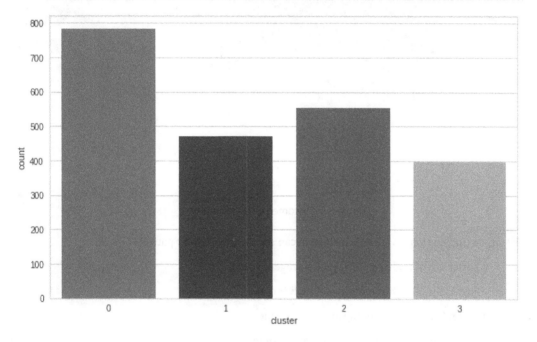

Figure 8.15: Cluster count

The clusters are fairly distributed with a predominance of cluster 0. It can be clearly seen that cluster 1 is our biggest set of customers, closely followed by cluster 0.

2. We can explore what each cluster is spending on for the targeted marketing strategies using the following code:

```
f, ax = plt.subplots(figsize=(12, 8))
pl = sns.scatterplot(data = data,x=data["Spent"],
y=data["Income"],hue=data["Clusters"], palette= colors)
```

```
pl.set_title("Cluster vs Income And Spending")
plt.legend()
plt.show()
```

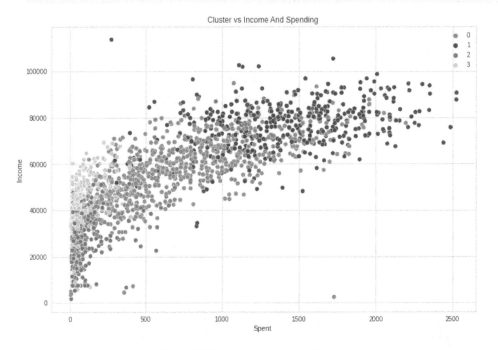

Figure 8.16: Income versus spending

In the income versus spending plot, we can see the next cluster patterns:

- Cluster 0 is of high spending and average income

- Cluster 1 is of high spending and high income

- Cluster 2 is of low spending and low income

- Cluster 3 is of high spending and low income

3. Next, we will see the detailed distribution of clusters of the expenditure per product in the data. Namely, we will explore expenditure patterns. The code is illustrated here:

```
f, ax = plt.subplots(figsize=(12,6))
sample = data.sample(750)
pl = sns.swarmplot(x=sample["Clusters"],
y=sample["Spent"], color= "red", alpha=0.8 ,size=3)
```

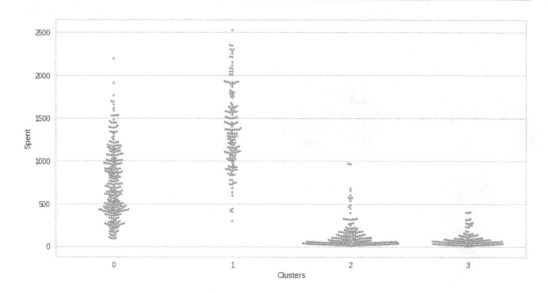

Figure 8.17: Spend distribution per cluster

From *Figure 8.17*, it can be seen how the spend is evenly distributed in cluster 0, cluster 1 is centered on high expenditure, and clusters 2 and 3 center on low expenditure.

4. Next, we will use Seaborn to create Boxen plots of the clusters to find the spend distribution per cluster:

```
f, ax = plt.subplots(figsize=(12, 6))
pl = sns.boxenplot(x=data["Clusters"], y=data["Spent"],
palette=['red','blue','green','orange'])
```

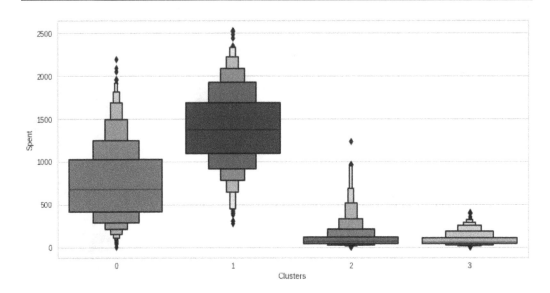

Figure 8.18: Spend distribution per cluster (Boxen plot)

We can visualize the patterns in a different way using a Boxen plot.

5. Next, we will create a feature to get a sum of accepted promotions so that we can model their relationships with the different clusters:

```
data["TotalProm"] = data["AcceptedCmp1"]+
data["AcceptedCmp2"]+ data["AcceptedCmp3"]+
data["AcceptedCmp4"]+ data["AcceptedCmp5"]
```

6. Now, we will plot the count of total campaigns accepted in relation to the clusters:

```
f, ax = plt.subplots(figsize=(10, 6))
pl = sns.countplot(x=data["TotalProm
"],hue=data["Clusters"], palette=
['red','blue','green','orange'])
pl.set_title("Total Promotions vs Cluster")
pl.set_xlabel("Cluster")
pl.set_ylabel("Count")
```

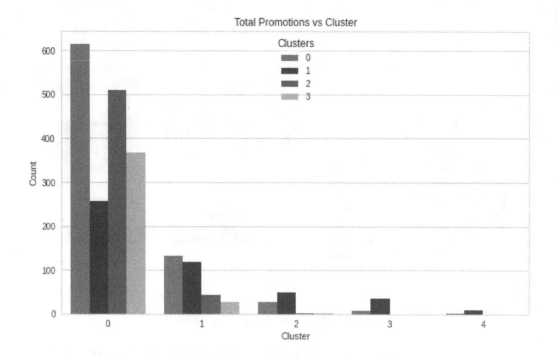

Figure 8.19: Promotions applied per cluster

We can see that although there is no characteristic pattern in the promotions per cluster, we can see that cluster 0 and cluster 2 are the ones with the highest number of applied promotions.

7. Now, we can visualize the number of deals purchased per type of cluster:

```
f, ax = plt.subplots(figsize=(12, 6))
pl = sns.
boxenplot(y=data["NumDealsPurchases"],x=data["Clusters"],
palette= ['red','blue','green','orange'])
pl.set_title("Purchased Deals")
```

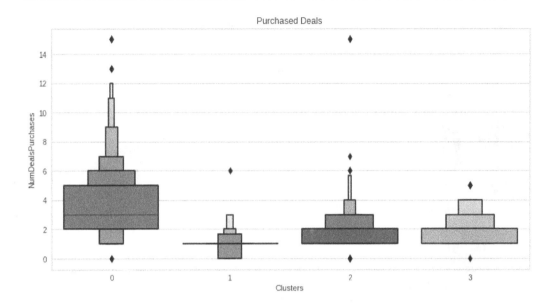

Figure 8.20: Purchased deals per cluster

Promotional campaigns failed to be widespread, but the transactions were successful. The results from clusters 0 and 2 are the best. Cluster 1, one of our top clients, is not interested in the promotions, though. Nothing draws cluster 1 in a strong way.

Now that the clusters have been created and their purchasing patterns have been examined, let us look at everyone in these clusters. To determine who is our star customer and who requires further attention from the retail store's marketing team, we will profile the clusters that have been developed.

Considering the cluster characterization, we will graph some of the elements that are indicative of the customer's personal traits. We will draw conclusions based on the results.

8. We will use a Seaborn joint plot to visualize both the relationships and distributions of different variables:

```
sns.jointplot(x=data['Education'], y=data["Spent"],
hue =data["Clusters"], kind="kde",
palette=['red','blue','green','orange'],height=10)
```

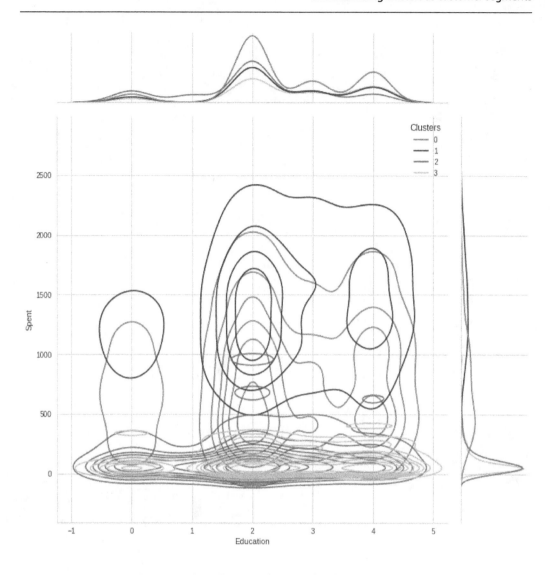

Figure 8.21: Spend versus education distribution per cluster

Cluster 0 is centered on medium education but with a peak in high education. Cluster 2 is the lowest in terms of education.

9. Next, we will look at family size:

```
sns.jointplot(x=data['Family_Size'],
y=data["Spent"], hue =data["Clusters"], kind="kde",
palette=['red','blue','green','orange'],height=10)
```

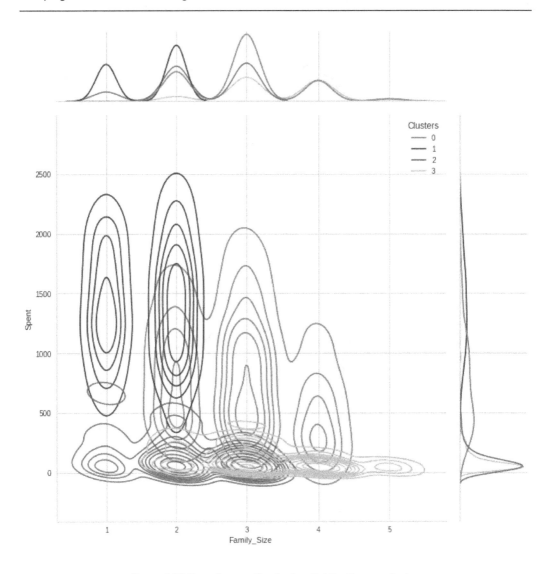

Figure 8.22: Spend versus family size distribution per cluster

Cluster 1 represents small family sizes, and cluster 0 represents couples and families. Clusters 2 and 3 are evenly distributed.

10. We'll now look at the spend versus customer cluster:

```
sns.jointplot(x=data['Customer_For'],
y=data["Spent"], hue =data["Clusters"], kind="kde",
palette=['red','blue','green','orange'],height=10)
```

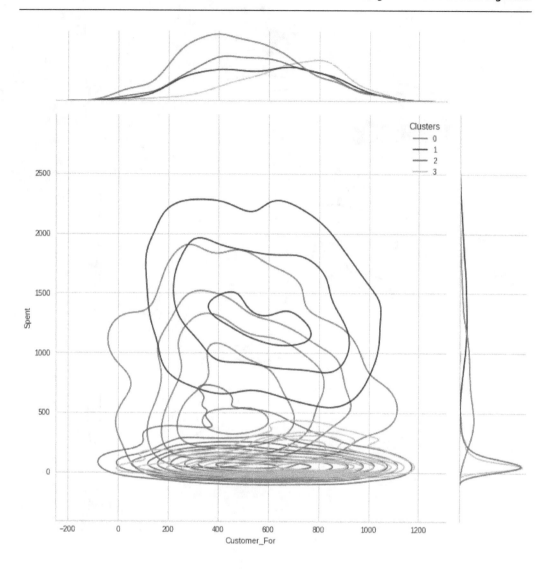

Figure 8.23: Spend versus customer distribution per cluster

Cluster 3 is the group with older clients. While it is interesting to see that although cluster 0 is the one with the highest spending, it is skewed to the left in terms of days since the user has been a customer.

```
sns.jointplot(x=data['Age'], y=data["Spent"],
hue =data["Clusters"], kind="kde",
palette=['red','blue','green','orange'],height=10)
```

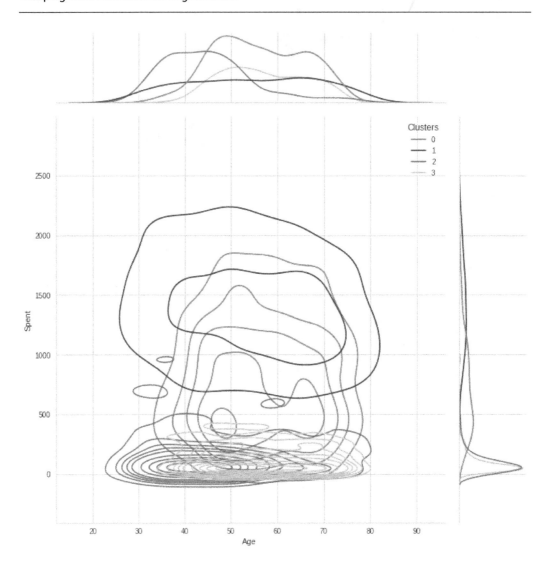

Figure 8.24: Spend versus age distribution per cluster

Cluster 0 is the one with older customers, and the one with the youngest clients is cluster 2.

Summary

In this chapter, we have performed unsupervised clustering. After dimensionality reduction, agglomerative clustering was used. To better profile customers in clusters based on their family structures, income, and spending habits, we divided users into four clusters. This can be applied while creating more effective marketing plans.

In the next chapter, we will dive into the prediction of sales using time-series data to be able to determine revenue expectations given a set of historical sales, as well as understand their relationship with other variables.

9

Using Historical Markdown Data to Predict Sales

Many retailers have no choice but to follow the industry trend of increased use of discounts and special marketing to maintain a competitive edge in today's oversaturated market. This is because most of the new customers are more price-sensitive and will check prices across websites to discover the bests offers for specific products.

Discounting, however, has its drawbacks. While promotions can speed up sales, businesses also run the danger of further profit loss when offering discounts without conducting adequate research. One challenge of modeling retail data is the need to make decisions based on limited history. If Christmas comes but once a year, so does the chance to see how strategic decisions impacted the bottom line.

In this chapter, we delve deeper into the most recent markdown and discount marketing tactics used by industry leaders and show you how to implement them while maintaining profit margins. We will use historical sales information from 45 supermarkets spread across several areas. Although it is well recognized that these markdowns have an influence on sales, it can be difficult to foresee which departments will be impacted and how much, so our goal will be to forecast the sales for each department in each store, which has multiple departments. Selected holiday markdown events are included in the dataset to increase the difficulty.

In this chapter, we will learn how to do the following:

- Determine sales performance considering all the factors that impact it
- Explore the sales data to determine factors that affect sales
- Study the effect of promotional markdown on sales during holidays
- Predict the sales given specific markdowns applied

We will be using data that reflects actual real data to try to get as close as possible to real-life situations.

Technical requirements

To be able to follow the steps in this chapter, you will need to meet the next requirements:

- A Jupyter notebook instance running Python 3.7 and above. You can use the Google Colab notebook to run the steps as well if you have a Google Drive account.

- An understanding of basic math and statistical concepts.

Creating effective markdowns

A markdown is a devaluation of a product because it cannot be sold at the original selling price. An example of a discount would be if you have an item that after a month of slow sales you decide to discount by 20%. Even if you just lost revenue, it also invites more people to buy it at a lower price. Since the item didn't originally sell well, offering a good discounted price can often lead to sales that otherwise wouldn't have happened. However, you will often find that you need to pursue your markdown strategies based on slow sales, moving products from 20% to 30%, 40%, and more as needed. Timing is particularly important because you want to sell the product while it is still relevant to the season, trends, and more.

Markdowns need to be differentiated from discounts. In retail, a discount is a reduction in the price of an item or transaction based on the type of customer who is buying. The employee discount, senior discount, and frequent shopper discount are a few examples. Because of the discounts they receive, many retailers believe that this makes the customers more likely to return to their store than to one of their competitors.

In this chapter, we will use historical sales information from stores located in various locations in the US. Each store has a range of departments, and we will forecast the department-wide sales. Additionally, the company hosts a number of promotional markdown sales all year round, out of which the Super Bowl, Labor Day, Thanksgiving, and Christmas are the four biggest holidays.

In addition, Walmart runs several promotional markdown events throughout the year. These markdowns precede prominent holidays, the four largest of which are the Super Bowl, Labor Day, Thanksgiving, and Christmas. The weeks including these holidays are weighted five times higher in the evaluation than non-holiday weeks. Part of the challenge presented by this competition is modeling the effects of markdowns on these holiday weeks in the absence of complete/ideal historical data.

In the next section, we will analyze the data to understand the variables, its distribution, and we will structure it for better visualization and for use in machine learning.

Analyzing the data

We are provided with 3 files, which contain anonymized information about the 45 stores, indicating the type and size of the store, historical training data, which covers 2010-02-05 to 2012-11-01, and a file that contains additional data related to the store, department, and regional activity for the given dates.

In the next example, the following Python modules were used:

- pandas: A Python package for data analysis and data manipulation
- NumPy: This is a library that adds support for large, multi-dimensional arrays and matrices, along with an ample collection of high-level mathematical functions to operate on these arrays
- Seaborn and Matplotlib: Python packages for effective data visualization

1. We will start the analysis by importing the libraries, and we will start to analyze the data by reading all the files and parsing the Date column using the parse_date option of the read_csv pandas function:

```python
import pandas as pd # data processing
import matplotlib.pyplot as plt # visualization
import seaborn as sns # visualization
train=pd.read_csv("/content/train.csv",
        parse_dates=["Date"])
features=pd.read_csv("/content/features.csv",
        parse_dates=["Date"])
stores=pd.read_csv("/content/stores.csv")
```

2. Now that all the files are loaded, we can start by looking at the first rows of the train file:

```python
train.head()
```

	Store	Dept	Date	Weekly_Sales	IsHoliday
0	1	1	2010-02-05	24924.50	False
1	1	1	2010-02-12	46039.49	True
2	1	1	2010-02-19	41595.55	False
3	1	1	2010-02-26	19403.54	False
4	1	1	2010-03-05	21827.90	False

Figure 9.1: Train file with weekly sales for the store, day, and department

The file contains weekly sales data for each store and department, flagging also whether this day is a holiday or not.

We will also introduce some date variables to make the analysis easier:

```
train['Year']=train['Date'].dt.year
train['Month']=train['Date'].dt.month
train['Week']=train['Date'].dt.week
train['Day']=train['Date'].dt.day
```

3. The next file we will look at contains information about each story in terms of type and size. We can use this information later to assess if the effects of markdown vary depending on the store characteristics:

```
stores.head()
```

	Store	Type	Size
0	1	A	151315
1	2	A	202307
2	3	B	37392
3	4	A	205863
4	5	B	34875

Figure 9.2: Store type and size data

4. We can start to visualize the data by looking at the distribution of sales types and sizes using the boxplot from Seaborn. In the next block of code, we create a subset of data concatenating the **Type** and **Size** columns of the store's data. Then, we create a figure, using Matplotlib, of 8x6 inches, which will contain the seaborn figure:

```
data = pd.concat([stores['Type'], stores['Size']],
axis=1)
f, ax = plt.subplots(figsize=(8, 6))
fig = sns.boxplot(x='Type', y='Size', data=data)
```

The code will show us the distribution of the store size.

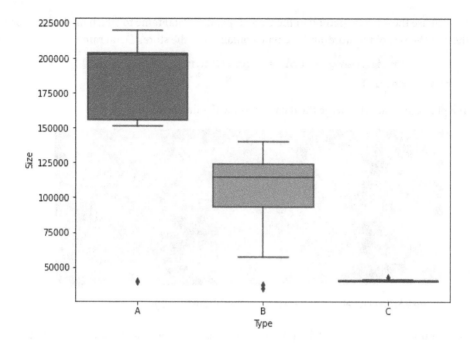

Figure 9.3: Store type and size data

Within size, we can see that there are three types of stores, out of which type A is the biggest. It is interesting to see the variation between the quantiles as well as the outliers.

5. Finally, the next file contains more contextual data about each day and store. This information is about temperature, fuel price, and the different markdowns applied divided into five types, consumer price index, unemployment, and information about whether the day was a holiday or not:

```
features.head()
```

	Store	Date	Temperature	Fuel_Price	MarkDown1	MarkDown2	MarkDown3	MarkDown4	MarkDown5	CPI	Unemployment	IsHoliday
0	1	2010-02-05	42.31	2.572	NaN	NaN	NaN	NaN	NaN	211.096358	8.106	False
1	1	2010-02-12	38.51	2.548	NaN	NaN	NaN	NaN	NaN	211.242170	8.106	True
2	1	2010-02-19	39.93	2.514	NaN	NaN	NaN	NaN	NaN	211.289143	8.106	False
3	1	2010-02-26	46.63	2.561	NaN	NaN	NaN	NaN	NaN	211.319643	8.106	False
4	1	2010-03-05	46.50	2.625	NaN	NaN	NaN	NaN	NaN	211.350143	8.106	False

Figure 9.4: Contextual data by store

We will use the `merge` method in the `train` pandas DataFrame to attach information about the day, the size of the store, and the type contained in the store's DataFrame:

```
train=train.merge(stores, on='Store', how='left')
train.head()
```

The previous code will merge the data and show the first few lines.

	Store	Dept	Date	Weekly_Sales	IsHoliday	Type	Size
0	1	1	2010-02-05	24924.50	False	A	151315
1	1	1	2010-02-12	46039.49	True	A	151315
2	1	1	2010-02-19	41595.55	False	A	151315
3	1	1	2010-02-26	19403.54	False	A	151315
4	1	1	2010-03-05	21827.90	False	A	151315

Figure 9.5: Weekly sales data with information about holidays, store type, and size

We can now visualize the distribution of weekly sales by type of store. We will create a subset of data using the **Type** and **Weekly_Sales** column, creating a Matplotlib figure of 8x6 inches, which then is filled with a seaborn boxplot:

```
data = pd.concat([train['Type'], train['Weekly_Sales']],
axis=1)
f, ax = plt.subplots(figsize=(8, 6))
fig = sns.boxplot(x='Type', y='Weekly_Sales', data=data,
showfliers=False)
```

This will generate boxplot visualizations by type of store.

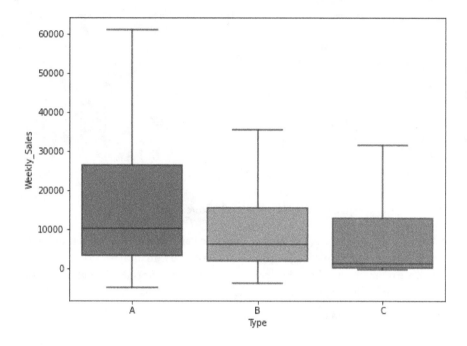

Figure 9.6: Boxplot of weekly sales by type

In relation to the type of store, we can see that although the A is the smallest one, it is the one with the highest median sales.

6. We will now create a boxplot of the distribution of sales data by store ID. We create a subset of data with the columns **Store** and **Weekly_Sales** from the train data, create a Matplotlib figure of 25x8 inches, and show a seaborn boxplot where the x-axis is the store ID and a color differentiation by type:

```
data = pd.concat([train['Store'], train['Weekly_Sales'],
train['Type']], axis=1)
f, ax = plt.subplots(figsize=(25, 8))
fig = sns.boxplot(x='Store', y='Weekly_Sales', data=data,
showfliers=False, hue="Type")
```

The code will generate boxplots of the weekly sales by store.

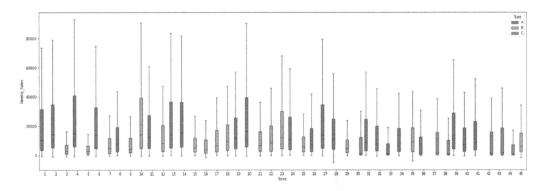

Figure 9.7: Weekly sales data by store ID and type

From the boxplot, we can see that store can be the variable giving information on sales, as there is a consistent pattern of high upper boundaries sales in all types. This is an indication that there are moments in which the demand increases in a short amount of time. Also, there are no indications of having moments in which the demand falls drastically under the median.

Much intrinsic information on type, size, and department is included in the store data. Therefore, we will look at how the holidays impact sales.

7. We repeat the same pattern of creating a subset of data, a Matplotlib figure, and a seaborn boxplot, but now the hue variable is set to the **IsHoliday** column:

```
data = pd.concat([train['Store'], train['Weekly_Sales'],
train['IsHoliday']], axis=1)
f, ax = plt.subplots(figsize=(25, 8))
fig = sns.boxplot(x='Store', y='Weekly_Sales', data=data,
showfliers=False, hue="IsHoliday")
```

This code will show us the distribution of sales with even more levels of information.

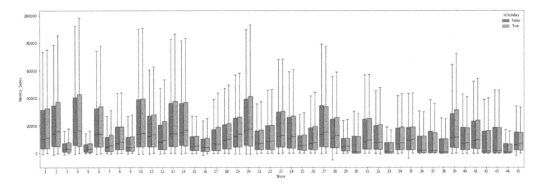

Figure 9.8: Weekly sales data by store ID during and excluding holidays

We can see from the data that **Holiday** and **Store** do not show significant relations except for a small higher sales soaring during the holiday day. This may imply that most of the sales are done days before the holiday itself.

8. Now, let us dive into the difference in sales by type of department. To do this, we will create a subset of data as the grouping of the weekly sales per department, then apply the mean, and reset the index. We show the data using a bar plot because otherwise, it would be impossible to see at glance any difference in a boxplot because of the number of departments:

```
data= train[['Dept','Weekly_Sales']].groupby('Dept').
mean().reset_index()
f, ax = plt.subplots(figsize=(25, 8))
fig = sns.barplot(x='Dept', y='Weekly_Sales', data=data)
```

This visualization will give us a perspective of sales by department.

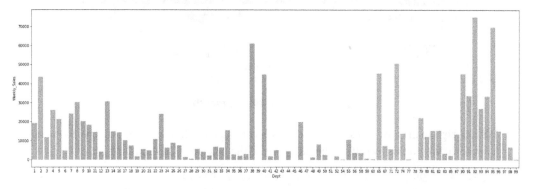

Figure 9.9: Weekly median sale by department

We can see that there is variation between the sales of different departments. We have a high concentration of revenue in some of them, which could lead us to consider excluding the ones with smaller sales. This may not be appropriate as these departments may allow customers that just look for those items to go to that store and then buy other items. You could study this further using analysis such as the Apriori algorithm.

9. Next, we will visualize the weekly sales by month to glimpse at the seasonality of the data. We create a subset of data with the columns and visualize the data with a boxplot:

```
data = pd.concat([train['Month'], train['Weekly_Sales']],
axis=1)
f, ax = plt.subplots(figsize=(8, 6))
fig = sns.boxplot(x='Month', y="Weekly_Sales", data=data,
showfliers=False)
```

The following is the distribution of monthly sales.

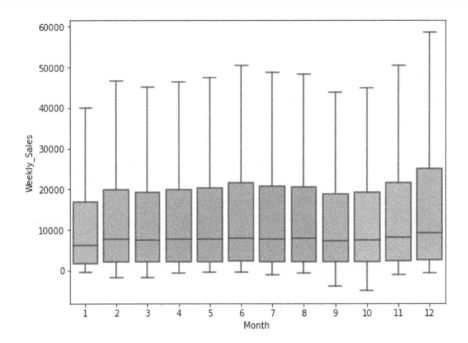

Figure 9.10: Weekly sales by month

We can explore the monthly sales further by visualizing the behavior of the holidays in the sales by month. We do this by setting the hue value of the boxplot to IsHoliday:

```
data = pd.concat([train['Month'], train[
        'Weekly_Sales'],train['IsHoliday']], axis=1)
f, ax = plt.subplots(figsize=(8, 6))
fig = sns.boxplot(x='Month', y="Weekly_Sales", data=data,
showfliers=False, hue='IsHoliday')
```

The following plot is the distribution of sales by month and holidays.

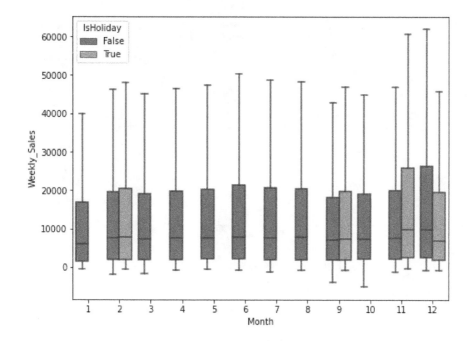

Figure 9.11: Weekly sales by month differentiating holidays

For most of the holidays, the sales on the day of the holiday are slightly higher than on regular days, apart from Christmas, which is in December.

Now, we can create a seaborn relplot to visualize the data per week:

```
data = pd.concat([train['Week'], train['Weekly_
Sales'],train['Type']], axis=1)
sns.relplot(x='Week', y="Weekly_Sales", data=data, hue='T
ype',kind='line',height=8, aspect=2.2)
```

This plot shows us the median and the confidence intervals.

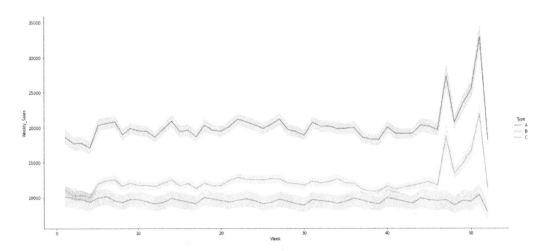

Figure 9.12: Weekly sales through time

By looking at the relplot, we can see the sharp increase in sales between weeks 40 and 50.

10. We can visualize the weekly sales data by using a boxplot with `Week` on the x-axis and the `Weekly_Sales` column on the y-axis :

```
data = pd.concat([train['Week'], train['Weekly_Sales']],
axis=1)
f, ax = plt.subplots(figsize=(20, 6))
fig = sns.boxplot(x='Week', y="Weekly_Sales", data=data,
showfliers=False)
```

This plot shows us the median and the confidence intervals by week of the year.

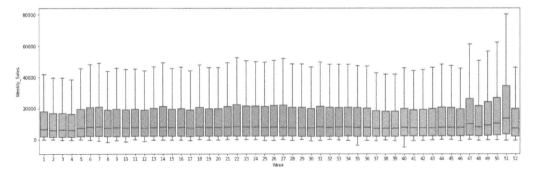

Figure 9.13: Weekly sales by the week of the year

We can see now that the holiday in the first month of the year produces a minor increase, while the ones in the last part of the year have the biggest increase in sales, including a sudden drop in the week after.

11. We can plot the data now using a seaborn relplot using the dates and the weekly sales as well as making a differentiation by type of store with the hue parameter:

```
data = pd.concat([train['Date'], train[
        'Weekly_Sales'],train['Type']], axis=1)
sns.relplot(x='Date', y="Weekly_Sales", data=data, hue='T
ype',kind='line',height=8, aspect=2.2)
```

The preceding code plots the data with a confidence band.

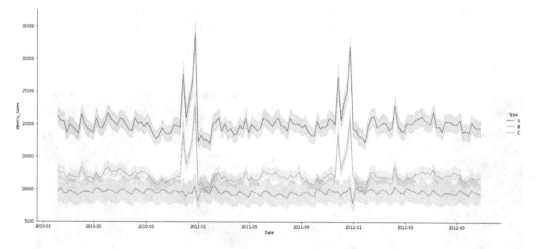

Figure 9.14: Weekly sales through time

We can observe that the same patterns repeat in the two years of data contained, which could be further explained if we would look at the seasonality of the data, which are the recurring patterns that happen every certain period of time. The cycles of buying patterns repeat during the last part of the year, showing a sharp increase during the weeks before Christmas.

12. Our next step will be to analyze the mean values of weekly sales, making a differentiation by week and markdown applied. To do this, first, we will group the weekly sales by week and apply the mean, and we print the shape as a sanity test:

```
data_store = train[['Week','Weekly_Sales']].
groupby(['Week']).mean().reset_index()
data_store.shape
>>>(52, 2)
```

Then, we can get the information from the features DataFrame about markdowns applied in that specific week and apply the mean as well:

```
data_features = features[['Week','MarkDown1','MarkDown2',
'MarkDown3','MarkDown4','MarkDown5']].groupby(['Week']).
mean().reset_index()
data_features.shape
>>>(52, 6)
```

13. We can now merge both DataFrames and obtain information about the median sale per week as well as the type of markdown applied:

```
data_store = data_store.merge(data_features,on=['Week'],h
ow='left').fillna(.0)
data_store.index = data_store['Week']
data_store = data_store.drop(['Week'],axis=1)
data_store.head()
```

Week	Weekly_Sales	MarkDown1	MarkDown2	MarkDown3	MarkDown4	MarkDown5
1	14862.139543	3613.161444	22830.517889	69.137241	670.903803	4055.353222
2	14030.667886	3337.716889	11027.824444	40.445904	478.737838	3394.079444
3	14077.870442	3842.447222	3219.526111	42.761316	793.230649	2533.178111
4	13530.033667	2047.044333	1580.932247	54.269474	279.501867	2465.213889
5	16029.516788	24089.612333	1943.950444	198.031818	24865.942619	4185.380333

Figure 9.15: Median weekly sales and markdowns per week

Using this information, we can now plot the data to see the impact of discounts in comparison with the weekly sales:

```
data_store.plot(figsize=(20,8))
```

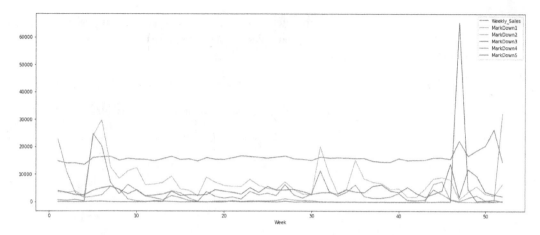

Figure 9.16: Median weekly sales and markdowns per week

We can see from the data that many markdowns are applied immediately before Christmas and then in the weeks that follow it. The answer may be that these markdowns are applied to reduce the stock of products that were not bought during the holiday period.

14. Now, we will look at the relationship between sales and the features describing the conditions for each day and store. To do this, we group the sales data by week and apply the mean. We then do the same for the features data and finally merge both DataFrames:

```
data_features = features.drop(['Store','Date','MarkDown1',
'MarkDown2','MarkDown3','MarkDown4','MarkDown5'],axis=1).
groupby(['Week']).mean().reset_index()
data_store = train[['Week','Weekly_Sales']].
groupby(['Week']).mean().reset_index()
data_store = data_store.merge(data_features,on=['Week'],h
ow='left').fillna(.0)
data_store.head()
```

The previous code will show us the merged data.

	Week	Weekly_Sales	Temperature	Fuel_Price	CPI	Unemployment	IsHoliday
0	1	14862.139543	35.689407	3.242504	173.272421	7.558659	0.0
1	2	14030.667886	36.157111	3.284378	173.375978	7.558659	0.0
2	3	14077.870442	37.254000	3.294252	173.492335	7.558659	0.0
3	4	13530.033667	38.076222	3.295563	173.601897	7.558659	0.0
4	5	16029.516788	38.019611	3.174667	172.216315	7.823822	0.0

Figure 9.17: Median weekly contextual data

15. We can now use the information to construct a seaborn pair plot to visualize any relationship. We exclude the Week and IsHoliday variables, the latter because categorical variables are difficult to visualize with this type of plot:

```
sns.pairplot(data_store.drop(['Week','IsHoliday'],axis=1))
```

The code will create a plot with the relationship between the numerical variables.

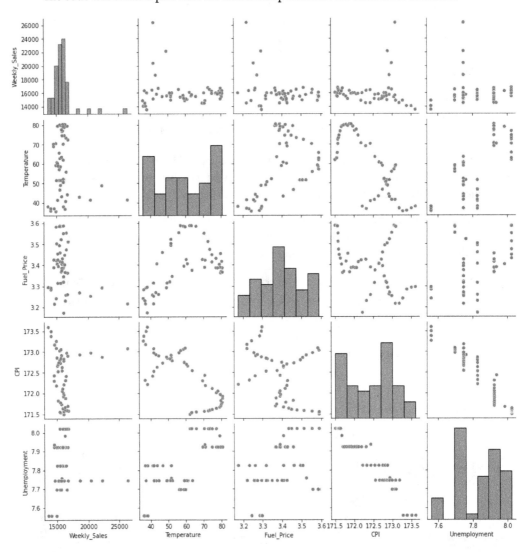

Figure 9.18: Feature pair plot

We can see that although we would be able to better appreciate the relationships, most of the weekly sales have a similar mean per week, making it difficult to differentiate meaningful relationships with CPI, unemployment, or fuel price. We should repeat the exercise without grouping the data, which would consequently give us more information but would take a bit more processing time.

16. To predict the sales, first, we need to manipulate the data and make some decisions. The first is at which level we want to make the predictions in terms of time. In our case, we will use `predict` for weekly sales. We will group all the data into a single DataFrame in which each data point is enriched with information about both the store as well as the conditions of that day.

We also transform the Type column into a one-hot vector representation using the `pd.get_dummies` function:

```
data = train.drop(['Year','Month'
,'Week'],axis=1).merge(features.
drop(['IsHoliday','Week'],axis=1),on=['Store','Date'])
data = pd.concat([data.drop(['Type'],axis=1),
        pd.get_dummies(data['Type'])],axis=1).fillna(0)
data['IsHoliday'] = data['IsHoliday'].astype(int)
data.head()
```

We can see the created columns in the DataFrame.

	Store	Dept	Date	Weekly_Sales	IsHoliday	Size	Day	Temperature	Fuel_Price	MarkDown1	MarkDown2	MarkDown3	MarkDown4	MarkDown5	CPI	Unemployment	A	B	C
0	1	1	2010-02-05	24924.50	False	151315	5	42.31	2.572	0.0	0.0	0.0	0.0	0.0	211.096358	8.106	1	0	0
1	1	2	2010-02-05	50605.27	False	151315	5	42.31	2.572	0.0	0.0	0.0	0.0	0.0	211.096358	8.106	1	0	0
2	1	3	2010-02-05	13740.12	False	151315	5	42.31	2.572	0.0	0.0	0.0	0.0	0.0	211.096358	8.106	1	0	0
3	1	4	2010-02-05	39954.04	False	151315	5	42.31	2.572	0.0	0.0	0.0	0.0	0.0	211.096358	8.106	1	0	0
4	1	5	2010-02-05	32229.38	False	151315	5	42.31	2.572	0.0	0.0	0.0	0.0	0.0	211.096358	8.106	1	0	0

Figure 9.19: Dataset with no encoded variable

This configuration of data allows us to extend the exploration to the analysis of correlations between the variables, which in turn sets the stage to start using the data to predict sales.

The next block of code will use the `corr()` method of the `pandas` DataFrame to analyze the correlation between variables, and we will use the `numpy` package to mask the redundant values and finally plot the data using the seaborn `heatmap` visualization:

```
import numpy as np
df_corr = data.drop(['Date'],axis=1).corr()
mask = np.triu(np.ones_like(df_corr, dtype=bool))
df_corr = df_corr.mask(mask).round(3)
fig, ax = plt.subplots(figsize=(16,16))
sns.heatmap(df_corr, annot=True,ax=ax)
```

The preceding code will create the correlation plot of the variables.

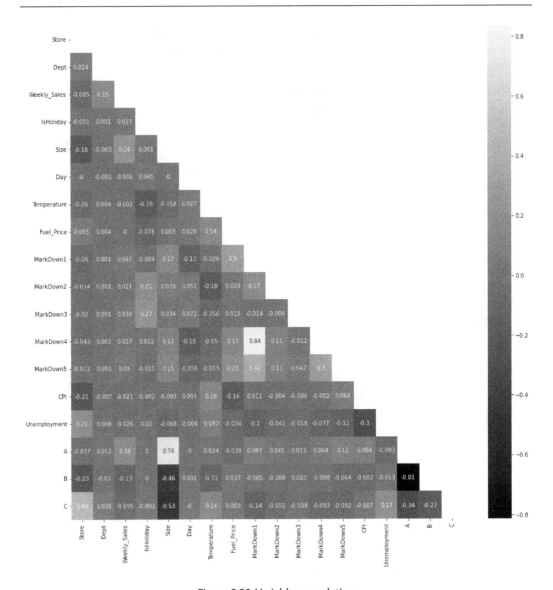

Figure 9.20: Variables correlation

We can see some interesting correlations, for example, the positive correlation between the size of markdown 2 and 3 and the size of the store, and the positive correlation between the size of markdown 1 and 4.

17. Finally, we can show the degree of correlation between the variables and the weekly sales:

```
f, ax = plt.subplots(figsize=(20, 6))
data = df_corr['Weekly_Sales'].dropna().sort_
```

```
values(ascending=False)
sns.barplot(x=data.index,y=data)
```

The following barplot will show us the most correlated variables.

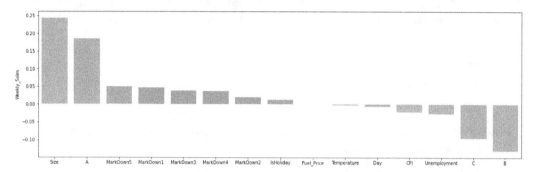

Figure 9.21: Variables correlation sorted

We can see that the weekly sales are highly influenced by the size of the store positively, followed by markdowns 5 and 1. It is negatively correlated with unemployment and **Consumer Price Index (CPI)**, which makes sense.

Now that we have a better understanding of the data, we will start the process of making predictions on weekly sales.

Predicting sales with Prophet

Forecasting a time series can be a challenging task if there are many different methods you can use and many different hyperparameters for each method. The Prophet library is an open source library designed to make predictions for univariate time series data sets. It is easy to use and designed to automatically find a good set of hyperparameters for the model to make competent predictions for data with standard trends and seasonal structure. We will learn how to use the Facebook Prophet package to predict the weekly sales time series:

1. First, we will import the library and create a dataset that contains all the features described as either continuous variables or one-hot representations:

```
from fbprophet import Prophet
data = train.drop(['Year','Month'
,'Week'],axis=1).merge(features.
drop(['IsHoliday','Week'],axis=1),on=['Store','Date'])
data = pd.concat([data.drop(['Type'],axis=1),
       pd.get_dummies(data['Type'])],axis=1).fillna(0)
data['IsHoliday'] = data['IsHoliday'].astype(int)
```

2. Filter results for Store 1, as we will train a model that learns the behavior of each specific store:

```
data = data[data.Store==1]
```

3. For the Prophet package, we need to prepare some expected column names with a specific data type. In this case, we need to pass ds and y variables, the first being a datetime type of column:

```
data['ds']= pd.to_datetime(data['Date'])
data =  data.sort_values(['ds'],ascending='True')
data['y']=data['Weekly_Sales']
```

Now that we have created the columns with the proper data types, we can drop the redundant columns and show the first lines:

```
data = data.drop(['Date','Weekly_Sales'],axis=1).reset_
index(drop=True)
data.head()
```

	Store	Dept	IsHoliday	Size	Day	Temperature	Fuel_Price	MarkDown1	MarkDown2	MarkDown3	MarkDown4	MarkDown5	CPI	Unemployment	A	B	C	ds	y
0	1	1	0	151315	5	42.31	2.572	0.0	0.0	0.0	0.0	0.0	211.096358	8.106	1	0	0	2010-02-05	24924.50
1	35	3	0	103681	5	27.19	2.784	0.0	0.0	0.0	0.0	0.0	135.352461	9.262	0	1	0	2010-02-05	14612.19
2	35	4	0	103681	5	27.19	2.784	0.0	0.0	0.0	0.0	0.0	135.352461	9.262	0	1	0	2010-02-05	26323.15
3	35	5	0	103681	5	27.19	2.784	0.0	0.0	0.0	0.0	0.0	135.352461	9.262	0	1	0	2010-02-05	36414.63
4	35	6	0	103681	5	27.19	2.784	0.0	0.0	0.0	0.0	0.0	135.352461	9.262	0	1	0	2010-02-05	11437.81

Figure 9.22: Data to be used for model training

We can now split the data into train and test data sets.

```
x_train = data[:-1000]
x_test = data[-1000:]
```

4. Finally, we can define the model that we will use. In this case, we need to establish linear growth with multiplicative seasonality. In this case, we have also included weekly seasonality:

```
model = Prophet(changepoint_prior_scale=0.05,
                interval_width=0.95,
                growth = 'linear',
                seasonality_mode = 'multiplicative',
                weekly_seasonality=True,
                changepoint_range=0.9)
```

Before training the forecaster, we can add regressors that use the additional variables.

Here, the `add_regressor` argument is the column name of the additional variable in the training DataFrame:

```
for c in ['Dept','IsHoliday',
        'CPI','Fuel_Price','MarkDown1',
    'MarkDown2','MarkDown3','MarkDown4','MarkDown5',
    'Unemployment']:
    print(c)
    model.add_regressor(name=c, prior_scale=None,
standardize='auto', mode='additive')
```

Note that here we are adding additional variables as regressors to the model. These variables should have values for your future (test) data. One key factor is that we are using the same parameters for all of the variables, while fine-tuning these parameters for each one of the variables is advised instead of this method. Although, the selection of each one of these parameters in consideration of the specifics of each variable is beyond the scope of this analysis.

Finally, we can fit the model:

```
model.fit(data[['ds','y','Dept','IsHoliday','CPI',
    'Fuel_Price','MarkDown1','MarkDown2','MarkDown3',
    'MarkDown4','MarkDown5', 'Unemployment']])
```

5. After the model has been trained, we can use it to make forecasts on the test data to evaluate the performance of the prediction:

```
forecast = model.predict(x_test[['ds','Dept','IsHoliday','
CPI','Fuel_Price','MarkDown1','MarkDown2','MarkDown3',
    'MarkDown4','MarkDown5', 'Unemployment']])
```

We can access the resulting forecast that shows us the predicted values for each date, along with the upper and lower boundaries:

```
print(forecast[['ds', 'yhat', 'yhat_lower',
        'yhat_upper']].head())
```

```
            ds          yhat    yhat_lower    yhat_upper
0  2012-07-27  36069.587113  -12322.507744  87218.507871
1  2012-07-27  24210.667108  -26059.891558  73319.931131
2  2012-07-27  23881.252664  -27559.281764  73969.300074
3  2012-07-27  23222.423774  -25101.013603  72494.483064
4  2012-07-27  22234.180441  -25967.218063  71437.863666
```

Figure 9.23: Forecasted data

6. Now, we can concatenate these results with the actual values for y in the test data to visualize the results. The resulting curves are softened using a rolling average with a window of seven lags for visualization purposes:

```
forecast_data = pd.concat([forecast[['yhat',
'yhat_lower', 'yhat_upper']],
x_test['y'].reset_index(drop=True)],axis=1)
forecast_data.rolling(window=7).mean().
plot(figsize=(20,8))
```

The preceding code will generate a visualization where we can see the actual sales versus the actual results.

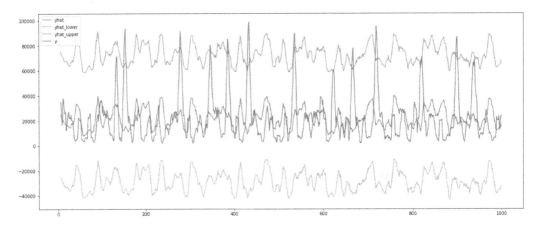

Figure 9.24: Forecasted data against actual values

We can see that, apart from certain cases, most of the time the predicted value has been close to the actual values, in rare times surpassing the upper boundary but never the lower.

Summary

In this chapter, we have dived into the details of sales analysis and markdown applications. As discussed, there is a trade-off between reducing the price of items to increase sales and reduce stock-related costs and the amount of revenue that is lost due to that decrease in price. In the case of retail, these outcomes are impacted by multiple factors, among which are the location of a given store, the environmental and economic conditions, and seasonality, as we saw with the analysis of sales during different holiday seasons.

The analysis and prediction of sales and markdowns can be applied to fine-tune the price reductions applied to maintain the equilibrium between profitability and sales, as well as to have a deep understanding of the variables involved and their relative impact that can lead to the design of better markdown strategies.

In the next chapter, we will dive into the specifics of learning the consumer behavior at e-commerce retailers, understanding consumer segmentation, predicting consumer lifetime value, and predicting which users will eventually buy.

10

Web Analytics Optimization

A data-driven marketing optimization is an analytical approach to marketing that values decisions that can be supported with trustworthy and verifiable data. It places high importance on choices that can be substantiated by empirical evidence, whether traffic sources, page views, or time spent per session. The effectiveness of data collection, processing, and interpretation to maximize marketing results are key components of the data-based approach's success.

In this chapter, we will be learning about the following:

- Understanding what web analytics is
- How web analytics data is used to improve business operations
- Calculating the user's **customer lifetime value** (**CLV**) based on web analytics data
- Predicting the user's CLV based on this historical data

Let's determine what the requirements will be for understanding these steps and following the chapter.

This chapter covers the following topics:

- Understanding web analytics
- Using web analytics to improve business decisions
- Exploring the data
- Calculating CLV
- Predicting customer revenue

Technical requirements

In order to be able to follow the steps in this chapter, you will need to meet the next requirements:

- A Jupyter Notebook instance running Python 3.7 and above. You can use the Google Colab notebook to run the steps as well if you have a Google Drive account.

- Understanding of basic math and statistical concepts.

Understanding web analytics

For e-commerce, understanding user base behavior is fundamental. Data from web analytics is frequently shown on dashboards that can be altered on the basis of a user persona or time period, along with other factors. These dashboards are then used to make product and market decisions, so the accuracy of this data is of paramount importance. The data can be divided into groups, including the following:

- By examining the number of visits, the proportion of new versus returning visitors, the origin of the visitors, and the browser or device they are using (desktop vs. mobile), it is possible to understand audience data

- Common landing pages, commonly visited pages, common exit pages, the amount of time spent per visit, the number of pages per visit, and the bounce rate can all be used to study audience behavior

- Campaign data to understand which campaigns have generated the most traffic, the best websites working as referral sources, which keyword searches led to visits, and a breakdown of the campaign's mediums, such as email versus social media

This information can then be used by sales, product, and marketing teams to gain knowledge about how the users interact with the product, how to tailor messages, and how to improve products.

One of the best and most potent tools available for tracking and analyzing website traffic is Google Analytics. You can learn a ton about your website's visitors from this, including who they are, what they are looking for, and how they found you. Google Analytics should be used by every company that wants to develop and improve its online presence.

The most crucial information that Google Analytics will provide you with is listed here:

- Where your visitors are coming from – very important if you're targeting a specific audience.

- How people find your website is crucial information for figuring out whether your efforts are successful. It indicates whether users arrived at your site directly, via a link from another website (such as Twitter or Facebook), or via search engines.

- Browsers used by your visitors – by understanding which browsers they use, you can decide which ones you should concentrate on.

- Which search engine terms people used to find your website are essential information for SEO. Finding out what search terms people use to find your website helps you gauge your progress.

In the next section, we will dive into how we can use Google Analytics data to understand our customer bases.

Using web analytics to improve business operations

By utilizing insights from digital analytics and user input, we can increase the performance of our websites and apps through conversion rate optimization. This is done by using the current traffic and maximizing it, with the intention of leading to a rise in sales, leads, or any other goal.

With the help of digital analytics dashboards and analysis, we can monitor user activity, including their source, where they go on our website or app, and how they move around the various pages. We can determine where there is the most potential and what needs to be changed to meet the specified aims and objectives thanks to the content and user behavior analysis.

Tagging for a business's website or app has context thanks to the definition and execution of a measurement plan. This enables companies to perform a **strengths, weakness, opportunities, and threats (SWOT)** analysis, which will lead to fixing your goals and objectives and indicate which user segments must be targeted with particular content and messaging both inside and outside the website or app.

An A/B or multivariate test is also possible when the opportunity or threat has been identified. With this, we may display two (or more) different iterations of a website's functionality to various user groups and then assess which one performs better. We can make data-driven decisions using this method while ignoring factors such as seasonal impacts.

Now that we have the context of the application, let's start by looking at the dataset and understanding our needs, our objectives, and the limitations of the analysis.

Exploring the data

We will use the following Python modules in the next example:

- **pandas**: Python package for data analysis and data manipulation.
- **NumPy**: This is a library that adds support for large, multi-dimensional arrays and matrices, along with a large collection of high-level mathematical functions to operate on these arrays.
- Statsmodels: Python package that provides a complement to SciPy for statistical computations, including descriptive statistics and estimation and inference for statistical models. It provides classes and functions for the estimation of many different statistical models.
- **Seaborn and Matplotlib**: Python packages for effective data visualization.

We'll get started using the following steps:

1.   The following block of code will load all the required packages, as well as load the data and show the first five rows of it. For readability purposes, we will limit the maximum number of rows to be shown to 20, set the limit of maximum columns to 50, and show the floats with 2 digits of precision:

```
import pandas as pd
pd.options.display.max_rows = 20
pd.options.display.max_columns = 50
pd.options.display.precision = 2
df = pd.read_csv('google_analytics_clean_data.csv')
df["date"] = pd.to_datetime(df["date"], format="%Y%m%d")
# seting the column as pandas datetime
df.head()
```

The preceding code will load the file, convert the date column into the correct data type, and prompt us to the first rows.

	channelGrouping	date	fullVisitorId	sessionId	socialEngagementType	visitId	visitNumber	visitStartTime	device.browser	device.op
0	Organic Search	2016-09-02	27294437909732085	27294437909732085_1472822600	Not Socially Engaged	1472822600	2	1472822600	Chrome	
1	Organic Search	2016-09-02	982320996976275749	982320996976275749_1472849434	Not Socially Engaged	1472849434	1	1472849434	Safari	
2	Organic Search	2016-09-02	9876750586615598787	9876750586615598787_1472801099	Not Socially Engaged	1472801099	1	1472801099	Chrome	
3	Organic Search	2016-09-02	3982295596181714479	3982295596181714479_1472825889	Not Socially Engaged	1472825889	1	1472825889	Chrome	
4	Organic Search	2016-09-02	7155698260250055490	0715569826025005549_1472864193	Not Socially Engaged	1472864193	1	1472864193	Chrome	

Figure 10.1: Google Analytics sample data

We can see that it's a demo of the data that we can obtain from Google Analytics, as some columns are not available.

2.   We will explore the set of columns:

```
df.columns
```

This line will show us the name of all the columns in the file.

```
df.columns

Index(['channelGrouping', 'date', 'fullVisitorId', 'sessionId',
       'socialEngagementType', 'visitId', 'visitNumber', 'visitStartTime',
       'device.browser', 'device.operatingSystem', 'device.isMobile',
       'device.deviceCategory', 'geoNetwork.continent',
       'geoNetwork.subContinent', 'geoNetwork.country', 'geoNetwork.region',
       'geoNetwork.metro', 'geoNetwork.city', 'geoNetwork.networkDomain',
       'totals.visits', 'totals.hits', 'totals.pageviews', 'totals.bounces',
       'totals.newVisits', 'totals.transactionRevenue',
       'trafficSource.campaign', 'trafficSource.source',
       'trafficSource.medium', 'trafficSource.keyword',
       'trafficSource.isTrueDirect', 'trafficSource.referralPath'],
      dtype='object')
```

Figure 10.2: Column names

From the information that we obtain about the columns and the data from the Kaggle competition, we can describe the columns in the dataset:

- `fullVisitorId`: Identifier for each user.

- `channelGrouping`: The channel from which the customer was redirected.

- `date`: The date of the visit.

- `Device`: Type of device used.

- `geoNetwork`: Location of the customer.

- `socialEngagementType`: Is the customer socially engaged?

- `trafficSource`: This shows the source of the traffic.

- `visitId`: Identifier of the specific visit.

- `visitNumber`: Count of sessions for the specific customer.

3. Now that we have the information about the columns, we can plot the revenue columns to look at their distribution:

```
df['totals.transactionRevenue'].plot(figsize=(12,4))
```

This line will use pandas `plot` methods to show the distribution of the column.

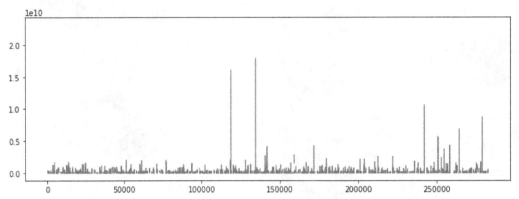

Figure 10.3: Revenue distribution

Many companies have found the 80/20 rule to be true: only a tiny proportion of clients generate the majority of the revenue, and we can verify this by looking at the data, with a small proportion of clients generating the most amount of revenue. The problem for marketing teams is allocating the proper funds to promotional activities. In this instance, the ratio is significantly lower.

4.   The statistical link between the data points is depicted using a relational plot. Data visualization is crucial for spotting trends and patterns. This graphic gives users access to additional axes-level functions that, using semantic subset mappings, can illustrate the relationship between two variables. Passing the entire dataset in long-form mode will aggregate over repeated values (each year) to show the mean and 95% confidence interval.

Here, we use the `seaborn` package to create a relation plot with 95% confidence interval areas for the revenue column:

```
import seaborn as sns
sns.relplot(x='date', y='totals.transactionRevenue',
data=df,kind='line',height=8, aspect=2.2)
```

This showcases the distribution of the transactions with a confidence interval as follows:

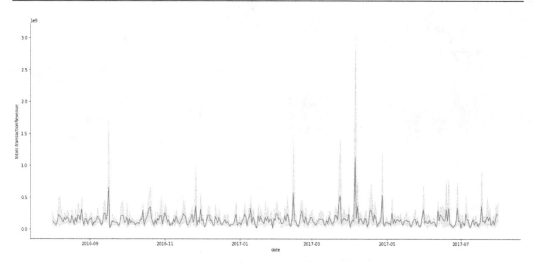

Figure 10.4: Revenue distribution with a confidence interval

One of the problems we see here is that because of the difference in value, the data is difficult to see, so we will implement a logarithmic scale. When examining a wide range of values, a nonlinear scale called a logarithmic scale is frequently utilized. Each interval is raised by a factor of the logarithm's base rather than by equal increments. A base ten and base e scale are frequently employed.

Sometimes, the data you are displaying is much less or greater than the rest of the data – when the percentage changes between values are significant, logarithmic scales also might be helpful. If the data on the visualization falls within a very wide range, we can use a logarithmic scale.

Another benefit is that when displaying less significant price rises or declines, logarithmic pricing scales perform better than linear price scales. They can assist you in determining how far the price must rise or fall in order to meet a buy or sell target. However, logarithmic price scales may become crowded and challenging to read if prices are close together. When utilizing a logarithmic scale, when the percent change between the values is the same, the vertical distance between the prices on the scale will be equal.

5.   Here, we will implement the logarithmic scale using the numpy library on the revenue column:

```
import numpy as np
df['totals.transactionRevenue'] = np.log(df['totals.
transactionRevenue'])
df['totals.transactionRevenue'].plot(figsize=(12,4))
```

Here, we can see the transactions on a logarithmic scale.

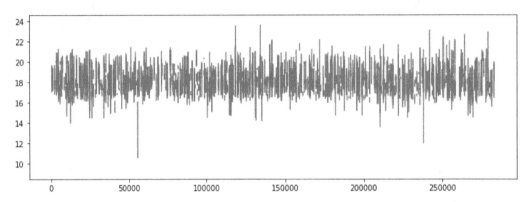

Figure 10.5: Logarithmic scale revenue

6. We can now use the relationship plot to visualize the logarithmic transaction values with their confidence interval better:

```
sns.relplot(x='date', y='totals.transactionRevenue',
  data=df,kind='line',height=8, aspect=2.2)
```

We can get better visibility with `relplot`, which will plot the mean data as a line and show the confidence intervals where 95% percent of the data exists.

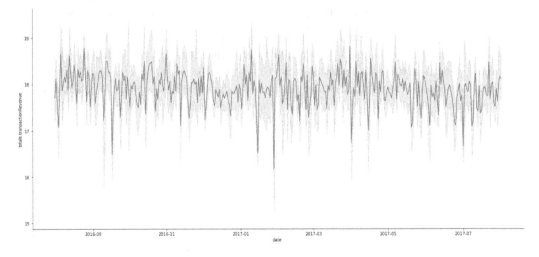

Figure 10.6: Logarithmic scale revenue with a confidence interval

7. Another way to visualize this is by using scatter plots, which will be helpful for identifying outliers:

```python
import matplotlib.pyplot as plt # visualization
data = df.groupby("fullVisitorId")["totals.
transactionRevenue"].sum().reset_index()
f, ax = plt.subplots(figsize=(12, 6))
fig =sns.scatterplot(x='fullVisitorId', y='totals.
transactionRevenue',size=4,alpha=.8,color='red',
data=data)
```

The scatter plot shows us that there are some outliers.

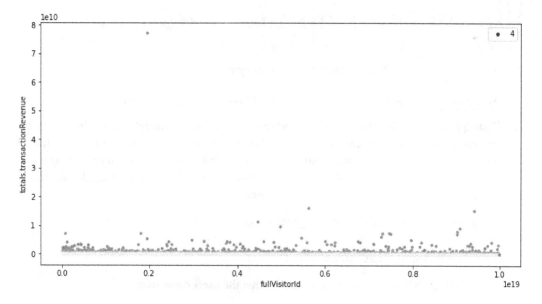

Figure 10.7: Transactions as scatter plot

Here, we can see more clearly that there are just a couple of users who generate an incredibly high amount of revenue with their orders.

8. Now, we can look at the expenditure patterns of the top 50 clients:

```python
top_50_customers = data.sort_values(['totals.
transactionRevenue'],ascending=False).head(50)
top_50_customers['totals.transactionRevenue'].plot.
bar(figsize=(15,6))
```

The next is a barplot of the top customers.

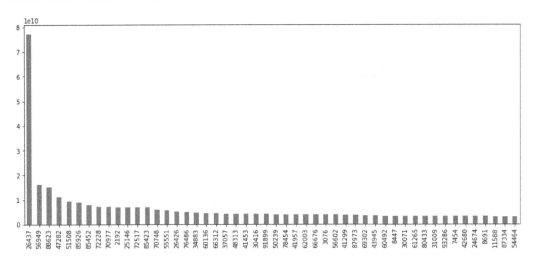

Figure 10.8: Users with the highest revenue

We can confirm from this graphic that user **26437** is our biggest customer.

9. Finding potential markets for your goods and services with Google Analytics is another fantastic application of the tool. You can check the number of visits and conversion rates separately by country to choose where to focus your efforts and which locations are worth expanding into if your business runs on a worldwide scale or if you are considering becoming global. Here, we can analyze the top countries in our user base:

```
global_countries = df['geoNetwork.country'].value_
counts().head(20)
global_countries.plot.bar(figsize=(16,6))
```

The preceding code will show us the countries that the users come from.

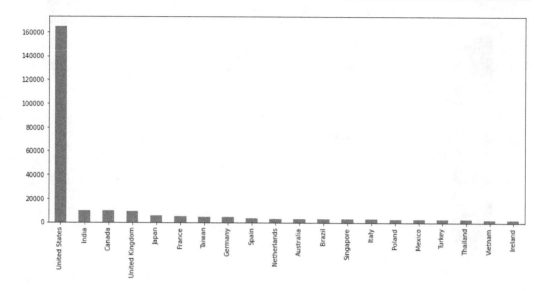

Figure 10.9: Total countries

We can see that the vast majority of users are concentrated in the US.

10. Let's now focus on our top clients and see where they come from. We can do this by masking the users that are in our top 50 users list and then replicating the preceding graphic:

```
top_50_data = df[df.fullVisitorId.isin(top_50_customers.
fullVisitorId)]
top_50_countries = top_50_data['geoNetwork.country'].
value_counts()
top_50_countries.plot.bar(figsize=(12,6))
```

The preceding code will show us the top countries in a barplot.

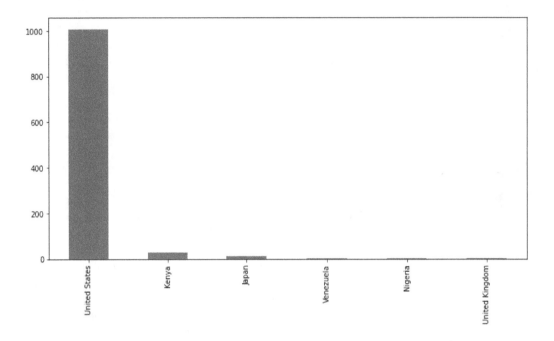

Figure 10.10: Countries of biggest customers

Again, we can determine that our biggest clients come from the US, followed by Kenya and Japan.

11. Now, we will analyze how many of our visitors actually converted, meaning that they actually bought something:

```
zero_revenue_users = (data["totals.
transactionRevenue"]==0).sum()
print("Number of unique customers with non-zero revenue:
", len(data)-zero_revenue_users, "and the ratio is: ",
zero_revenue_users / len(data))
>>> Number of unique customers with non-zero
revenue:  6876 and the ratio is:  0.9264536003080478
```

The ratio is that almost 8% of our users have actually bought from the website, which is good.

12. Now, we will start the process of cleaning the data, so we will look for categorical columns with just a single value. These are columns that don't provide any data, so we will get rid of them:

```
const_cols = [c for c in df.columns if df[c].
nunique(dropna=False)==1 ]
Const_cols
```

```
>>> ['socialEngagementType', 'totals.visits']
df = df.drop(const_cols, axis=1)
```

13. Now, we will simplify the data by removing some of the columns that we will not be using:

```
drop_cols = ['sessionId','visitId','visitStartTime',
'geoNetwork.continent','geoNetwork.subContinent',
'geoNetwork.region','geoNetwork.metro',
'geoNetwork.city','geoNetwork.networkDomain']
df = df.drop(drop_cols, axis=1)
df.columns
```

The following screenshot shows the columns we have now:

```
df.columns

Index(['channelGrouping', 'date', 'fullVisitorId', 'visitNumber',
       'device.browser', 'device.operatingSystem', 'device.isMobile',
       'device.deviceCategory', 'geoNetwork.country', 'totals.hits',
       'totals.pageviews', 'totals.bounces', 'totals.newVisits',
       'totals.transactionRevenue', 'trafficSource.campaign',
       'trafficSource.source', 'trafficSource.medium', 'trafficSource.keyword',
       'trafficSource.isTrueDirect', 'trafficSource.referralPath'],
    dtype='object')
```

Figure 10.11: Final set of columns

14. Our columns have now been reduced to the ones that we actually need. Now, let's explore the campaign column to find which campaign was more successful:

```
df['trafficSource.campaign'].value_counts().plot.
bar(figsize=(10,6),rot=30)
```

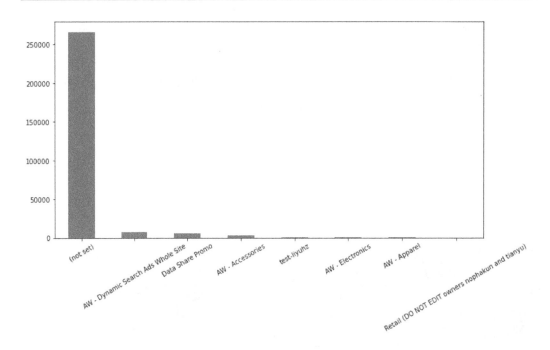

Figure 10.12: Campaign data

We can see from the campaign data that most of the traffic doesn't come from campaigns, and some of them actually perform poorly. This is information that could help the marketing team to optimize these campaigns and save money.

Calculating CLV

Customer lifetime value (CLV) is a metric used to describe how much money a company can expect to make overall from a typical customer during the duration that person or account stays a customer. CLV is the total amount a company makes from a typical customer during the term of that customer's relationship with the company and it is used in marketing to forecast the net profit that will be generated over the course of a customer's entire future relationship.

Knowing the CLV of our clients is crucial since it informs our choices regarding how much money to spend on attracting new clients and keeping existing ones. The simplest way to calculate CLV is by multiplying the average value of a purchase by the number of times the customer will make a purchase each year by the average length of the customer relationship (in years or months).

Numerous benefits can be derived from calculating the CLV of various clients, but business decision-making is the key one. Knowing your CLV allows you to find out things such as the following:

- How much you can spend and still have a lucrative connection with a similar consumer
- What kinds of products customers with the highest CLVs want

- Which products have the highest profitability

- Who your most profitable types of clients are

Spending your resources on selling more to your present client base is the key since the odds of selling to a current customer are 60 to 70 percent, compared to the odds of selling to a new customer, which are 5 to 20 percent. Several strategies will make it more likely for a consumer to make additional purchases from a company. Some of these methods are as follows:

- Make returning things that they have purchased from you simple for your clients, as making it difficult or expensive for a user to return a product will drastically lower the likelihood that they will make another purchase.

- Set expectations for delivery dates with the goal of exceeding expectations by establishing a safety margin. Promise delivery by May 20 and deliver it by May 1 instead of the other way around.

- Create a program with attainable and desired incentives for users to repeat purchases.

- To encourage customers to stick with your brand, provide incentives.

- Maintain contact with long-term clients to assert that you are still thinking of them. Give them a simple way to contact you as well.

- Focusing on acquiring and keeping repeat consumers who will promote your brand, as well as long-term clients.

More concretely, the steps to calculate the CLV are as follows:

1. Slice the data into chunks of 3 months.

2. Sum the revenue for each customer in the last 3 months.

3. Generate columns such as days since the last buy, average number of days between buys, and so on.

We'll run this using the following steps:

1. To apply this, we will define some helper functions that we will use along with the aggregate method in pandas to determine the CVL of our users:

```python
def groupby_mean(x):
    return x.mean()
def groupby_count(x):
    return x.count()
def purchase_duration(x):
    return (x.max() - x.min()).days
def avg_frequency(x):
    return (x.max() - x.min()).days/x.count()
```

2. We want to establish the time frame of analyses as 3 months, so we will create a variable to establish this:

```
clv_freq = '3M'
```

3. One thing to note is that we will be using the __name__ property to determine the function name in Python and to keep the column names tidy. To access the __name__ property, just put in the function name without parentheses and use the __name__ property. It will then return the function name as a string:

```
groupby_mean.__name__ = 'avg'
groupby_count.__name__ = 'count'
purchase_duration.__name__ = 'purchase_duration'
avg_frequency.__name__ = 'purchase_frequency'
```

4. Now, we can create our summary DataFrame by applying the groupby method and aggregating the values using our previously defined functions:

```
summary_df = df.reset_index().groupby('fullVisitorId').
agg({
    'totals.transactionRevenue': [min, max, sum, groupby_
mean, groupby_count],
    'date': [min, max, purchase_duration, avg_frequency]
})
```

5. Lastly, we will make some corrections to the column names for readability:

```
summary_df.columns = ['_'.join(col).lower() for col in
summary_df.columns]
```

We can check the final size of the DataFrame:

```
summary_df.shape
>>> (93492, 9)
```

We can also check the distribution of the values with the describe method:

```
summary_df.describe()
```

Here, we are calling a statistical summary from pandas:

```
summary_df.describe()
```

	totals.transactionrevenue_min	totals.transactionrevenue_max	totals.transactionrevenue_sum	totals.transactionrevenue_avg	totals.transactionrevenue_count
count	6876.00	6876.00	93492.00	6876.00	93492.00
mean	17.78	17.91	1.61	17.84	0.09
std	1.14	1.20	7.20	1.15	0.39
min	9.21	9.21	0.00	9.21	0.00
25%	17.03	17.12	0.00	17.09	0.00
50%	17.69	17.83	0.00	17.77	0.00
75%	18.43	18.57	0.00	18.50	0.00
max	23.50	23.86	582.40	23.50	33.00

Figure 10.13: Calculated user CLV

6. Now, let's filter the ones that have actually bought something by looking at the purchase date:

```
summary_df = summary_df.loc[summary_
    df['date_purchase_duration'] > 0]
```

After this, we have widely reduced the number of users in our dataset:

```
summary_df.shape
>>> (66168, 9)
```

7. We can visualize these results by plotting the grouped results using the transaction count:

```
import matplotlib.pyplot as plt
ax = summary_df.groupby('totals.transactionrevenue_
count').count()['totals.transactionrevenue_avg']
[:20].plot(
    kind='bar',
    color='blue',
    figsize=(12,7),
    grid=True
)
ax.set_ylabel('count')
plt.show()
```

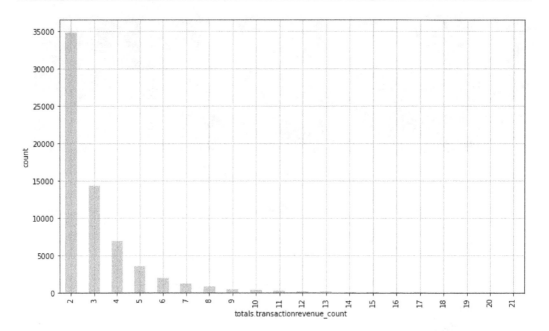

Figure 10.14: Transaction revenue count

8. Now, the most common number of transactions made is **2**, reducing in a parabolic manner. This gives us enough information to be able to offer customers incentives to keep buying after their second transaction.

Now let's take a look at the number of days between transactions:

```
ax = summary_df['date_purchase_frequency'].hist(
    bins=20,
    color='blue',
    rwidth=0.7,
    figsize=(12,7)
)
ax.set_xlabel('avg. number of days between purchases')
ax.set_ylabel('count')
plt.show()
```

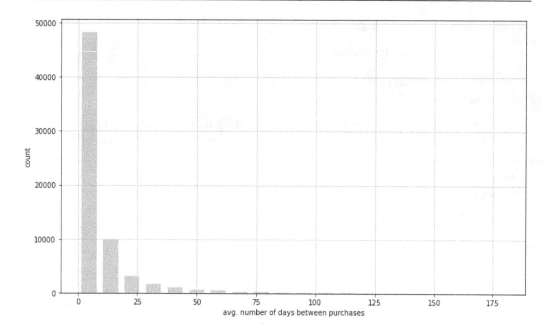

Figure 10.15: Time between purchases

This information shows us that it's rare for customers to make another purchase after 25 days, so we can use this information to keep our users engaged in case the number of times between transactions is higher than a given threshold. This allows us to reduce customer churn and improve loyalty.

Now, we have determined how we can calculate the CLV, which will allow us to craft better marketing strategies, knowing exactly what we can spend to acquire each customer.

Predicting customer revenue

By utilizing the historical transactional data from our company, we are attempting to forecast the future revenue that we will get from our clients at a given time. Planning how to reach your revenue goals is simpler when you can predict your revenue with accuracy, and in a lot of cases, marketing teams are given a revenue target, particularly after a funding round in startup industries.

B2B marketing focuses on the target goals, and here is when historical forecasting, which predicts our revenue using historical data, has consistently been successful. This is because precise historical revenue and pipeline data provide priceless insights into your previous revenue creation. You can then forecast what you'll need in order to meet your income goals using these insights. Things that will allow us to provide better information to the marketing teams can be summarized into four metrics before you start calculating your anticipated revenue:

- How long you take to generate revenue
- The average time deals spend in each pipeline stage

- The number of previous deals

- The revenue generated for the time period

These metrics form the basis of your predicted revenue in most cases and will allow the creation of better-defined marketing plans.

Questions such as how long it takes for a user to start making money require you to gather these metrics. Knowing your user's time to revenue (the length of time it takes a deal to generate a paying customer) is the first step. This is due to the fact that time to revenue determines the framework for how long it typically takes you to create revenue and earn back the investment made into gaining this customer, from the moment an account is created to the user making a purchase. If these metrics are omitted, your revenue cycle and your estimates will be out of sync without this parameter, which may cause you to miss goals and allocate money incorrectly. The fact is that you must be aware of your time to revenue.

Equally, the only way to measure it precisely is to gather data starting from the instant an anonymous user first interacts with you until the moment this account converts to a client. If you don't identify first contact, you're measuring incorrectly and, once more, underestimating how long it actually takes you to make an income:

1. We will start the analysis by importing the packages that we will be using, including the LightGBM classification. It's important to note that we will the transaction NaN values with zeros:

```
from sklearn import model_selection, preprocessing,
metrics
import lightgbm as lgb
# Impute 0 for missing target values
df["totals.transactionRevenue"].fillna(0, inplace=True)
y = df["totals.transactionRevenue"].values
id = df["fullVisitorId"].values
```

To make categorical data available to the various models, categorical data must be translated into integer representation first through the process of encoding. Data preparation is a necessary step before modeling in the field of data science – so, how do you handle categorical data in data science? Some of the methods used are as follows:

- One-hot encoding using Python's category_encoding library

- Scikit-learn preprocessing

- get_dummies in pandas

- Binary encoding

- Frequency encoding

- Label encoding

- Ordinal encoding

When data cannot be transported across systems or applications in its existing format, this method is frequently employed to ensure the integrity and usefulness of the data. Data protection and security do not employ encoding because it is simple to decode.

A very effective method for converting the levels of categorical features into numerical values is to use labels with a value between 0 and n classes - 1, where n is the number of different labels. Here, we are encoding the variables using `LabelEncoder`. A label that repeats assigns the same value as it did the first time.

2. We will list the categorical columns that we want to encode. Here, the list is hardcoded, but we could have used `pandas` data types to determine the object column:

```
cat_cols = ['channelGrouping','device.browser','device.
deviceCategory','device.operatingSystem','geoNetwork.
country','trafficSource.campaign','trafficSource.
keyword','trafficSource.medium','trafficSource.
referralPath','trafficSource.source','trafficSource.
isTrueDirect']
```

3. Now, we will iterate over them and encode them using `LabelEncoder`:

```
for col in cat_cols:
    print(col)
    lbl = preprocessing.LabelEncoder()
    lbl.fit(list(df[col].values.astype('str')))
    df[col] = lbl.transform(list(df[col].values.
astype('str')))
```

4. Now that the categorical columns have been converted, we will continue to convert the numerical columns into floats to meet the requirements of LightGBM.

The next are the columns that we will be working with:

```
num_cols = ['totals.hits',
            'totals.pageviews',
            'visitNumber',
            'totals.bounces',
            'totals.newVisits']
```

5. As the next step, we use the `astype` pandas method to cast these data types into floats:

```
for col in num_cols:
    print(col)
    df[col] = df[col].astype(float)
```

6. Now, we can split the training dataset into development (`dev`) and valid (`val`) based on time:

```
import datetime
dev_df = df[df['date']<='2017-05-31']
val_df = df[df['date']>'2017-05-31']
```

7. Apply the log to the revenue variable:

```
dev_y = np.log1p(dev_df["totals.transactionRevenue"].
values)
val_y = np.log1p(val_df["totals.transactionRevenue"].
values)
```

8. Next, we concatenate the categorical and numerical columns:

```
dev_X = dev_df[cat_cols + num_cols]
val_X = val_df[cat_cols + num_cols]
```

The final shape of the development DataFrame can be found as follows:

```
dev_df.shape
>>> (237158, 20)
```

The final shape of the validation DataFrame can be found as follows:

```
val_df.shape
>>> (45820, 20)
```

In order to predict the CLV of each user, we will use the LightGBM regressor as specified before. This algorithm is one of the best-performing and it's a decision tree algorithm.

A decision tree is a supervised machine learning tool that can be used to classify or forecast data based on how queries from the past have been answered. An example of supervised learning is a decision tree model, which is trained and tested on datasets that have the desired category. The non-parametric approach used for classification and regression applications is the decision tree. It is organized hierarchically and has a root node, branches, internal nodes, and leaf nodes.

LightGBM is a gradient-boosting algorithm built on decision trees that improves a model's performance while using less memory. An open source gradient boosting implementation in Python, also called `LightGBM`, is made to be as effective as existing implementations, if not more so. The software library, machine learning method, and open source project are all referred to collectively as LightGBM.

The benefits of LightGBM include faster training rates and greater effectiveness: LightGBM employs a histogram-based approach, which accelerates the training process by bucketing continuous feature values into discrete bins. This technique also converts continuous values into discrete bins, which use less memory.

9. To simplify the training pipeline, we will implement a custom function to run the LightGBM model. This function has predefined parameters that we can change according to the performance obtained. These parameters are passed as a dictionary and the documentation can tell you a bit more about them:

```python
def run_lgb(train_X, train_y, val_X, val_y):
    params = {
        "objective" : "regression",
        "metric" : "rmse",
        "num_leaves" : 50,
        "learning_rate" : 0.1,
        "bagging_fraction" : 0.7,
        "feature_fraction" : 0.5,
        "bagging_frequency" : 5,
        "verbosity" : -1
    }
    lg_train = lgb.Dataset(train_X, label=train_y)
    lg_val = lgb.Dataset(val_X, label=val_y)
    model = lgb.train(params, lg_train , 1000,
    valid_sets=[lg_val ], early_stopping_rounds=100,
    verbose_eval=100)
    pred_val_y = model.predict(val_X,
    num_iteration=model.best_iteration)
    return model, pred_val_y
```

Here, the function loads the training and development datasets using the Dataset method and trains the model using the specified parameters during 1,000 steps. The development dataset is used for validation, as it will give us information about the overall performance of the model.

10. Now, we can train the model:

```python
model, pred_val = run_lgb(dev_X, dev_y, val_X, val_y)
```

```
Training until validation scores don't improve for 100 rounds.
[100]    valid_0's rmse: 0.413213
[200]    valid_0's rmse: 0.413032
[300]    valid_0's rmse: 0.413314
Early stopping, best iteration is:
[201]    valid_0's rmse: 0.412934
```

Figure 10.16: RMSE values for the revenue per user

The result shows us that the performance of the model can be improved, which would require us to fine-tune the parameters until we reach a level of performance that is within our interval of confidence.

Summary

Web analytics allows us to optimize the performance of the products and services sold online. The information obtained enables us to improve the way in which we communicate with clients, thanks to a deeper understanding of our customers and their consumption patterns. In this chapter, we have dived into a basic understanding of this data and how it can be used to determine the CLV of our customers, understand their characteristics, and identify key metrics to establish a successful digital marketing plan.

The next chapter will look into the considerations made by several industry experts on how data, machine learning, and BI can be used in real-life business contexts to improve operations.

11

Creating a Data-Driven Culture in Business

Transforming organizations into data-driven ones requires more than just recipes that can be implemented to solve certain problems. There is a lot that we can learn from those who have already walked the path of changing organizations to become more efficient and successful when using data. In this chapter, we will dive into the experience of data leaders and learn about the following:

- How they started their careers in data

- What skills they had to master to become successful data leaders

- What technology and data mean and how they are used in the context of business

- How data-driven cultures can be implemented in organizations

Hopefully, their experience can guide both your transformation to become a data leader, as well as the organizational transformation required to become data-driven.

The invited leaders that will be sharing their perspectives are:

- **Patrick Klink**: Managing director and founder of ONBRDNG, a Dutch company that helps companies digitally transform, he is a seasoned data leader and pioneer. Patrick's experience makes him one of the most sought-after digital transformation and growth experts in the Dutch market and abroad, as he helps companies transform from traditional businesses into all-around digital companies:

Before ONBRDNG, Patrick was the director of product and technology at RTL and an international leader in broadcast, content, and digital, with interests in 60 television channels. He also supported several companies as chief of product/data/tech or CTO. Patrick serves as a supervisory board member and provides venture capital for several scale-ups.

- **Michael Curry**: He is a general manager, chief product officer, strategy leader, and brand and product storyteller. With 30 years of experience in all aspects of enterprise business-to-business software, he is a technology product expert with skills and experience in product management, marketing, development, implementation, and sales. To complement this, he is also an expert in the financial services and healthcare industry, as well as an accomplished speaker, being a guest lecturer at Harvard and Penn State:

Michael has been at IBM for 17 years, working as vice president of IBM Watson Health. Leading the divestiture of Watson Health business to Francisco Partners, he helped simplify business from 30+ products to six major product areas and restructured development under a single development leader, reducing the development run rate and SaaS operations costs by double digits. He also led the shift to a public cloud, improved EBITDA by triple digits while improving NP, and led the divestiture of Watson Health business to Francisco Partners.

- **Florian Prem:** With more than 20 years of experience in data and analytics, Florian is the **Chief Data Officer (CDO)** at Deloitte Technology in Zurich, Switzerland:

Florian is part of the Deloitte Technology leadership team as the inaugural CDO. Deloitte Technology is the department of Deloitte Consulting, which is a globally integrated technology organization that spans more than 85 countries and has more than 10,000 professionals.

Before becoming the global CDO, Florian was the first CDO for Deloitte Switzerland with a mandate for data strategy, governance, risk and security, data management, data analysis and AI, automation, collaboration, and document and records management platforms.

- **Micaela Kulesz:** A behavioral data scientist with experience in AI, experimental economics, and consumer behavior. She is a lead data scientist, a leader in data and innovation, and a machine learning engineer (on the AI team). Now, she is the lead data scientist for data and innovation, with a focus on retail tech, developing solutions for the retail sector:

With a background in economics from the University of Buenos Aires, she received her Ph.D. at the University of Bremen in experimental and behavioral economics, applied game theory, and experiment metrics. After this, she worked as a researcher at the Swedish University of Agricultural Sciences, before transitioning to a data scientist position.

She chooses to work with honest, direct, and kind people and has a vision of data science as a pseudo-art that involves having creative conversations with colleagues and everyone in general.

- **Jack Godau**: Data Leader, currently **Chief Technical Officer (CTO)** at Doctorly in Berlin, Germany. He enjoys talking about startups, healthcare, recruiting, the future of work, and digital transformation:

Jack is an empathetic, cooperative, and passionate leader who has built on a strong career of being a technical expert with strong sales skills. He has worked with organizations of all types and sizes to manage their digital evolution by providing technical and strategic leadership, guidance, and coaching. Highly proficient in team building and in fostering an inclusive culture to enable local and remote teams to succeed, Jack has successfully built and grown strategic partnerships at an international level.

- **Julio Rodriguez Martino**: A dynamic leader with more than 15 years in establishing, developing, and directing high-performing, globally diverse teams. Julio is an analytics/data science/machine learning/artificial intelligence professional, with skills and experience in team management, as well as being a writer and mentor:

Julio has leveraged a strong educational background in physics to solve overly complex problems resulting in the development of innovative solutions. He is a team leader across various functions, including analytics, artificial intelligence, machine learning, data science, and engineering. Julio is a compelling communicator, well-versed in engaging key stakeholders, translating business requirements into technical requirements, and advising C-level executives as technical SMEs. With a strong aptitude for driving innovation and knowledge-sharing across cross-functional internal departments, Julio is a lifelong learner with a passion for research and development while remaining up to date with the latest developments within the field of AI and ML.

- **Agustina Garcia Hernandez**: Data and strategy director for Anheuser-Busch InBev. She is an economist and analytics pioneer, with a great strategic thinking mindset that brings business and technical data together. Her focus is to empower teams from diverse cultures and profiles so that they achieve impact results for the commonwealth. She has experience and skills having developed deep management and directing expertise in multinational companies. She has also led local projects as well as international ones, creating solid expertise in project management, which has given her the extra mile in her management career:

Agustina's key strengths are leveraged by bringing business knowledge and data together; she has experience bringing teams of people from diverse cultures together, leading projects, and obtaining integrated results. She focuses on creating opportunities without losing the big picture. Empathetic, she understands the need and converts it into a solution. She bridges teams and stakeholders under the same goals with attractive oral and graphic presentations that inspire actions and results. Her processes align intuitive business knowledge with data-based insights to improve the decision-making process while connecting the dots from different areas of expertise, transforming complexity into simple and executable answers. Agustina leverages different methodologies such as focus groups, polls, segmentation, and machine learning/artificial intelligence to arrive at business solutions that optimize the usage of diverse disciplines.

- **Bob Wuisman**: With a background in human resources and business, Bob has leveraged his experience in business processes to become the data operations director at Ebiquity Digital Innovation Center in Utrecht, Netherlands:

Building on his years of experience as a business process consultant, Bob has successfully built business intelligence environments in various businesses. With a holistic vision and process-driven mindset, Bob thrives on building teams and sustainably growing data-driven operations, and with skills and experience in professional competencies including people, process, and project management.

- **Wim van der Meer**: With a focus on sustainability and water management, Wim is the CDO of Waterschap Vallei & Veluwe in Apeldoorn, Netherlands:

Wim has been part of the Water Board Vallei en Veluwe as program manager for digital transformation. He was responsible for the development of a data-driven network organization. As project leader implementer, Wim has overseen the Environment Act Permit, supervision, and enforcement, as well as having been a water board inspector. His background is in water management, law, and agile organization.

Let us start by looking at the path that these leaders made to start working with data.

Starting to work with data

Starting the journey to become a data leader requires improving your skill set to incorporate certain capabilities that allow you to not only understand descriptive visualizations, basic statistical concepts, as well as tech and data concepts but also create the skills to lead teams and understand business requirements.

This section consists of answers that our data leaders gave when asked about which skills and capabilities were required to become successful data leaders.

Julio Rodriguez Martino

- How did you get into data science and engineering?

  I have a degree in science, and I focused my scientific career on experimental physics. Having experience in data analysis, statistics, and problem-solving made data science a natural choice when moving to the industry.

- Which are the areas in which you needed to work the most to get there?

  Machine learning and Python. I had little experience in both.

- If you were to start your journey to become a data leader again, how would you tackle it?

I would not change a single thing.

Michael Curry

- Can you tell us why you became interested in working with data?

Early in my career, I took a product role in a data integration company. In this role, I saw firsthand how much of an impact a strategic focus on data has on businesses. The companies that excelled in integrating, curating, and analyzing data were the companies that performed the best in their market. They were better at serving customers, better at selling, better at building products, and better at managing their investments. From this experience, I realized that data would be a critical tool for every step of my career.

- Which skills did you have to develop to become a data leader?

Data cataloging and curating, data analytics, data visualization, and data governance.

- How can business decision-makers and analysts prepare themselves to use data science and analytics?

Business decision-makers need to define the problem spaces that will yield the biggest returns on data. Where can specific insights help the most to impact the business? Is it better to help your sales organization to better target new customers, or to streamline product development? Where are the data blind spots that can be removed to help improve decisions and operations? These are the types of questions that business decision-makers need to answer so that they can define the outcomes they are hoping to achieve.

Micaela Kulesz

- How did you get into data science and engineering?

I have a background in applied quantitative methods, with a Ph.D. in economics. It was a natural step to get into data science, and then into data engineering to advance toward innovation.

- Can you tell us why you became interested in working with data?

Data is factual. Loose interpretations are feasible, but not scalable. "What are the facts?" is the first question to ask ourselves. And only after comes what we read from the facts. This is a general attitude that drives prosperous societies.

There are words hidden in the data, and you can dig as much as time exists. Data is magic.

- Which skills did you have to develop to become a data leader?

Dedication and discipline are the keys to becoming an expert. To become a leader, however, I had to develop patience and focus. Data teams need a purpose, as does any team. Yet as data can acquire important volumes, it is easy to get lost in it: the leader needs to ensure focus at every point in time.

- Which are the areas in which you needed to work the most to get there?

I would say my "multi-purpose" programming skills. I could program very well in R, STATA, and bash (sh, zsh), but to grow within the data science field, a multi-purpose language helps enormously. It helps to be able to communicate with people from other teams and backgrounds, but mostly to let our ideas grow with the field.

- How can business decision-makers and analysts prepare themselves to use data science and analytics?

Once the discussion opens the door to data – thus, facts – innovative ideas will come in, and little by little the change will start. This is the best preparation: discussing and listening.

- If you were to start your journey to become a data leader again, how would you tackle it?

I would participate more in meetups and hackathons.

Bob Wuisman

- How did you get into data science and engineering?

I was good at Excel and as a business analyst, I was involved in an implementation program for a new CRM system (Microsoft Dynamics AX). No one had thought about the reports that had to be built to keep track of the operations. I raised my hand, pointed out this missing part of the program, and got the project. A month later, I realized I did not know what I signed up for but loved it and started to Google what a SQL server is.

- Which are the areas in which you needed to work the most to get there?

Learning SQL Server, QlikView, data warehouse concepts, ETL, and data in general. Everything that was tech and data-related.

- If you were to start your journey to become a data leader again, how would you tackle it?

From the domain perspective – if your role is extracting business value from data.

- Can you tell us why you became interested in working with data?

The insights I got from data enabled me to get a clear picture of overly complex topics, such as end-to-end supply chains, from the first coffee drink to the invoice.

- Which skills did you have to develop to become a data leader?

Mostly technical skills and concepts, because I already had a strong organizational background in business processes, culture, architecture, and more. I learned SQL to extract data, transform it, and load it into the databases, as well as to query and combine data. Data modeling helped me learn how data can be joined and provided me with data visualization tools such as QlikView and PowerBI. The basics of Python, the main language these days, and understanding the full implications of each decision and code on each downstream step also helped.

- How can business decision-makers and analysts prepare themselves to use data science and analytics?

It is not a goal per se. First, figure out why you want to use data science and analytics and what it will bring you. Having data science is no shortcut to success.

Wim Van Der

- Can you tell us why you became interested in working with data?

As a governmental organization in the water domain, we face huge challenges when it comes to climate change and water quality, especially in a country such as The Netherlands, where we live one-third under sea level. We need data and technology to help us understand the complexity and to model future solutions.

- Which skills did you have to develop to become a data leader?

Basic technical knowledge. Change management. Ethics. The dos and don'ts.

- How can business decision-makers and analysts prepare themselves to use data science and analytics?

Start training people that know your business and make them aware of the possibilities that data and technology have. From there, start expanding with, for example, DevOps teams.

Florian Prem

- Can you tell us why you became interested in working with data?

It was the best way to solve business topics and get insights/find root causes in my professional work.

- How did you get into data science and engineering?

By applying hands-on cross-domain knowledge (for example, within finance doing analytics more than 20 years ago), with a background in law, IT and management on compliance/governance, and delivering a series of digital transformations, AI/ML, data management, and IT modernization programs.

- Which areas did you need to work in the most to get there?

I had to do constant work to stay up to date with technology and regulatory matters.

- Which skills did you have to develop to become a data leader?

Data governance, compliance, regulatory knowledge; data management and analytics/AI and ML/technology skills; program, project, and product management skills, and change management skills and soft skills.

- How can business decision-makers and analysts prepare themselves to use data science and analytics?

  Become more tech-savvy and learn the importance of data/using data within their operations, decision-making, products, and processes.

Most of today's data leaders transition from distinct roles into positions that require them not only to create systems that gather and display data but also to manage highly specialized data teams. In their answers, we can see how each one of them, in their journey to become leaders, was able to reinvent themselves and learn the skills required to thrive in these leadership positions.

In the next section, we will get their perspective on how data is being leveraged today in organizations and what their focus has been.

Using data in organizations

Each of the interviewed leaders currently holds a position where they need to either transform their organizations into data-driven ones or improve how they currently extract value from them.

Let us see their perspective on the current state of data in companies and organizations.

Florian Prem

- How are companies using data to improve their operations?

  End-to-end in their business and operating model with a customer, operations, and employee focus, but most still only in silos.

- How important is it for companies to become data-driven?

  Today, very; tomorrow, it is a survival topic.

- What is the benefit that businesses get from storing large volumes of data?

  There is no direct benefit from storing large volumes of data. Value comes only from insights and contexts that become assets.

- In your experience, are businesses aware and open to exploring new uses for their data?

  Some are, and most are just starting – the leaders have built their business and operation models around it.

- What infrastructure is needed for companies?

  There is not one answer for this besides: do not start with the infrastructure/technology – the technology is defined by the business needs.

- Which business areas more often need to process big volumes of data?

  It depends on your industry – operations and finance and customers/products.

- What is the frequency at which this data needs to be updated?

  It depends on the data and the insights/use case you want to achieve – from real-time to daily/weekly/monthly/yearly or per case (for example, address change).

Micaela Kulesz

- What is the benefit that businesses get from storing large volumes of data?

  So far, this is only a current cost and a potential benefit. Unfortunately, data science resources are very scarce, and developments in the field are driven by non-structured data, which, in turn, attracts the few resources there.

- In your experience, are businesses aware and open to exploring new uses for their data?

  Not enough to drive a consistent change.

- How do companies deal with the complexity of creating data teams and maintaining complex infrastructure?

  This depends on the size and the focus of the company.

- What infrastructure is needed for companies?

  It depends on the scale and the industry.

- Which business areas more often need to process big volumes of data?

  They all need to; always.

- What is the frequency at which this data needs to be updated?

  It depends on how they use it.

- Which areas in these companies can benefit the most from using data science and engineering?

  Innovation and discovery. This area can work in parallel with the rest of the firm. A blue/green development focused on increasing the data-driven culture.

- How can data be used to drive revenue in the context of economic contraction?

  To increase the margins of profitability. In the meantime, there is no need for much effort to maintain and even increase profits. In times of crisis, we need to work within the limits. Here, data is key.

- How can data be used to reduce costs in operations in the context of rising costs in the supply chain?

  I would like to improve the performance of the current models. Yet to build new ones, I do not think volume is necessary.

- How are companies using data to improve their operations?

  They are starting to try small products that improve user experience.

- How important is it for companies to become data-driven?

  Crucial. I think this will define their place in the market in the next 5 years.

- How are companies using data to understand customers' behavior patterns?

  A/B tests are very widespread and are the main tool for approaching behavior. However, as I mentioned previously, when it comes to structural data, there is much room for improvement.

Wim Van Der

- How are companies using data to improve their operations?

  In this phase, mostly to make processes more efficient, reduce energy use, get better output, create new software, and create models for climate scenarios.

- How important is it for companies to become data-driven?

  It is not. It is important to stay human-driven, but humans need to learn how data can help.

Julio Rodriguez Martino

- What benefit can businesses get from storing large volumes of data?

  Quality is more important than quantity. A lot of bad data will not help solve any problem.

- In your experience, are businesses aware and open to exploring new uses for their data?

  They are aware and open, but not always able to do it. Businesses often need help to get started.

- How do companies deal with the complexity of creating data teams and maintaining complex infrastructure?

  I have seen diverse ways of dealing with data teams at various times. Many years ago, companies were hiring data scientists without knowing what their value was. Later, they realized it was easier to hire third-party teams to do specific projects. When it was clear that the knowledge that was created was not kept in the company, there was a shift toward a hybrid approach: small in-company teams helped by external professionals.

- What infrastructure do companies need?

  Having access to cloud computing, I do not think there is a need for specific infrastructure in most cases.

- Which business areas often need to process big volumes of data?

  Any business unit dealing with transactional data. Other areas usually manage smaller amounts of data.

- What is the frequency at which this data needs to be updated?

It depends on the type of analysis. In some cases, the frequency will be low; in other cases, almost real-time frequency might be needed.

Michael Curry

- How are companies using data to improve their operations?

I have seen data used effectively in all aspects of operational management. In my career, I have used data to drive transformation, pinpointing areas that most needed improvement. I have used data to inform on areas of new opportunity in new markets or even within existing customer bases. I have also used data to predict where products were likely to see increased demand over time.

- How important is it for companies to become data-driven?

The more data-driven an organization is, the more successful they tend to be. This is a straight-line relationship that has been proven in study after study. Working on assumptions and intuition rather than data will usually lead to wasted time and money. Today, with the power of machine learning, we can get more use out of data than ever before. The companies that stay at the forefront of these investments are the ones that will outperform their peers.

- What are the main challenges of creating a data-driven culture in business?

Data is challenging to obtain and often has quality or timeliness issues. In addition, people often struggle to understand what they are looking at in the data. As such, it is often easier to base decisions on assumptions and intuition. The last conversation they had with a customer, for example, can oversteer many decisions. Creating a culture where the default is to turn to a deeper analysis of data in decision-making requires that there be a strong focus on making the necessary data available, easily understandable, and trustworthy. These require large investments that many companies are not willing to make.

- Digital companies have been born with data analytics and ML embedded at the core of their business. Are more traditional companies lagging in the adoption of these technologies in their day-to-day operations?

Certainly, some are. However, even traditional companies have been making large investments in data, analytics, and ML. Purely digital companies have an advantage in that often, their entire supply chains are digitized, making it easier to access the data needed for decision-making, but more traditional companies often have more directly relevant data, larger existing customer bases, and more history to work with, so effective investments in data analytics and AI can sometimes yield superior results. The issue is really whether traditional companies can overcome the cultural inertia to become data-driven.

- Which areas in these companies can benefit the most from the use of data science and engineering?

  There are not any areas that cannot benefit from data science and engineering. The most progress, however, has happened on the marketing and sales side of businesses. Using analytics to understand customer behavior and better pinpoint offers to customers has become very commonplace. A lot of recent data science investment has focused more on the production side of businesses, and this could yield even bigger returns – helping pharmaceutical companies speed up drug discovery, helping agricultural companies to improve crop yield, and helping chemical companies to produce novel new compounds faster. Using data to reduce long, expensive investments and improve their yield has the potential to dramatically improve productivity across all industries.

Bob Wuisman

- What benefit can businesses get from storing large volumes of data?

  None. It only costs money. It is about the quality and value of the company.

- In your experience, are businesses aware and open to exploring new uses for their data?

  Yes, but there is always the political complication when you make actual results transparent with data analysis and point out someone polished their results a bit too much. This happens everywhere – internally and externally.

- What infrastructure do companies need?

  Elite and high-performance teams are all on the cloud or multiple cloud platforms; check out the Dora research done by Google.

- Which business areas often need to process big volumes of data?

  All industries with data streaming components.

- What is the frequency at which this data needs to be updated?

  No general rule can be applied to this. Sometimes, every nanosecond; sometimes, once a year.

Jack Godau

- What benefit do businesses get from storing large volumes of data?

  I am on a slightly different track than you. It starts with the vision, the organizational goals, and strong alignment on those. Once that exists, only then should the effort be made to determine the information required to make decisions and only after that to discover the data sources and pull the required information.

  The analogy I would use is mining (not data but digging in the ground for stuff). We do not simply pull down forests and mine entire mountains to "see what we can find." We set out to specifically extract the resources needed at the minimum cost and effort – this is something that "data teams" miss, so a huge effort is poured into "let's keep it all," "let's run some analysis, and see what it tells us." That is not useful or viable from a business point of view.

There is only a benefit if there is a purpose. Hoarding data – especially things that have no value – can be a costly mistake.

Data should not be confused with information.

You need to be truly clear about what goals you are pursuing organizationally and then determine what information you need; then, you can determine the data sources for such information. This is, of course, much harder than just "hiring a data team and letting them work it out."

Now that we have a perspective on how teams work in implementing successful data-driven strategies in companies, in the next section, we will focus on why these companies will find it relevant to implement successful data strategies.

Benefits of being data-driven

Transforming organizations into data-driven ones is not an easy task. It requires a clear focus on the objectives we want to achieve, as this transformation requires a lot of resources and creates a lot of inconveniences when changing the current process to make use of data for informed decision-making.

Wim Van Der

- Which areas in these companies can benefit the most from the use of data science and engineering?

  It depends on the company and its identity; I do not think there is one solution that suits all.

- How can data be used to drive revenue in the context of economic contraction?

  Economic revenue should no longer be the core drive for companies. Value in a wider perspective is. So, do not stare at huge piles of economic revenue; also look at ecological revenue.

- How can data be used to reduce costs in operations in the context of rising costs in the supply chain?

  Start with a DevOps team to analyze your business processes and give them an open task to make it more efficient.

- How are companies using data to understand customers' behavior patterns?

  Process mining is still a successful tool to make customer journeys.

Michael Curry

- How can data be used to drive revenue in the context of economic contraction?

  Even in slowing market conditions, money is being spent by companies, governments, and individuals. Data is the secret to uncovering where and why that money is being spent so that businesses can more effectively compete for it. Understanding how priorities are changing as economic conditions change, for example, is something that data can uncover. Data can also be used to help fine-tune pricing and packaging to optimize the changing needs of buyers.

- How can data be used to reduce costs in operations in the context of rising costs in the supply chain?

Optimizing supply chains has long been a focus of data analytics. Better predictions of demand and better allocation of resources can help minimize costs without sacrificing revenue.

- How are companies using data to understand customers' behavior patterns?

Customer behavior analytics have been some of the largest investments that companies have made over the past decade. This has been accelerated by the natural data footprints that people leave behind in a digital setting. These footprints can give a much deeper understanding of the behaviors and motivations of individuals than could be achieved in purely analog settings. Therefore, digital tracking has become so ubiquitous (along with the backlash to it). Home insurance companies, for example, are interested in knowing when people might be house hunting in a new ZIP code so that they can target offers to them.

- More traditional companies are used to outsourcing their market research to consultancy companies. Is the use of social media, web analytics, and search engine data replacing these approaches?

To a considerable extent, this is becoming true. The tools that used to be available to only a few very skilled data analysts (and thus concentrated by consultancies) are now much more available to a much broader population of people. In addition, data analytics has become a much more common skill that a much larger percentage of businesspeople are learning, and the data that is used to enrich internal data is now more accessible to even casual business analysts. As a result, the reliance on expensive external consultants has been reduced.

Jack Godau

- In your experience, are businesses aware and open to exploring new uses for their data?

No.

- How important is it for companies to become data-driven?

Zero percent – we need data to make decisions, BUT the business must drive the vision and strategy. Purely working just from the data and "bubbling up" is not a viable strategy. Sure, Amazon uses its data to help sell more products – but its vision is to be the best online store. Data enables this but data by itself does not do it. The strategy and vision must be there first and must be well articulated.

Bob Wuisman

- How do companies deal with the complexity of creating data teams and maintaining complex infrastructure?

  This highly depends on C-level data literacy and company culture. Not unimportant is the number of attempts that they made to transform into a data-driven organization. On the first try, there is a lot more freedom and delegated responsibility than on the next try.

Florian Prem

- Which areas in these companies can benefit the most from the use of data science and engineering?

  Customer, people, and products – across the board with every company being different and having different pain points.

- How can data be used to drive revenue in the context of economic contraction?

  Be better than your competitors, know your customers, and apply cost savings.

- How can data be used to reduce costs in operations in the context of rising costs in the supply chain?

  It depends on your industry and supply chain – not one answer is possible.

- How are companies using data to understand customers' behavior patterns?

  The best way IMHO is data-driven end-to-end customer journeys.

We now have a perspective of how these leaders would think that organizations can benefit from implementing data-driven strategies. In the next section, we will dive into the challenges that come with these transformations.

Challenges of data-driven strategies

There are no out-of-the-box strategies that we can implement to champion a data-driven transformation in a company, so each of these strategies needs to be tailor-made according to the needs of these organizations.

We asked the data leaders about the usual challenges they faced when transforming these organizations into fast-paced, data-driven companies.

Bob Wuisman

- What are the main challenges of creating a data-driven culture in business?

  70 percent of the time, such an attempt fails. Culture and politics. Siloed departments that do not want to collaborate and a power-oriented culture. The lack of sufficient technology. Data quality is not safeguarded, and technology is centralized instead of organization performance.

A project is led by a CIO, CTO, or CFO. A CDO or a similar position should lead and report to the CEO or COO.

- What are the main technical challenges of creating a data-driven culture in business?

Become stable, reliable, and trustworthy. Deliver what you promise and point out the advantages of the needed investments.

Florian Prem

- How do companies deal with the complexity of creating data teams and maintaining complex infrastructure?

Not very well – they're better off hiring and empowering a tech and business-savvy CDO and starting digital transformation programs with exec endorsement.

What is the best way for business decision-makers to collaborate with highly specialized data teams to serve the company's needs?

Combine the data teams into a CDO/corporate data office and let the CDO and their team lead deal with it – different skills than what are normally used in data teams are required for that.

- What are the main challenges of creating a data-driven culture in business?

Politics, people, processes, and solutions, and lack of exec endorsement/driving.

- What are the main technical challenges of creating a data-driven culture in business?

People but also existing solutions/technical debt/silos.

- Digital companies have been born with data analytics and ML embedded at the core of their business. Are more traditional companies lagging in the adoption of these technologies in their day-to-day operations?

Yes, data must be incorporated into their operating and business model.

- More traditional companies are used to outsourcing their market research to consultancy companies. Is the use of social media, web analytics, and search engine data replacing these approaches?

No, but end-to-end analytic platforms might make it easier soon – you still need the competencies and tools to understand the data and market insights, and so on.

Wim Van Der

- What are the main challenges of creating a data-driven culture in business?

Start bottom up and create small successes. Make people tell their success stories. Do not start with the newest technology; people need to learn first and get in the right mindset.

- Digital companies have been born with data analytics and ML embedded at the core of their business. Are more traditional companies lagging in the adoption of these technologies in their day-to-day operations?

    The question remains: what are your business values, and what is the identity of what you strive for? After that, start with technology. The ones that seem to be ahead now, might be behind soon – not on technological levels but ethical levels.

Jack Godau

- What are the main technical challenges of creating a data-driven culture in business?

    The question is wrong – nobody in the real world wants a data-driven culture. Here is the great misalignment between data and business. Take healthcare, for example – data mining for the right information can be a huge benefit to the treatment of patients. But in the real world, everyone understands that it should be the focus of the organization to treat the patient, not to have the data. Making information from data easily accessible and visible to enable treatment is a good thing, but it is not a data-driven culture.

Micaela Kulesz

- What are the main technical challenges of creating a data-driven culture in business?

    Large companies need processes, and processes take time to incorporate at scale. Small firms are more flexible, but also lack the budget to invest in innovative technologies. Quite a challenge! But, in general, the answer is "people."

- What are the main challenges of creating a data-driven culture in business?

    Employees fear losing jobs to automation, human rights are being challenged by algorithmic fairness, and companies fear losing rights over the use of their data. There is a lot of fear. Exposing the company to more data-driven action will help to overcome this fear.

- Digital companies have been born with data analytics and ML embedded at the core of their business. Are more traditional companies lagging in the adoption of these technologies in their day-to-day operations?

    Larger non-digital companies are the ones most lagging. On the one hand, their scale makes changes intrinsically complex. On the other hand, until now, the data had a specific usage and destiny, whose sense and purpose are starting to be challenged.

- More traditional companies are used to outsourcing their market research to consultancy companies. Is the use of social media, web analytics, and search engine data replacing these approaches?

    I do not think so: it increases their competitive landscape and forces them to innovate.

Julio Rodriguez Martino

- What infrastructure is needed for companies?

  Having access to cloud computing. I do not think there is a need for specific infrastructure in most cases.

- What are the main technical challenges of creating a data-driven culture in business?

  I do not think the challenge is technical. The most important challenge is to change the way the whole organization thinks about the data. It is extremely important to show everyone the value of the data so that they know how important it is to generate quality data and keep it safe.

Having a vision of the challenges that we will face when championing data initiatives helps us plan a strategy that will foster the adoption and continuity of our data strategy.

In the next section, our questions will focus on how we can create data teams that support the transformation of our organizations.

Creating effective data teams

Data initiatives require the implementation of data teams with specialized skills, as well as a multidisciplinary approach as the technology that supports the data strategy sits on top of the commercial strategy.

We asked the data leaders their perspective on data teams; here are their answers.

Florian Prem

- What does a good data team look like?

  It depends on the mandate of the CDO. I normally organize into governance, data analytics, and data value creation/product. Then, I build cross-domain teams for agile product delivery (IT, business, and data).

- What are the most important topics to consider when leading a data team?

  Understand your team, understand your business, and understand your technology.

- What are the best practices for business decision-makers to collaborate with highly specialized data teams?

  See what I stated previously, hire a tech and business-savvy CDO, and build enterprise-wide/ multiple linked data offices.

Michael Curry

- What are the best practices for business decision-makers to collaborate with highly specialized data teams?

The most important best practice is to establish a data organization. The goal of this organization should be to define and execute the curation process for data across the business, the alignment of data to business needs, and the governance of how data is being used.

Micaela Kulesz

- What does a good data team look like?

Three or four members: a lead data scientist, a junior/semi-senior data scientist, a data engineer from an IT background, and a product manager if possible. This team composition is very dynamic and can tackle many – if not most – business problems. I find it important to emphasize that at least one of the members must come from an IT background and another one from a business one.

- What are the most important topics to consider when leading a data team?

- Ensure dynamism within the team.

- Understanding is a privilege. Research about the latest developments is ca. 15% of the time of the team, and it is mostly carried out by juniors/semi-seniors.

- Seniors are responsible for providing a clear context for the projects, and they must be able to code.

- Spend the necessary time to discuss and make the problem to tackle clear, and don't depart from it.

- What is the best way for business decision-makers to collaborate with highly specialized data teams to serve the company's needs?

Business decision-makers have a noticeably clear focus and optimization functions. Here, the data team can provide data services to the business and help them to increase their focus, or not. If they do, they become an operative service of the firm with no life on its own. However, as data teams are new and thus finding their identity within the firm as well, placing themselves as "data operatives" or "data providers" is not what they want. If they accept themselves as "data servers," I think it optimal that the business takes the time to explain the problems and the pains until they are truly clear, and the data team must bring specific solutions for these pain points. No more, no less.

Bob Wuisman

- What does a good data team look like?

  A good data team is a team that has a clear view of the company strategy and knows how to contribute to that in a fast way. Everything they do has a clear business objective, even if it is at the infrastructure level. Having adopted a DevOps methodology is key.

- What are the most important topics to consider when leading a data team?

  Have a transparent organized backlog that is supported, appreciated, and recognized by senior managers and executives. Make sure engineers have no constraints in doing their work. Ideally, they can work without any external support. Results need to be celebrated and "errors" must be taken as learning opportunities.

- What are the best practices for business decision-makers to collaborate with highly specialized data teams?

  Adopt DevOps as well as have a clear strategy, objectives, KPIs, processes, and IT to capture the right data. Become familiar with data concepts and dive into business administration. Do not oversell or over-ask.

Jack Godau

- What is the best way for business decision-makers to collaborate with highly specialized data teams to serve the company's needs?

  Having clarity of vision and needs, transporting this to the teams, and making sure they understand the organizational goals. Regular feedback loops, working with the teams to understand their outcomes, and validating those against real-world cases. After that, all the standard stuff – classic enablement of the teams, no micromanagement, providing good tools, and more should be undertaken.

Julio Rodriguez Martino

- What does a good data team look like?

  A good mix of different profiles, coming from diverse backgrounds. They should be eager to learn and teach by helping each other.

- What are the most important topics to consider when leading a data team?

  Leading by example. The leader must understand firsthand the challenges each member faces: learning new topics and working with colleagues with different backgrounds and experiences. The leader should also be aware of the details of each project, at least up to their knowledge of the subject.

- What is the best way for business decision-makers to collaborate with highly specialized data teams to serve the company's needs?

  To help identify business problems that can be solved with data and will return value. In addition, to be ready to work together with the data team to understand and explain the results of the analysis.

Wim van der

- What are the best practices for business decision-makers to collaborate with highly specialized data teams?

  The extended reality, blockchain, and digital twins, but this depends on the business. However, DevOps teams are known for success when positioned well.

Creating and supporting efficient data teams to develop a successful data strategy in an organization is of crucial importance and requires more than simply hard skills.

In the next section, we will ask the data leaders their perspectives on what the future looks like for these organizations in terms of data.

Visualizing the future of data

Data has become a central pillar for companies that want to uncover the possibilities of value for the business, which is why modern technologies will shape the future of organizations.

We asked the data leaders what their perspectives are on the future in terms of technologies.

Michael Curry

- What future technologies do you think will shape the future of data being used in business?

  Data integration, data quality, and data governance continue to be expensive and overly manual, and yet they remain the biggest barriers to companies being able to get full leverage from their data. I expect to see dramatic improvements in these areas, using new AI-based approaches to reduce manual effort.

Florian Prem

- What future technologies do you think will shape the future of data being used in business?

  Explainable AI, device-to-device comms/IoT -> predictive analytics, automation, end-to-end analytics platforms, and new NLP and image/video processing models – once these technologies are available as products and platforms, they will be more broadly used.

Bob Wuisman

- What technologies do you think will shape the future of data science and engineering?

  The next big step will be quantum computing. Until that time, there are more and faster cloud platforms that have increased niche services.

Micaela Kulesz

- What technologies do you think will shape the future of data science and engineering?

  In data science, these come in line with increasing the understanding and modeling of big structural data.

  In engineering, this involves improving the algorithms; we already know how to perform fast and easy tasks.

Julio Rodriguez Martino

- What technologies do you think will shape the future of data science and engineering?

  I guess that no-code and AutoML technologies will become increasingly popular. Only sophisticated analyses will require coding in the future.

Shaping the future of data in organizations will require being nimble to adapt to new challenges and technologies. Hopefully, the perspective of our data leaders has provided you with an idea of which technologies will shape the future of data.

The next section will dive specifically into the experience of data leaders who have specialized in championing digital and data transformations in several organizations.

Implementing a data-driven culture

Data has gained center stage in the table of discussion for company leaders and managers. The opportunity to improve operational performance and engage in an optimized manner with the customers to find new sources of revenue are promising goals to achieve by implementing a data strategy, but these transformations do not come without hassle.

For this section, we have interviewed Patrick Flink, a data leader who has a company that focuses on transforming organizations into digital organizations, and Agustina Hernandez, who has built global data teams from scratch in some of the biggest companies in the world.

Agustina Hernandez

With a background in econometry, Agustina had previous experience as an econometric modeler and decided to follow her passion early on in her career, even if it meant having a reduction in pay. Her other passions are coaching and photography. She worked on several projects, creating insights for top FMCG companies, and leading the teams that would create insights on topics such as brand equity, media ROI, assortment, and more. One of her main focuses has been to understand the client's needs in depth to achieve the objectives of business revenue and EBITA.

After working for several client accounts, she joined a top cosmetic company as head of Global Data Analytics and was tasked with building the data team for this company, to deliver data-driven solutions and create a cultural change in the organization to be more focused on data.

Her leadership strategy can be regarded as setting in the table of discussion all the different stakeholders of a data team, regardless of their domain and backgrounds. She fosters communication within the team without imposing a specific view, rather than working to get to know the client's requirements to focus on the task to deliver, making sure that the team has all the resources to continue while focusing on improving this communication.

The vision she has of a data team is that it is a team in charge of changing realities and that companies can improve their operations by understanding that creating a data-driven culture is necessary to improve skills and have a top-down approach. Most of the time, this requires a team that gets to be attached to the current organization and pushes these changes through a lot of work, and focuses on changing behaviors. For Agustina, the eruption of data in companies can be seen as a technology that will drive any kind of change, magically solving and improving all metrics. The data strategy sits on top of the current strategy to be able to increase the reach of the knowledge that we can use to make better decisions.

- What are the approaches to effectively implementing a data-driven transformation in an organization?

  There are several types of approaches to achieving an effective transformation. The creation of lighthouse groups, which are aspirational teams, examples of the transformation that they want to achieve, to guide the transformation is not enough because later, these teams collide with a reality different from the conditions in which they work. This is because these teams have more resources than the others, and it differs from the real situation in which the rest of the company finds itself.

  The Lighthouse model is opposed to the one set up by a parallel organization, which is in charge of transforming the company's processes. It strongly implements them by establishing transformation objectives and clear incentives such as variable bonuses in the middle. This generates internal conflicts but is maintained for the time that a new culture lasts. This also implies that resources are required and that this transformation hurts as if it were organizational adolescence.

Some organizations have large margins that allow them to duplicate resources by creating transformation teams for each of the departments, which then end up joining those teams and departments that are seeking to improve. The problem with this is that it duplicates resources but not all the equipment in those resources to carry out this transformation.

- What is the perspective of management on these transformations?

Middle management is the hardest to convince because by adopting a new strategy, they end up doing two things at once. While there are middle managers excited about change, everything is defined with hands and resources, and carrying out the transformation requires diverting change processes and diverting resources from operations, which affects the performance metrics by which these middle managers are judged. Implementing an effective data strategy collides with reality when those who should be using the data do not change their processes to incorporate these metrics or insights into their decision-making and daily operations. These individuals are middle managers who are closer to operations and do not have the time or the skills to lead the transformation or drive the use of data.

- What benefits can these organizations expect from becoming data-driven?

The data is nothing if the processes are not changed; if you do not think about equipment and processes, the data that's collected will not have a use or an impact. Data-driven does not have fewer resources. This is a misconception that arises from the spirit of IT, which always seeks to improve its operating costs. The data-driven strategy must focus on what generates revenue in the company. The CDO, who depends on IT or operations, aims to save costs and that does not work. Data is neither less cost nor less time – it involves finding value opportunities. An example is that of promotions or price reductions, which, if applied without sufficient data on customers and products, generate that subsidy for those who were already about to buy. If we used data, we could calculate promotion elasticities and customize them to give each of the buyer segments what they want most by making them buy more than they would have but not generating trade spend savings. Once the organization matures and understands the true role of the data strategy, that data strategy becomes the responsibility of either the sales department, the strategy department, or the general manager. Alternatively, you will need to do a C-level.

- How does data storytelling fit into a data-driven transformation?

This data strategy must have storytelling that supports this strategy and communicates what each of the organization's participants' roles is. This strategy must be implemented from the top down because if, on the contrary, it arises from each team or department, atomization is generated, which is why an alignment is necessary that effectively shows and communicates the benefits obtained step by step.

- What are the ingredients for a successful data-driven strategy?

The ingredients of the data strategy are clear purposes that are tangible objectives, a culture that aligns everyone behind those objectives, and the resources and perseverance necessary to carry out this transformation within the organization.

- How do people fit in the data-driven strategy?

  In the case of people, it is important to think about the skills and abilities of each of them. Some people are good at analysis, some people are good at bringing strategies to reality, and there are a few who do both things well. Typically, data teams have strategy development capabilities and domain knowledge to carry out the data strategy. This is because hard knowledge is not enough and data is complementary to a reality that needs to be known, so there is a need to have field knowledge to complement the use of data to make effective decisions. This field knowledge lives in these middle ranks close to operations, who must learn from the data scientists doing the parts of the team with a CDO that coordinates these developments throughout all the teams. This does not work if there is a single centralized department that provides data to the entire organization.

- What is the role of technology in this transformation?

  In the case of technology, this is an enabler that allows the strategy to be carried out, but this technology is built on the data strategy, which, in turn, is built on a commercial strategy, not the other way around. Solutions of minimum complexity should always be sought to solve a data problem that solves a business problem. This is carried out with a team of data engineers, MLOps, DataOps, and others, always controlling the quality of the development to ensure the reliability of information and the rules and abilities of systems.

Patrick Flink

Patrick is an expert in transformative strategy implementation. He places enormous focus on extracting actionable value from data with a minimal approach that can deliver value fast. His company, ONBRDNG, is a Dutch company that specializes in digital transformation, with an accent not only on strategy for being data-driven but also on execution.

With a background in business and management, he had a multidisciplinary approach to learning the tools and skills necessary to extract value from data, prioritizing actionable outcomes. He has been a CTO and CDO and has worked with media companies in the Netherlands to develop innovative products and solutions.

Patrick is both pragmatic and creative. He is a results-driven strategist who enjoys communicating with every level of an organization and rebuilding companies from traditional businesses into all-around digital companies.

- How did you prepare yourself to have the skills to be a data leader?

  Yes, well, I am a lifelong learner. So, of course, I did some stuff myself but also spent a lot of time with our developers and analysts. I spend a lot of time just sitting next to them. So, it is always good to be multidisciplinary; then, you can see the value of working with other professionals from different domains. Often, this involves asking a lot of questions, looking from different perspectives, and so on. So, yes, that is where I started. We also did a lot of stuff surrounding media, the benefit of which is that media companies are always focused on how we can engage our customers and our consumers increasingly. The latest features, functionality, and products are also presented here because everybody knows that they are incredibly open to new stuff. They generate a lot of data in terms of behavior, what they like, what they do not like, and so on. You can use this information to be able to produce a proper strategy.

- Which kind of methodologies do you use to uncover value in the data?

We have an approach that is moving toward a methodology. But in my experience, most of the time, everybody has the same examples. And they do not take everything important to be successful in that area into account and forget to dive into the whole story. And then it is not only about collecting all kinds of data and then getting better because of it. It is just to see and understand how they do it – more than what they do because you know that can differ. And what we like about our approach is that we make it small, and quite simple. We use data to tell us what is happening, and then we see what we can do, and everybody says data-driven or data decision-making or whatever. But it is much more on the human aspect and creativity. And if you also look at the most, you know, data-driven companies, of course, they use data, but it is also still about creativity, intuition, and betting while being very honest. I have seen too many companies that hire a lot of data engineers, data and data scientists, and more while spending a lot of money on infrastructure. We use data to see if our bet is right and if we are moving the needle. We use a lot of it, and without customers, we work a lot on data sprints, also to make it focused.

We follow the journey of a customer, from beginning to end. All of this is possible, yet everybody's busy with so much stuff, so we try to make it simple. That's why we do a lot of stuff in data sprints for a couple of weeks – nobody tells you that a lot of times, to use data and get value from data, you don't need a lot of people.

- What kind of challenges have you faced when working with data teams in a company?

One of the challenges is that companies that hire too many people. I experienced this myself; I asked a data manager who is responsible for customer insights to say we need a churn prediction model, and then a couple of weeks later, or months, we ask how it is going. They say that it's not clear what the business requirements are, but that we can do facial recognition. However, that is not what we asked for. We can build a recommendation engine, but we already have a recommendation, so this is not where we need it now. So, it is not our biggest issue to have more people. There are a lot of companies with so many people working on a topic that it's not beneficial or actionable, and we do not get real value from it either.

- What is your approach to creating successful data projects?

What we are doing is trying to make it exceedingly small. So, start with a number. Say, for example, we are going to work data-driven. Okay; what is the answer? What is our first assumption? Let us see what we are, what we are discovering, and what we are experiencing – this 90 percent is data cleaning. We are structuring data and getting the right labels, the right data, and the right definitions. But nobody talks about it. So, we might try to make it simple, and then really get real about it. This concept of data sprints is a view of the landscape of where we work on it. Is it sometimes very fragmented; for example, or it is a monolithic system or a landscape? Then, we ask, what is the business? What are we promising to the customer? How are we earning our money? Then, we try to get a view of the end-to-end journey of a customer. We start from here. What are our main challenges? What is the key question? Is it growth? Is it churn? Is it process automation? This is also related to the decision. Do we want to automate all kinds of stuff? Then, we must start with the hypothesis and work from there. We must always try to get some value out of it in 6 weeks – 6 weeks only. We evaluate the infrastructure and the business model, and we look at the channels in the customer's journey. Then, we must set ourselves a goal based on those 6 weeks, with a small team. This team should be multidisciplinary and part of the company. It is your team. Well, of course, we do it for the customers. And it is always, of course, a hybrid multi-disciplinary team.

- How do you set priorities and collaborate with data teams in a company?

The focus of the team depends, of course, on the top management. If it is concerned with digital process automation, the objectives will be of a certain kind. If it is a factory, for example, or an e-commerce company, it will focus on conversion. It is, of course, a little bit of a different question when it comes to experience or where the focus is, depending on the company. So, that sometimes changes a little bit, but we always assist and work with the customer. We use main and we have our data platform also, so it is our customers are difficult with five legacy systems. Then, we have our data platform, where we do the landscape analysis on the data in certain systems. Then, we can say, "give us the elements from this system so that we can create some sort of initial view." We use a lot of the global stack as well as some tooling, such as scripting. There are also experts on that platform. However, our data platform is used to ensure that we can accelerate.

- What should be the goals of a data-driven transformation?

So, on average, I think that if you talk about data-driven, you should talk much more to your customers. Then, you should talk about what you see in the data, as well as what everyone else sees. After, you should talk about your revenue, costs, and the results you wish to obtain. In the end, a lot of companies are only talking about those components. If you are data-driven, then you can already predict what your result will be because you already see it in the behavior of customers. You will see what the outcome will be somewhere further along the line than the next quarter. I think that, in the end, you will always end up committing to delivering on your promise, which is important to your customers.

Transforming companies into data-driven organizations requires a profound cultural change that needs to be implemented with a top-down approach, championed by leaders who can create a narrative to support the data strategy and adapt to the needs and objectives of the organization. This transformation is not just about technology, but mostly about people and processes. I am thankful for the perspective of both Agustina and Patrick and hope that their experiences can help you create effective cultural transformations.

Summary

In this chapter, we explored the distinct parts that constitute a data transformation for companies that want to become data-driven by leveraging the perspective and experience of data leaders with extensive knowledge and experience in leading digital and data transformations.

These approaches allow not only companies to transform but also leaders and managers to adapt to the new skills and processes required to implement a successful data strategy. By doing so, they have a clear goal of how the company will benefit from these efforts, how to create and lead data teams, as well as how to consider the implications of enabling digital and data transformation.

Overall, the objective of this book has been to help business leaders, managers, and enthusiasts implement ready-to-use recipes that seek to undercover insights about consumers, their behavior patterns, how they perceive prices, how they effectively make recommendations, and, in general, how to complement the commercial strategy with managerial economics applied in Python.

I have leveraged the knowledge of coders, managers, and specialists from whom I got the inspiration to author this book. All the code and data that's been modified and used in this book belong to their respective owners and producers, to whom I am grateful. Most of all, I want to thank the data leaders, who, amid their incredibly busy day-to-day lives, have taken the time to answer the questions presented in this chapter.

I am thankful for the time you took to read this book, and hopefully, it has inspired you to use data and achieve your objectives while having fun and enjoying the process.

Index

Packt.com

Subscribe to our online digital library for full access to over 7,000 books and videos, as well as industry leading tools to help you plan your personal development and advance your career. For more information, please visit our website.

Why subscribe?

- Spend less time learning and more time coding with practical eBooks and Videos from over 4,000 industry professionals

- Improve your learning with Skill Plans built especially for you

- Get a free eBook or video every month

- Fully searchable for easy access to vital information

- Copy and paste, print, and bookmark content

Did you know that Packt offers eBook versions of every book published, with PDF and ePub files available? You can upgrade to the eBook version at packt.com and as a print book customer, you are entitled to a discount on the eBook copy. Get in touch with us at customercare@packtpub.com for more details.

At www.packt.com, you can also read a collection of free technical articles, sign up for a range of free newsletters, and receive exclusive discounts and offers on Packt books and eBooks.

Other Books You May Enjoy

If you enjoyed this book, you may be interested in these other books by Packt:

Data Cleaning and Exploration with Machine Learning

Michael Walker

ISBN: 978-1-80324-167-8

- Explore essential data cleaning and exploration techniques to be used before running the most popular machine learning algorithms
- Understand how to perform preprocessing and feature selection, and how to set up the data for testing and validation
- Model continuous targets with supervised learning algorithms
- Model binary and multiclass targets with supervised learning algorithms
- Execute clustering and dimension reduction with unsupervised learning algorithms
- Understand how to use regression trees to model a continuous target

Data Science for Marketing Analytics - Second Edition

Mirza Rahim Baig, Gururajan Govindan, Vishwesh Ravi Shrimali

ISBN: 978-1-80056-047-5

- Load, clean, and explore sales and marketing data using pandas
- Form and test hypotheses using real data sets and analytics tools
- Visualize patterns in customer behavior using Matplotlib
- Use advanced machine learning models like random forest and SVM
- Use various unsupervised learning algorithms for customer segmentation
- Use supervised learning techniques for sales prediction
- Evaluate and compare different models to get the best outcomes
- Optimize models with hyperparameter tuning and SMOTE

Packt is searching for authors like you

If you're interested in becoming an author for Packt, please visit `authors.packtpub.com` and apply today. We have worked with thousands of developers and tech professionals, just like you, to help them share their insight with the global tech community. You can make a general application, apply for a specific hot topic that we are recruiting an author for, or submit your own idea.

Share Your Thoughts

Now you've finished *The Art of Data-Driven Business*, we'd love to hear your thoughts! Scan the QR code below to go straight to the Amazon review page for this book and share your feedback or leave a review on the site that you purchased it from.

https://packt.link/r/1-804-61103-4

Your review is important to us and the tech community and will help us make sure we're delivering excellent quality content.

Download a free PDF copy of this book

Thanks for purchasing this book!

Do you like to read on the go but are unable to carry your print books everywhere?

Is your eBook purchase not compatible with the device of your choice?

Don't worry, now with every Packt book you get a DRM-free PDF version of that book at no cost.

Read anywhere, any place, on any device. Search, copy, and paste code from your favorite technical books directly into your application.

The perks don't stop there, you can get exclusive access to discounts, newsletters, and great free content in your inbox daily

Follow these simple steps to get the benefits:

1. Scan the QR code or visit the link below

https://packt.link/free-ebook/9781804611036

2. Submit your proof of purchase
3. That's it! We'll send your free PDF and other benefits to your email directly